MEDIA EDUCATION IN THIRD WORLD

Media Education in Third World

C.S.H.N. MURTHY
Assistant Professor
in Mass Communication (Reader)
Amity School of Communication
AMITY UNIVERSITY LUCKNOW/NOIDA
(U.P.)

KANISHKA PUBLISHERS, DISTRIBUTORS
NEW DELHI-110 002

KANISHKA PUBLISHERS, DISTRIBUTORS
4697/5-21 A, Ansari Road, Daryaganj
New Delhi-110 002
Phones : 2327 0497, 2328 8285
Fax : 011-2328 8285
e-mail: kanishka_publishing@yahoo.co.in

First Published 2007

ISBN 978-81-7391-985-5

PRINTED IN INDIA

Published by Madan Sachdeva for Kanishka Publishers, Distributors, 4697/5-21A, Ansari Road, Daryaganj, New Delhi-110 002, Typeset by Sunshine Graphics, Delhi, and Printed at Nice Printing Press, Delhi.

Preface

The book is an outcome of my original research which I carried out during 2003-05 as an assignment at the instance of the Director General Mr. Gebrezghi Dimam (popularly known as *Acha* in Asmara, Eritrea), Department of Adult and Media Education, Ministry of Education, Government of Eritrea where I was appointed for the first time as Assistant Professor in Media Technology though I was also on the faculty of Eritrean Institute of Technology which is modelled on the lines of Indian Institute of Technology (IIT) in India.

I was asked to develop and design strategic theoretical (discourse) and technical document—*Media Education in Eritrean Education*—that would enable the Ministry of Education, Government of Eritrea to establish a state of the art Media Educational Technology both at national level and regional level in order for achieving rapid educational transformation and poverty reduction to ensure an equitable and sustainable growth besides narrow down the gap between the developed and the developing world.

In fact, I never did such a work earlier to any foreign government, though I was well-conversant with several such policy documents of my own and other countries across the globe as a journalist for over two decades. As such the task appeared to be stupendous and it called for a primary understanding of the socio-economic, cultural and political history of Eritrea.

Eritrea has a lot of similarities with India. It has about nine officially recognized languages, each signifying an ethnic group. Topographically the country has a long coastal line on its eastern side (Red Sea), hilly and plain areas in the middle of the country similar to India. Hence, it took a lot of time for me to read the history of Eritrea, its 30 years armed struggle for independence and subsequent formation of the Republic of Eritrea in 1991.

It was after perusing a number of documents of the Ministry of Education, Government of Eritrea and the World Bank, besides other development partners such as UNICEF, USAID, UNESCO, etc., and other stakeholders that I could arrive at conceptualizing the outline of the strategic document that I was assigned to develop. Following this, I had to develop an appropriate methodology before going into the detailed chapters of the document. This was no simple task by itself for there were limited number of books available both in our Department library as also in the library of Asmara University, British Library and American Library. I had to refer to a number of books and journals online which again a struggle was given the poor internet facility access the country had at this time.

Against all the odds, I struggled to complete the first draft nearly in seven months' time. At every stage, after finishing each chapter, I had the opportunity to discuss with my immediate superior and Director of Media Education, Mr. Baslios Zemos.

By September 2004, I had finished the final draft after receiving the first round of comments from all the Directors—Mr. Baslios, Mr. Woldu and Mr. Tocabbo—including the Director, General Gebrezghi Dimam. I submitted the final copy to the Ministry of Education, Government of Eritrea in October, 2004.

Subsequently, I had no look back as there was a very good appreciation of my work from all the corners of the Ministry of Education. It helped me intensely to be confident in carrying forward similar assignments. Based on the document—*Media Education in Eritrean Education*— I developed several other strategic documents like *Launching of Educational Television Channel, Teacher Development Programmes for Primary Teachers in English,* and *Designing Supporting Education for Girls via Bana Radio.*

Parts of this work—*Media Education in Eritrean Education*—have already been published in peer reviewed international journals, most important and prestigious one among them being *Journal of Adult and Continuing Education (a NIACE, UK publication)* edited by Professor Mike Osborne, University of Sterling, UK. Another such internationally renowned journal is *Educational Media International* edited by Professor John Hedberg, University of Macquarie, Australia.

The book offers a comprehensive and analytical discussion of the global media educational and ICT (Information and Computer Technology) strategies being pursued in a number of third world countries including Asia, South America and Africa. The discussion includes how initially the technologies of the first world (US, Japan and the Europe) guided the formulation of media technologies and educational strategies of the third world and how they failed also to deliver. The book offers in essence that the educational strategies of each third world country could be formulated based on its own socio-economic, cultural and political settings and could not be copied straight from the East or the West.

I hope that the academicians, fellow journalists and the students of journalism would find the book useful at least to the point of appreciating the fact that media professionals can design media strategies for any country in the world, given an opportunity. It is no longer an area exclusive to engineers and telecommunication professionals.

It was my privilege and pleasure to be first Indian to do this kind of strategic development work in Media for a Sub-Saharan African nation on African continent.

Further, I place on record all my deep indebtedness to Mr. Gebrezghi Dimam, the Director-General and Mr. Baslios Zemos, the Director Media Education Division for all their continued love and encouragement, besides useful discussions which enhanced the quality of the work presented inside.

I also thank Ms. Timinit and Ms. Woonush for their secretarial assistance throughout. I can hardly forget the beautiful sketches drawn for my work by Ms. Yodit Mehri, the artist of the Department.

C.S.H.N. Murthy

Contents

1
Introduction

The State of Eritrea is liberated as an independent nation on May 24, 1993 and has been admitted to the full membership of the United Nations as the 182nd member nation on May 28 of the same year. Eritrea (Italians adopted this name from the Greek word *Erythraea*—literally meaning *"Red"* is located in the Horn of Africa to the North of the Equator between latitudes 12° 22′ N and 18° 02′N and longitudes 36° 26′22″ E and 43° 23′ E. It has a vast area of 1,22,000 square kilometers* (in the report compiled by the Ministry of Education *"Eritrea-Basic Education Statistic – 2000/01"*, it is mentioned as 1,23,000 square kilometers approximately: page 11) with a population density 29 per square kilometer. On the Eastern side the country is adjoined by the Red Sea, with the presence of a number of islands called Dahlak islands on it, which runs into a long 1,212 kilometers of coast line from Ras Kasar in the North to Dar Elwa in the South East. Whereas the Republic of Djibouti (formerly a French Somaliland) forms its Southeastern most border, Ethiopia forms its Southern most border with Sudan as its Western and Northern borders.

Administratively the country is divided into 6 Zobas (regions) namely: Anseba, Debub, Debubawi Keih Bahri (South Red Sea), Gash Barka, Maekel and Semenawi Keih Bahri (North Red Sea). Eritrea is a country with a splendid variety of land contrasts

---

* *As per the geographical data given in "Eritrea – Demographic and Health Survey-2002." – National Statistics and Evaluation Office, Asmara, Eritrea: ORC Macro, Calverton, Maryland and USA, May 2003, p. 1.*

ranging from below sea level to above sea level comprising such an expanse as deserts, the forests of Equatorial Africa and the severe volcanic ecology of South Arabia and Djibouti zone. For the sake of convenience and understanding one can look at Eritrea from three physiographic zones such as the Western Lowlands, the Central and Northern Highlands and the Eastern Lowlands also referred as Coastal plains. Most of the Western Lowlands and the Coastal Plains have extreme hot and cold climatic conditions leaving the Highlands with moderate temperatures and clouds that render the environment pleasant and cool throughout the year.

The geography of any country personifies its economy. The economic conditions act as torchbearer of the country in leading it on a progressive path with respect to education and self-reliance.

Table–1
Eritrea Economic and Social Sector Performance Indicators

Eritrea, Demographic Indicators Estimated for 2000 to 2020

	2000	*2005*	*2010*	*2015*	*2020*
Population in millions (% of increase)	4.10	4.60 (12%)	5.10 (24%)	5.60 (37%)	6.20 (51%)
Population Growth Rate (%)	2.3	2.1	2.0	1.9	1.6
Population by Age Groups ('000s)					
0-4	730	760	810	870	930
5-9	610	710	740	800	860
10-14	520	600	700	740	790
Sub-total	**1,860**	**2,070**	**2,250**	**2,410**	**2,570**
15-19	420	510	590	690	730
20-64	1,710	1,530	3,950	2,630	3,100
65+	110	120	140	170	198
Total	**4,100**	**4,650**	**5,220**	**4,880**	**6,610**
Dependency Ratio %*	100	97	91	81	74
Of which under 15 group %	**90**	**88**	**81**	**72**	**65**
Women of Childbearing Age (15-49)	21%	23%	24%	25%	26%
Labor Force Participation (15-60)	50%	51%	53%	55%	58%

* Dependency Ratio is population under 15 and over 64 divided by the 15-64 age group population.

Source: World Development Indicators, 2001.

The Eritrean economy lies in its vast variety of geographical and topographical resourcefulness. The vast open lands with relative fertility of soils coupled with milder climate render the Central Highlands a centre of rain-fed agricultural activity. Similarly during the monsoon season, the Western Lowlands offer a potential for cultivation and agro-pastoralism. The Coastal Plains harbored two major Ports—Massawa and Assab with a promise of a very good activity for commerce promotion.

Eritrea, Key Economic Indicators, 1993-2001

	1993 1997	*1998*	*1999*	*2000*	*2001*	*1998 2001*
Real GDP growth (%)	4.9	3.9	-1.5	-10.9	9.1	0.2
Inflation (% change, end of year)	9.1	9	10.6	26.8	7.7	13.5
Gross National savings/GDP (%)	39.4	12.0	13.7	19.1	21.1	16.5
Income per capita	200	207.6	191.7	173.8	175.0	187
Govt. Expenditure/GDP (%)	63.5	81.8	99.6	101.4	78.1	90.2
Govt. domestic debt (net)/GDP (%)	34.3	63.4	98.8	127.5	105.9	98.9
Net donor support/GDP (%)	**12.3**	**17.3**	**27.1**	**24.3**	**33.7**	**25.6**

Source: IMF, World Bank Database.

Eritrea Government and Donor Contribution to Education and Training Expenditure (US $M), 1993-2000

Spending on Basic and Secondary Education						*University of Asmara*		
Year	*Total Spending US$m*	*Capital Spending US$m*	*Donors' Contribution US$m*	*Donor Contribution % of Total Spending*	*Donor Contribution % of Capital Spending*	*Total Spending US$m*	*Donors' Contribution US$m*	*% Donors' Contribution*
1993	10.8	2.5	2.5	23.1	100.0	0.9	0.3	32
1998	33.9	9.3	7.1	20.9	76.3	3.6	1.7	46
1999	34.9	13.4	9.7	27.8	72.4	4.2	2.3	56
2000	26.8	8.3	7.1	26.5	85.5	3.5	1.8	51

Source: Eritrea Ministry of Education and Ministry of Finance.

The rainfall is another factor, which greatly influences the country's economy. The Central Highlands register a high rainfall to the tune of 1000 mm per annum in the area of Escarpment and on an average 450 mm to 600 mm in other areas per annum. On the contrary the Eastern Lowlands experience an average rainfall as low as 200 mm per annum. Compared to the Eastern Lowlands, the Southern

Table-2

Eritrea Demographic and Health Indicators—Projections

Indicators	*Actual*	*Projected*			
	2000	*2005*	*2010*	*2015*	*2020*
Population (millions)	4.10	4.60	5.10	5.60	6.20
Population change since 2000 (%)		12%	24%	37%	51%
Population Growth Rate (%)	2.3	2.1	2.0	1.9	1.6
Life Expectancy at Birth (years)	50	51	54	57	58
Total Fertility Rate	5.2	4.7	4.1	3.5	2.9
Infant Morality/1,000 live Births	61	57	52	47	43
Population by Age Groups					
Children under 15 years	0.7 (18%)	0.7 (16%)	0.8 (15%)	0.8 (14%)	0.8 (13%)
Youth under 15 years	1.9 (45%)	2.1 (45%)	2.2 (43%)	2.3 (40%)	2.3 (38%)
Labor Force Participation (15-60)	2.1 (50%)	2.3 (51%)	2.7 (53%)	3.1 (55%)	3.6 (58%)
Dependency Ratio					
Total (under 15 and over 60 years)	100	97	91	81	74
Youth only (under 15 years)	90	88	81	72	65

Source: World Development Indicators, World Bank, Washington, D.C., 2001.
Courtesy: Eritrea Education and Training Sector.
Note: World Bank Document No. 24448-ERI-A.

Western Lowlands experience a high rainfall to the extent of 600 mm on an average per annum. There are two major periods of monsoon in Eritrea: one commencing from June to September covering both the Western Lowlands and the Central Highlands, the other beginning in October and continues through upto March covering the Eastern Lowlands. Although surface water is available in lesser quantities, the ground water potential is good enough in the Western Lowlands and in some part of the Coastal Plains and this could be used for both household and industrial purposes.

Eritrea has abundant natural resources including arable land (26% of the total area) of which only about 4 per cent is under cultivation. Eritrea is also rich by possessing varied and abundant mineral resources including copper, gold, iron, nickel, silica, sulfur and potash. Good quality marble and granite also exist in large quantities. As for the means of resources the Agriculture and Pastoralism are the two main sources of livelihood for about 80 per cent of population. But for the centuries of colonialism unleashed by the Italians and the Britishers the fertility of soil in Eritrea could have a different promise for the native populations. However, an efficient resource management coupled with scientific approach to natural flora and fauna in the last one decade has resulted in the identification of 6 agro-ecological zones, which in turn are sub-divided into 55 sub-zones in Eritrea. This has helped retrieve the lost fertility of the soil and restore the water conservation techniques in agriculture. Even the migration of the soil fertility from the central Highlands to the Western Lowlands is successfully countred and put to effective utilization in the agriculture.

Here it is important to note that these are not to be viewed as mere scientific zones for some academic purposes. They are the decisive economic zones with sociological implications about which we deal extensively in the subsequent chapters. These topographical and environmental complexities posed a formidable challenge to the Government of Eritrea in implementing the educational and developmental programmes and as one gets to know more and more about it in the subsequent pages, it would become clear the enormity of these complexities. In short it is a difficult terrain on which one has to traverse with a great caution. Further, it is important to know that to a great extent the pastoralism transformed itself to sedentarism barring a few tribes from the immigrant groups. It is clear from the above that as on the date of liberation Eritrea is a much exploited country by the alien rulers and it is also not a land abundant country primarily. The available resources were unevenly distributed between the different regions some parts were densely populated, barren, mountainous, dry and uncultivable while others were fertile and well watered. The latter were suitable for cultivation and livestock production.

The agricultural sector by and large sustains mainly on rains as indicated above and with arable land being below 10 per cent of the cultivable land, the productivity is low and the agricultural sector including the livestock and fisheries accounts for only one-fifth of the nation's GDP, the per capita income being less than 200 dollar well below the average of 270 dollar per capita for the less developed countries. Eritrea is thus one of the poorest nations in the world.

The country's population, though not exactly determined by any scientific census operations on a national basis, is estimated to be around 3,615,050 (1994 as base year with a population growth rate at 2.7%) with many of them in the productive age group (see the Table 2. Eritrea, Demographic Indicators Estimated for 2000-20). As a result the population of Eritrea will continue to grow over the next twenty years. Thus, Eritrea's population is estimated to increase to 40,00,000 (4 million) by the end of 2000 with an annual growth rate of 2.3 per cent. By 2020 the population will touch the mark of 6.2 million with the majority population by then joining the adult age group. However in terms of absolute growth rate, by 2020 the population growth rate may decline to 1.9 per cent. Consequently the adult population will increase from the existing 50 to 58 per cent by 2020. This has its own sociological implications per se.

As to the literacy scenario of the country about 70 per cent male population and nearly 80 per cent female population are reeling under abject illiteracy. The socio-economic and political conditions coupled with the hard topographical realities of the country and centuries of alien rule had resulted in such high percentage of illiteracy. The efforts to transform this situation to a productive and constructive one in fact had begun way back 1960s, during the pre-independence armed struggle, when the then EPLF (The Eritrean Peoples'Liberation Front) conducted organized literacy camps to protect the educational interests of the budding generations across the country on the one side while battling with the Ethiopian army on the other side. It was, however, a beginning in the right direction though the context was different that time.

Historical Background

Historically Eritrea has been invaded by a number of races, which are related to those that are found in and around the Horn of Africa. The history dates back to the first invasion of the Ottoman Turkish rulers who after acquiring Massawa port began exercising the administrative control over the Eritrean lands during the period between 16th and 18th centuries. It was later replaced by the Egyptians who hoisted their flag around 1872. The Egyptian control over the Eritrean lands ended when the Italians came to colonize it after establishing a foothold at Assab through a maritime company, *Campagnia Maritimia Rubattino,* between 1890 and 1940. The Italian control, however, over the Eritreans did not last long. Italy went for a war on June 10, 1940 and the British defeated it by May 1941.

Table-3

Millennium Development Goals (MDG)

At the Millennium summit in September 2000 the states of the United Nations reaffirmed their commitment to working toward a world in which sustain development and eliminating poverty would have the highest priority. The Millennium Development Goals grew out of the agreements and resolutions of world conferences organized by the United Nations in the past decade. The goals have been commonly accepted as a framework for measuring development progress.

Millennium Development Goals:

Eradicate extreme poverty and hunger
Achieve universal primary education
Promote gender equality and empower women
Reduce child mortality.
Combat HIV/AIDS, malaria, and other diseases
Ensure environmental sustainability
Develop a global partnership for development
Improve maternal health

Eritrea's Millennium Development Goal Indicators	*Current*	*Target*
Poverty Rate (% of population below $1/day)	53%	22%
Net Primary Enrollment Rate (Grades 1-5)	38%	100%
Infant Mortality Rate (per 1,000 live births)	61	34*
Child Mortality Rate (per 1,000 live births)	94	52
Ratio of Girls to Boys in Primary & Secondary Education	85-72	Equal*
% Births Attended by skilled Health Personnel	29%	90%
Use of Contraception—Any Method (men)	NA	NA
Use of Contraception—Any Method (women)	8%	25*
% of population with Access to an Improved Water Source	7%	75%

* Target is inconsistent in various documents, requiring confirmation of actual targets.

Courtesy: Eritrea Education and Training Sector.

Note: World Bank Document No. 24448-ERI-A.

Ever since it was colonization of a different type by the Britishers and it brought a new experience in its fold to the Eritreans. The British rule over the Eritrean lands was a short lived one compared to the long tenure of Italians and it lasted until 1952 only. The Britishers while relinquishing their authority over Eritrea, tacitly conceded to the UN plan (UN General Assembly Resolution 390A(v) of 1950) in tune with the American imperialistic strategy to federate it with Ethiopia though the plan envisaged an autonomy of independent administration and constitution for Eritrea. However, the Ethiopian rulers wrecked havoc on the Eritrean economy and even went a step ahead by unilaterally abrogating the UN plan and integrating Eritrea with Ethiopia by 1962. This has led to the sowing of seeds for the armed struggle for the independence of the country and the first organization that formed to achieve it was the Eritrean Liberation Front (ELF).

In this context it is relevant to mention that the struggle for independence in Eritrea had actually started way back in 1940, much before most of the colonized nations in the African continent raised the banner of revolt against the respective alien rulers. It was in 1940s itself that Eritrea's democratic institutions (which represented its identity and expressed its nationalism) such as its flag, the governmental structure, political parties, trade unions, educational systems, industrial bases and free press came into existence. Though these were sought to be destroyed during the Ethiopian rule before and after the abrogation of federation, the roots of these institutions could never be removed totally and these roots in the collective conscience of the people had led to an armed struggle against Ethiopia for over three decades culminating in the process of liberation of Eritrea which symbolizes not mere physical victory but a triumph of right to self-determination and desire for a democratic order of life. It is altogether a different matter beyond this to know how the EPLF has emerged from the split of the ELF in 1970 but the armed guerilla warfare unleashed by the EPLF at last brought the desired liberation to the country in 1991. What began as a modest revolt with a few militants against the Ethiopian hegemony in 1961 initially culminated in a full-fledged war and realization of freedom to the country ultimately.

Whatsoever may be the ideological differences between ELF and EPLF, the latter came to stay as a symbol of the peoples' aspirations. The number of reforms brought in the peasant and agriculture sector and the liberation accorded to the women from the traditional strangleholds have made the EPLF a peoples' party which, after independence in 1993, has made an untiring effort to rebuild the war ravaged and drought affected nation into a modern society of knowledge and civilization in keeping with the Millenium Development Goals of the UN (See the Millenium Development Goals (MDG) and indicators in the Table-3).

In keeping with the commitments it had made to the people of Eritrea, the EPLF immediately after independence proclaimed its macro policy document of 1994 in which it set out its goals and educational policy. The Constitution of Eritrea included in its Chapter III an Article 21(1), under The Fundamental Rights, Freedoms and Duties, which states that *Every citizen shall have the right of equal access to publicly funded social services. The State shall endeavour, within the limits of its resources, to make available to all citizens' health, education, cultural and other social services.*

Accordingly the Ministry of Education is assigned the primary responsibility of identifying the priorities of the Education Sector both at national level and zoba level. It has to formulate the objectives and goals in transforming the country's educational scenario rapidly. It was no small task by itself. A fresh look has to be cast on the educational background of the bygone times as it had in store abundantly what one could describe as attacks of successive colonial rulers, beginning with the Italians of early nineteenth and twentieth centuries through British protectorate to Ethiopian rulers, who rendered the outcomes of their educational policies sub-servient to their governance.

The early Italian education of nineteenth century did not pave way for any progressive foundations of education in Eritrea. The Church and Mosque education of the past continued during the period of Italian administration too and at the most it produced pastors and clerics of non-conformist and orthodox churches. The Church education has of course provided for the spiritual means of individuals and to some extent proved to be a means of self-reliance. This apart, the Italians had established elementary schools some of which were Government and some of which were related to Church services. The Government Elementary Schools however had taught the children such topics as would make them eligible for the government service as clerks and as translators. Similarly the professional skills are acquired by means of transfer of know-how from person to person over generations and this process resulted in producing artisans and skilled labour for a variety of professional or native occupations. Looked from a modern angle of pedagogy and teaching methodology, there was neither an organized curriculum planning at any level nor was there any instruction based on scientific principles of learning. The whole Italian education did not go beyond elementary school and those who qualified through them (Church schools or Government schools) ended up either as pastors or clerics of the Orthodox Church or civil servants of the local administration.

Compared to the Italian legacy in education, the Britishers had done a little better in the sense they had extended the education up to the middle school and the extension was relatively better spread over entire Eritrea. But, whatever interest these little developments in education could arouse in the Eritreans was evaporated by the federation of Eritrea to Ethiopia which started imposing its cultural values on the Eritreams by implementing Amharic (a Semitic language with Geez alphabet: Geez is a language used in the Christian liturgy in orthodox church; Sem is son of Noah, a Biblical character) as medium of instruction upto the elementary school and a compulsory course upto high school.

Table–4
Macroeconomic Consequences of the War

	1993	*'94*	*'95*	*'96*	*'97*	*'93 -1997*	*'98*	*'99*	*2000*	*2001*	*'98-2001*
Income per capita*	NA	NA	180	200	220	200	207.6	191.7	173.8	175.0	187
Government Expenditure/GDP (%)	61.8	59.3	69.2	65.9	55.4	63.5	81.8	99.6	101.4	78.1	90.2
Government domestic debt (net)/GDP (%)	NA	NA	NA	NA	34.3	34.3	63.4	98.8	127.5	105.9	98.9
External public debt/GDP (%)	0.5	4.8	5.7	6.2	11.7	7.9	19.8	39.8	51.7	60.9	43.1
Private transfer/GDP (%)	40.5	56.7	37.6	38.9	54.6	43.7	34.7	36.9	32.2	26.5	32.6
Net donor support/GDP (%)	17.6	21.4	13.8	13.8	12.4	13.3	17.3	27.1	24.3	33.7	25.6

Source: IMF.
* World Bank Database, 2002.

Table–5
Comparative Aggregate Government Expenditure in Percent of GDP 1997-2001

	1993	*1998*	*1999*	*2000*	*2001*
Eritrea	61.8	81.8	99.6	101.4	78.1
Ethiopia	19.6	30.6	33.0	31.2	29.1
Uganda	18.6	19.0	20.5	21.1	19.6
Rwanda	23.9	18.9	19.7	18.9	21.4

Source: *World Bank Economic Country Reports.*
Note: World Bank Document No. 24448-ERI-A.
Courtesy: Eritrea Education and Training Sector.

It is pertinent to mention that the concern for languages and the medium of instruction is very high among Eritreans as Eritrea, as a country, is a culmination of composite culture of different races and languages and they look at the languages as their very cultural identity.

The high land Tigrinyans, for example, are culturally linked to Ethiopian Tigrinyans and both of them profess Coptic Christianity. (Coptic is an Egyptian language used in Christian liturgy till 16th century when they embraced Islam and made Arabic—a Semitic language their national language). The Southern stretch of the Coastal plain is occupied by the people called Afar, who are basically Muslims and speak in language called Afar, which is of Cushitic in origin. Similarly, the Western lowlands people speak Bidawet, a language which is spoken by the people on the Western border of Eritrea to Sudan. In all there are about nine languages spoken in the entire region of Eritrea by people belonging to various ethnic groups and communities. Most prominent them are Tigrigna and Tigre (spoken by the majority) and the other languages are Bilen, Bedawet, Afar, Kunama, Nara, Saho and Arabic. Some people still speak Italian in parts of Asmara and some speak Amharic of Ethiopia too. Given the complexity of these languages which are known as inter-related and falling under the group of Cushitic (Cush is son of Ham, who is a son of Noah) of Hamitic family of languages, the task of imparting education in their native languages in Eritrea has stood as an immense and colossal problem before the Ministry of Education.

Thus, it is very clear from the foregoing that however small the country is in its area and population, the heterogeneous topography climatic conditions, the various professions of the different communities, imbalances in the regional economic resources, cultural differences among different races and the variety of languages—the challenges it poses in its diversity to a Government are not small and all of them together render the task of decision making by the Ministry of Education and the Government of Eritrea highly difficult and complicated.

Yet the Ministry of Education has been trying to come to grips with the problems in the last one decade and to some extent has achieved a breakthrough undoubtedly. Ever since Independence the Eritrean Government had done a lot to improve the lot of Education System. In fact, during 1991-98, the Ministry has established a number of Elementary schools all over Eritrea (zoba-wise) with the nine native languages as the medium of instruction.

Unfortunately the war unleashed by Ethiopia in 1998 over a border dispute has caused a massive destruction of schools, besides bridges, villages and bungalows of Government and Private owners. The country's economy which has shown signs of improvement had taken a sudden nose dive (the GDP has plunged from 7 per cent to 3 per cent. See the Table-4—Macroeconomic Consequences of War) and thousands of people became refugees on their own land as a consequence of the war. The war came to an end by 2000 but the scars of the war have been too many and too hard to heal immediately. The impact of the 30 years of armed struggle could be overcome by the Eritrean Government by virtue of its hard work and dedication during 1991-98 during which time it has almost rebuilt and reconstructed the war torn economy and achieved a GDP of 7 per cent but the effects of ravage caused by the War of 1998-2000 are too hard to surmount and posed a formidable challenge to the Government of Eritrea.

As the things stood on 1999-2000, the Ministry of Education has taken a comprehensive view of the then scenario of education and has identified several gaping holes in the whole system. They are briefly presented here for a better understanding.

Access to education is not equitable over entire State and the efforts of over a decade barring the war period 1998-2000 has registered only a low level progress in general.

- The opportunity for higher education is also very low compared to the progress achieved at primary, middle and high school levels.
- The products of Education at any level are not qualitatively rich as to enter any professional careers.
- The existing system is giving a wide scope for wastage of resources including manpower resources.

The Ministry of Education having a close diagnostic look at these problems has then sat down in the exercise to reestablish and revamp the whole system to accelerate it as to meet the challenges of the rapidly changing world. After extensive deliberations over such a plan of recasting, with the President of the State presiding over in 1996, the Ministry has proposed the following principles of the reforms that would form the basis of the Government Policy Plan—*Rapid Transformation of the Eritrean Education System.* The principles enunciated therein are as follows:

- All wastage of manpower, resources, effort and the time must be dispensed forthwith.
- All avenues must be open to all age groups in order to help recognize and develop the latent potentials in them.
- Education must be made to meet the employment needs of the younger generations.
- The standards must be high enough as to enable them to compete with the global challenges.

Thus, the Government Policy document—*The Rapid Transformation of the Eritrean Education System*—has become a starting point of discussions for further reforms and refinements commensurate with the contemporary changes. It became a basis on which the modern education system of the country is going to establish itself. In other words, it is a foundation for many more educational developments that are going to come up in the future.

Constraints

Both the *Rapid Transformation of the Eritrean Education System (2002)* and the *National Educational Policy (2003),* outline the Government's ambitions to expand the present level of school education and establish new educational institutions at the Tertiary and Vocational level as to gear up the nation to meet the international standards in

Education. Towards achieving these ambitions the Government has identified the important areas where a lot of exercising of thinking, planning and manpower training besides mobilization of resources are required. They are:

- Expanding and improving the Comprehensive Early Childhood Care and Education as to allow a healthy process of child growth and to make it an integral part.
- Opening new primary (elementary) schools in those areas where schools are not either constructed or destroyed during war and to see that basic education for all is achieved by 2015 in line with the objectives of EFA.
- Opening of Middle schools and High schools further to see that the children educated in the elementary schools have continuity with next higher education (normal progression).
- Establishing specialized post-elementary, middle and high school vocational training centres to see that those who opt for a career after completing a particular level of education are imparted the skills related to the chosen career.
- To upgrade the existing Teacher Training Institutes to tertiary level institutes.
- To upgrade the present Business and Commerce college into a tertiary level institute.
- To establish 6 (six) new Universities of International Standards in 6 administrative zones in addition to completing the upcoming Dongollo Armed Forces College of Science and Technology as to facilitate the equitable access to those who complete their higher education.
- To increase the number of Junior Colleges to 13 (thirteen) by properly revamping and reshaping the existing Asmara Teacher Training Institute, Asmara Nursing and Medical Technology College, Asmara College of Business and Commerce, Pavonni Technical Institute, Hagaz Agricultural School.
- To start specialized elementary schools for the Gifted, the Disabled and for the Mentally Retarded.
- To found the Adults Craft Training and Primary Vocational Training Institutes to train the adults in vocational skills and handicrafts after their completion of elementary education.
- To establish Apprenticeship and Primary Vocational

Table–6
Eritrea: Education and Training Provision System

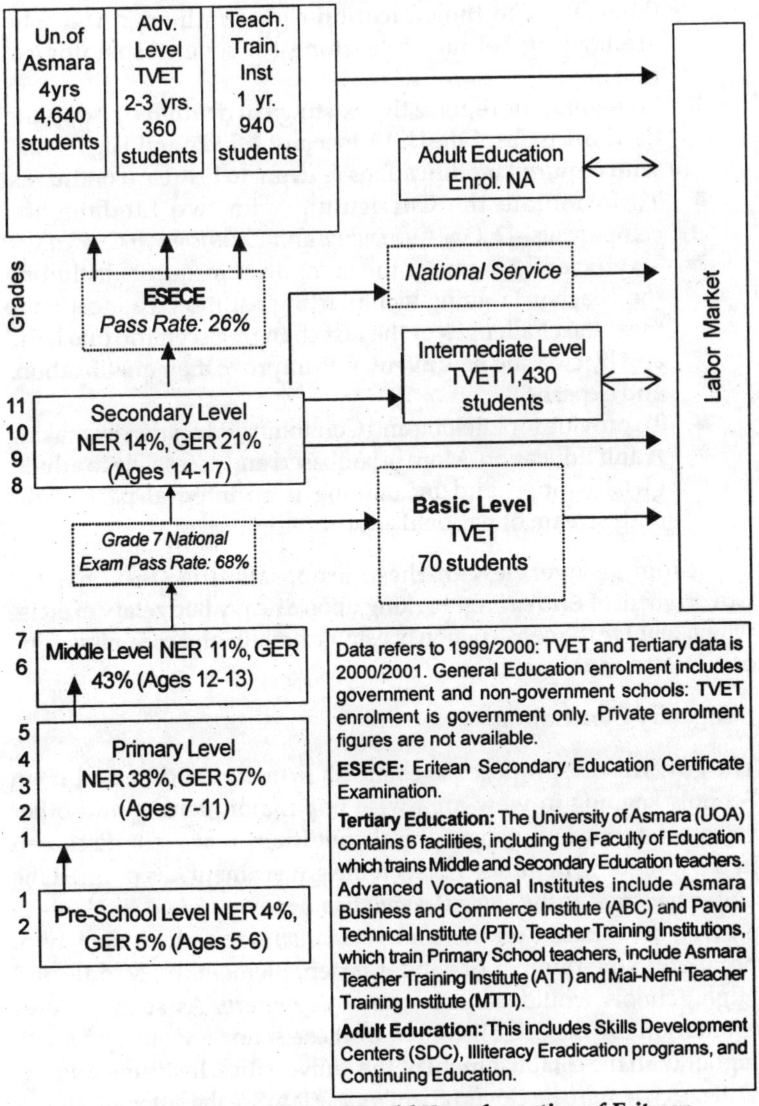

Scheme Evolved As Part of Rapid Transformation of Eritrean Educational System by MOE

Note: World Bank Document No. 24448-ERI-A.
Courtesy: Eritrea Education and Training Sector.

Training Institutes to enable the deprived and under-privileged children of the society who could not access themselves to the education right on the age and who are lagging behind in learning for several sociological reasons.

- To revamp or replace the existing curriculum by adapting the Curriculum of the US Elementary, Middle and High School with required modifications relevant to Eritrean conditions.
- To formulate the Curriculum with two fundamental components—1. *Core Curriculum* and 2. *Enrichment Curriculum.*
- To efficiently organize the manpower resources including the Teacher Training by imparting additional education to meet the challenges of the fast changing scenario one hand and by creating new avenues to improve their qualifications and expertise.
- To provide for Lifelong and Continuing Education by making Adult Education. More broadbased and accessible to adults, girls, women and by making it an integral part of the mainstream of national education.

From an overview of these proposals it is clear that the Government of Eritrea is embarking upon a heavy budgetary exercise which involve the construction of establishments and commissioning of infrastructural facilities.

Budgetary Constraints

The government proposes to establish Primary, Middle and High Schools keeping in view-area wise population density and other socio-economic and geographical conditions that were discussed in the foregoing in mind. As such the government has defined the *Unit population* as the *student population* per every 5,000 residents in a given area. Based on the *Unit population,* for a given density of population the number of Kindergarten, Elementary, Middle and High Schools would be uniforms everywhere. As such the cost estimation for the establishment of these schools would be much higher than the establishment of the Universities, Institutes and the Colleges wherein the Government's view is to see the latter are almost self-supportive right from their inception.

With a low per capita income beset with post-war devastation and serial drought over last three years, the country's economy is far from meeting the budgetary requirements of the establishment of above educational institutions and reforms.

However, since Independence, the financial constraints notwithstanding, the Eritrean Government has shown continuous upward growth in the Education sector in terms of its increase in the Gross Enrollment Ratio as also the number of Elementary and Secondary Schools.

A comparison of 1991/92 and 2001/02 academic year reveals that GER for elementary school has almost doubled from 36.3 per cent to 61 per cent; middle and secondary school GER has more than doubled from 20.1 to 44.6 per cent; and from 12.2 to 23.7 per cent respectively whereas the NER has increased from 22.4 to 42.7 per cent (Elementary), 7.0 to 12.3 per cent (Middle) and 8.4.to 14.1 per cent (Secondary) respectively.

Consequently, the number of Elementary and Middle Schools increased from 273 in 1991/92 to 747 in 2001/02 (174%). Similarly the number of Secondary Schools increased from 19 in 1991/92 to 44 in 2001/02 (132%). Moreover, the number of Technical Schools increased from 1 to 1991/92 to 10 in 2001/02 (900%). As a result the number of teachers also increased considerably from 4,504 in 1991/90 to 10,456 in the year 2001/02 (132%).

Despite all these, only 40 per cent of the school age children in Eritrea have privilege to Primary or Elementary education, 10.5 per cent have to Middle level and 13.6 per cent have to Secondary level education which only suggest that the current line of thinking of the Ministry of Education as outlined in its two important policy papers is the step in the right direction.

According to the estimates of the World Bank Document, in order for Eritrea to achieve Education For All (EFA) by 2015, all 7 years old (1,49,000) should be enrolled in the 2010 and must complete their Primary Schools by 2015/2016. Assuming that there is no more than 10 per cent inefficiency, the large over-aged children would move through the system. Compared to 1999, additional 73,000 places or 1,650 classrooms would be needed by 2010 with a teacher-student ratio being around 42.

In that case compared to 1999, around 12,000 additional primary teachers would be needed by 2015 as against the current 6,230 teachers. If the Primary or Elementary cycle would be brought more in line with the international practice by covering 5-6 year-old age groups, an additional 3,27,000 places would be needed by 2015. Compared to the situation in 2010, capacity of Grade I or Class I would have to be increased by 16 per cent in 2015. Expanding Primary or Elementary school provision to accommodate a 100 per cent Net Enrollment Ratio in all grades by 2015, the school system will have to grow roughly 165 per cent of its 1999 capacity. This is based on the assumption that there is only 10 per cent repetition rate among the grades and on over-aged students.

Table–7

Distribution of Government and Non-Government Schools by Region and Level of Schooling, 1999

Region	*Primary*			*Middle*			*Secondary*		
	Number of schools	*Govt.*	*Non-Govt.*	*Number of schools*	*Govt.*	*Non-Govt.*	*Number of schools*	*Govt.*	*Non-Govt.*
Anseba	107	69%	31%	18%	72%	28%	5%	80%	20%
Deb/Keih-Bahri	24	92%	8%	2	100%	0%	1	100%	0%
Debub	200	88%	13%	42%	83%	17%	8%	88%	13%
Gash-Barka	132	89%	11%	20%	100%	0%	4%	100%	0%
Maekel	112	81%	19%	34%	74%	26%	16%	81%	19%
Sem-Keih-Bahri	80	96%	4%	15	93%	7%	4	100%	0%

Source: Eritrea: Basic Education Statistics, 1999/2000.

Table–8

Eritrea: Students, Teachers and Schools by Level

	7 year-old estrants into grade 1	*Primary (NER)*	*Middle (NER)*	*Secon-dary (NER)*	*TVET**	*UN of Asmara**
Students	28,230	295,940 (38%)	74,320 (11%)	59,630 (14%)	1,860	4,640
Teachers		6,230	1,310	1,050	–	230
Schools		655	131	38	11	NA

* TEVT, UOA information is from 2000.

Source: Eritrea, Basic Education Statistics, 1999/2000.

Note: World Bank Document No. 24448-ERI-A.

Courtesy: Eritrea Education and Training Sector.

The Government's efforts to systematize and rationalize the education right from the grassroots is obvious and apparent when it has considered to establish more number schools that impart the Early Childhood Care and Education (ECCE) to the children of the age group 4 to 5 years and contribute to a healthy intellectual growth from that age itself.

As of now, according to an estimate of the Ministry of Education, there are about 91 Pre-Primary Schools in the entire country of which 5 are run by the Government and the rest belong to the NGOs. Even those are not equitably accessible to the children of all areas. The usual pattern of inequitable access reflects itself here too. Most of these schools are located in the Maekel zone while one school exists for the entire South Red Sea zone.

To counter this situation, the Government has been opening many KG schools and rural children's centres. Further, ECCE procedural Guidelines have also been developed. The initial in-service training for Kindergarten teachers and Community Care Teachers has been offered to increase the quality and relevance of the Teaching at the ECCE level. But whatever is done in this regard, according to Government's own appraisal and assessment, is far behind what is desired and as an effort to remedy this it proposes to establish the KG schools all over the country soon to offer a qualitative education.

The Eritrean Government has to some extent been receiving the aid for this programme under the Integrated Early Childhood Development Project (ICCDP) as an IDA credit of US $ 49 million of which US $ 13.6 million is earmarked for Pre-School Education. Under this project, 105 Kindergarten schools would be established in rural areas to improve the access to the Pre-School education, about 315 teachers, 735 assistants, 105 directors and 250 community caretakers would be given the training besides, learning materials, enhanced teaching materials, aids, supplies etc. This would enable the teachers to adapt the ECE programmes to their own local situations, introduce innovations and develop their own supplementary learning materials and aids.

The project also offers expertise in promoting good health and sanitation in 30 per cent rural Primary schools and Pre-school centres by establishing deep pit latrines and garbage disposal areas in each school and centre. The project further offers knowhow in building the institutional capacity for management and supervision of early childhood care and education. This positively enables a high enrollment rate at Primary level and discourages further dropouts or repetition rates in the vertical ascent on the ladder of education.

Another sagging phenomenon that is badly effecting the Government's efforts to achieve EFA by 2015 is the Education of Girls. It is a depressive scenario in more than one sense. Firstly, the country's orthodox traditions and ancient values of the family systems are a major stumbling block for the progress of the girl education. Secondly, the gender discrimination in favour of male sex contributed another major hindrance.

However, the EPLF government both during the freedom struggle and afterwards, made substantial efforts to bring the girls from the stranglehold of the traditions. As a result, a substantial improvement has been made in educating girls, the gender parity index being low notwithstanding.

The enrollment of girls has grown to 192,871 in 2000-01 compared to 96,272 of 1991-92 (100% increase). At the elementary level, the gross enrollment rate for girls rose from 33.8 to 55.5 per cent while that for boys increased from 38.7 to 61.2 per cent in the past decade (1991-92 to 2001-02). Gender disparity is more pronounced at the middle and secondary school levels. The gross enrollment for girls and boys for the middle school level rose from 20.3 to 41.5 per cent (girls) and 19.9 to 45.1 per cent respectively for the same period. Similarly for the Secondary Schools level girls enrollment rose from 12.1 to 16.9 per cent and that of boys rose from 12.2 to 27.2 per cent during the same period.

The gender disparity is more accentuated and uneven region-wise and varies vastly from region to region depending on the topographical and livelihood conditions, which have been, mentioned in the introduction itself as of sociological consequence. The girls' enrollment in the low lands areas suffer from low rate compared to the high lands. Poverty and the compulsions of the lower income groups have almost made it a mandate for the girls to take up domestic and agricultural chores by discontinuing education. This has put the Eritrean Government to find out immediate remedies and strategies to bring out the girl education from the clutches of these traditional boundaries in order to achieve the objectives of the EFA and Millenium Development Goals by 2015.

With regard to the Technical and Vocational Education and Training, there has been a single technical school as on the day of Independence. But in the last one decade the Government has established about nine more technical schools and a college of Commerce. In addition to 4-skill development centres have been established in various parts of the country where many adults, youngsters and dropouts have been trained in the various trades. In TVET sub-sector, efforts have been made to enroll the women and disadvantaged groups in technical and agricultural education and training. A quota of 30 per cent has always been allocated to ensure girls' participation.

The strategies for TVET development in the next phase include the establishment of Vocational Training Schools at three level as mentioned before, at each stage of Education such as Primary, Middle and Secondary, upgrade the status of the existing TVET centres, provide the relevant training to the learners' needs that are congruent to the national priorities and establish inter-sectorial co-ordination on the identification and provision of vocational training opportunities. This certainly calls for a lot of funding and recruiting qualified training professionals. Most of the donor funding goes to the TVET education.

The Government wants to make the TVET education a multi-track system as mentioned above, and at the centre of it lies its proposed Colleges of Further Education and Training (CFET) which would be offering training to the skilled human resources, consolidate the transition from school to work and provide the opportunities for continuous learning. In respect of gender parity in TVET only 19 per cent enrollment constitute women. The remote regions and young girls from the poorest households have not been at all represented to the desired level though these are indeed meant for those under privileged only.

Asmara holds the only two advanced level institutions and 37 per cent of total Intermediate level enrollment for the year 1999-2000. Asmara Technical School has the highest number of enrollment and trades offered. Similarly the Asmara Business and Commerce Institute which began in 1997 with 97 students has swollen to its full capacity by 2000. The Skill Development Centres (SDCs) operated by the Ministry of Education have enrollment risen from a modest of 71 in 1994 to 944 in 1996 and then declined to 208 in 1999. After the war there has not been a substantial improvement in rebuilding these SDCs. Even their efficacy in terms of providing wider employment opportunities has become dubious. The SDCs mostly offer a non-formal type of training, lasting from 6-9 months, without having any regard to the basic educational requirements. The Ministries too offer courses like Tailoring and embroidery through these SDCs and could only generate little interest and enthusiasm in the rural centres. But the SDCs are likely to continue in terms of the revised policy of the Government to establish them in the geographical areas wherein access to the other Technical and Vocational Education is more pointed.

However, a tracer study conducted by Atchoarena and Tekie (1997) has found that most of the trained work force under the TVETs and SDCs could be absorbed in the labor market immediately. It is a very encouraging sign to the Government's efforts. The TVET school graduates have been found to have relatively better absorption into the market (90%) compared to the graduates of SDCs (49%). Formal training presently is offered by the MOE at Basic, Intermediate and Advanced levels. Basic Training is currently being conducted by the Hagaz Agricultural School offering a 2-year Programme. Grade 7 is the pre-requisite for the admission into the school. Intermediate level begins after completion of grade 9. Programmes are three years in length. Advanced level accepts those who have completed grade 11. The courses are of 2 to 3 years duration. Of all the courses offered, by the other Ministries at the Basic level, the highest number of admissions is found in respect of Soil Conservation, Seed and Water, followed by the Typing and Computer applications, under the Ministry of Agriculture. Further courses like Animal Husbandry and other conservation programmes have found interest with the students under the same Ministry. In line with this the Government has evolved a strategy for the next Five Years during which the establishment Five Intermediate Technical and Vocational Schools and Seven Technical and Vocational Colleges is being planned.

This apart the Government is determined to raise the enrollment at the Post-Middle School level from 1700 to 6000, besides increasing the enrollment at Post-Secondary School level from 260 to 3000. The

Government also proposes to upgrade the 4 existing technical and vocational schools to college level. This is likely to be further strengthened when similar training is offered at the tertiary level (the University level) as part of the enrichment curriculum.

Approximately 12 or 13 areas have been identified as optional courses at higher secondary level (9th grade to 12th grade) which would add upto the expertise to be acquired. They include Agriculture Science and Technology Education, Business and Economics Education, Health Science and Technology, Mechanical Technology Education, Electrical Technology Education, Construction Technology Education, Industrial Technology Education, Home Economics Education, Information Technology Education, Environmental Science Education, Performing Arts Education, Visual Arts and Design Education and Physical Education. The Government has this year appointed a number of committees comprising Indian Expatriate Professors to hammer out the state of the art of these institutions which would come up in due course at various places in the State of Eritrea.

The Government's efforts to generate skilled force at all levels are perfectly in tune with the aspirations of the Society by and large. They are not only realistic but also commensurate with the market potential to absorb skilled force generated by bringing the above mentioned strategies and institutions in to play. It is true that there is a tremendous potential for better employment opportunities in Eritrea. Both the trade unions and the employers often emphasize that there is a lot of dearth for the skilled force at various levels in various trades.

It is estimated that 50,000-65,000 salaried employment will open up in the next one to two years. In the public sector 23,000 opportunities exist which need the specific qualifications to discharge the described job duties. In the private sector, there are innumerable jobs in the fields of Manufacturing, Trade, Service Sector, Construction, Agriculture and Fisheries. All these sectors have the potential to generate employment in tens of thousands in the next few years to come.

The Industrial Human Resource Development in the State of Eritrea of November 2000, states that 41 per cent of the enterprises surveyed (both small and large) needed more employees in the coming five years. When these survey statistics are extrapolated to the entire sector of the enterprises, the requirement that emerges out of the data would be in the range of 5,200 additional employees. Out of these opportunities, about 59 per cent relate to Technical cadre, 5 per cent to Ministerial cadre, 4.4. per cent constitute professional and Managerial cadre. The approximate projections of the requirement of the technical personnel in the next five years thus stands as: 19.5 per cent mechanist/metal, 12.4 per cent electrical/electronics, 12.3 per cent auto-mechanics, 7.8 per cent in wood works and other types of technicians come around 42.6 per cent.

At present the projected openings in the skilled and semi-skilled employment market and the admission rates in the various technical schools, other than those which the Government has planned now as part of I-PRSP and RTEES and is going to execute shortly as outlined above, are not compatible. The IDA has given a credit of 60 million US dollar through the World Bank in May 2002 to assist the Government of Eritrea to mobilize the soldiers under the project head Demobilization and Rehabilitation Programme (DRP). The programme is to be implemented during the years of 2002 and 2003. Though the programme began a little late, it is likely to reach its targets by the end of 2004. For Education and Training, the IDA Credit is under consideration and the MOE is optimistic to have it before the current IDA Credit for the DRP exhausts. However, about 2,00,000 soldiers will be entering the market through these educational programmes as skilled labour force in the next two years. The establishment of the Eritrean Institute of Technology, Maynofhi is a step in the right direction in realizing the above goals by the Government of Eritrea and the Ministry of Education.

On an average the expenditure of the Government as a percentage of the GDP on Education annually is 4 per cent in 1993 and has grown to 5 per cent between 1998-2000. The MOE's total spending on Education and Training during 2000 is about 26.8 million US dollars of which 8.3 million USD was spent on the Capital. Donor support for pre-tertiary education and training amounted to 85 per cent of the capital and 26 per cent of over all spending. The inequitable access to education and training as could be gauged from the above is a prognostic reflection of the Government's spending on the different levels of education in different degrees of measure. There are several reasons to it. Firstly, the Government dependence on Donor support, which sometimes selectively does funding to certain priority areas of the receptor country. As such the World Bank Document pointed out the need to harmonize the Donor coordination in bringing about the equitable distribution of the funds.

For instance the spending on the pupil at the tertiary level was the equivalent to 1,100 USD in 1999 (five times of the GDP per capita) and in TVET US dollar 880 compared to spending on basic and general secondary education of a pupil which is 55 dollar. It resulted in the paradox of helping the students from the economically rich families reach the University level and the poor ending up as dropouts.

Added to the above complications, the challenges with infrastructure and physical conditions of facilities create inequity in the education services provided. Roads in many areas outside the urban centre are non-existent. This has been a major stumbling block for the officials of the Education Ministry to keep their contacts with the Schools at the Zoba and rural level to the barest minimum. Except Asmara, the Capital of Eritrea, where the Telecommunications and Internet operate allowing an enhanced communication between the officials of the Ministry and the Schools, all other centres of Zoba and rural segments pose greater hurdles for smooth official transactions.

Lack of transportation is also a major problem. Children in rural areas have difficulties travelling long distances to reach their schools, which in fact contributed to absenteeism to a greater extent. Some schools are overcrowded with ever expanding population on the contrary. Lack of amenities like electricity, and drinking water and adequate sanitation plague majority of the schools in the rural centres. Many school buildings and classrooms are in need of substantial repair. The furniture in most schools is in need of repair. In some schools the students sitting per bench had been more than three against two and in some cases the students sitting on the benches are not compatible to sizes of the benches. There are about 100 schools still, which are running under the shades of the trees. All these make the Government of Eritrea to compete with its own priorities and for donor support.

The Ministry of Education does not count on the Private Sector for a major financial investment in the Sector of School Education or in the Technical Education for it believes that the Private Sector at present is not strongly founded and highly disorganized. Further, it believes that it cannot cope with the pace with which the reforms and new strategies are to be implemented. However, the Ministry of Education is toying with the idea of bringing in a comprehensive piece of legislation in Education and it includes establishment of the educational institutions in the private sector. It also would like to allow partnerships.

As such the external funding including donor support and funds from Diaspora keep playing a pivotal role in the rehabilitation and reconstruction programme of the Government of Eritrea. There were several donors with widely varying commitments in 2000. The majority of the funding came from 10 donors (see the list in the tables Donor and Diaspora Funds to MOE) and 73 per cent of commitments came from only 5 donors. DANIDA (a Danish Fund) is the single largest donor accounted for one-third of total external funding for the year 2000. External Donor funding of basic and secondary education is mainly used for capital spending. The World Bank is the main coordinator.

Since 1993, the public spending on education in Eritrea has risen dramatically. Basic and secondary education spending more than doubled between 1993 and 2000 which means an increase of 12 per cent on an average. With the recurrent budget being more than double during this period, the capital budget increased four times. Spending on basic and secondary education increased by 148 per cent over this period, which amounts to an increase of 18 per cent almost every year. The total public education and training expenditure as a per cent of GDP rose from 2.2 per cent, in 1993 to 4.9 per cent, in 2000 which means an average increase of 3.9 per cent. Spending on basic and secondary education increased from 2.0 to 4.3 per cent of GDP on an average 3.4. per cent annual increase of GDP. Recurrent expenditure in basic and secondary education also increased from 1.5 to 2.7 per cent of GDP. A huge amount of 72 per cent of total and recurrent spending on education was allocated to general education in 1999 of which a major chunk of 61 per cent goes to primary education, followed by 14 per cent to secondary education.

As such the above allocations in terms of GDP and otherwise suggest that the Primary Education has been fairly funded as a priority area by the Government and the MOE though it has led to an imbalance in the other two sectors namely middle and secondary education. But obvious concern of the Government is to realize the Universal Elementary Education and to get to the status of the *Fast Track* nations of the Wold Bank.

Though the Government achieved a great success in registering or enrolling a large number of students at the Primary level as reflected in the GER as 57 per cent, the NER has however dwindled to 37 per cent at the end of the efforts. This has made the Government to go into the intricacies of the working of the system which has thrown open several loopholes embedded in it so that the MOE could study and analyze them. As a result of this, it could clearly understand that there is a lot of wastage of human resources both on the students (dropouts and repeaters) and on the faculty side (poor expertise of faculty). This resulted in quickly going in for an *Interim–Poverty Reduction Strategy Paper* that is to be read with the Concept paper of *the Rapid Transformation of the Eritrean Educational System*. Both these papers reflect the Government's determination to do away with the inequitable access and distribution in the education system.

Against this the Government of Eritrea is considering to discourage or even dispense with the detention system to avoid repetition in the schools. As a result homogeneity of the classroom becomes possible, besides giving scope for enough space in primary schools. Therefore, the Government of Eritrea and the MOE together are planning for a dynamic and sustainable strategy for financing improvements in Education which would reduce the budgetary gap, likely to build-up by 2010, from 37 million US dollars to 23 million US dollar per year. To meet this challenging financial support the government has to make 16 per cent its GDP allocation per annum to Education as against the present allocation 5 per cent of the GDP in which case the Government has to register higher production and growth rates on all the fronts.

Academic Constraints

After the liberation of the country in 1993, the Government of Eritrea has an occasion to take a fresh look at the academic side of the country's education system precisely in terms of school hours and school working days, classroom student-teacher ratio, the age of admission into different levels of the schools and, the problem of repeaters and the over age of the students affecting the homogeneity of the classroom, teacher's teaching hours and counselling timings, teaching aids and teaching materials, low quality of teaching methods and the teachers' training, prescribing textbooks relevant to the Eritrean conditions, adopting suitable curriculum with relevance to the Eritrean sociological conditions and ensuring the continuity of education which is called as the *Normal Progression* by the Ministry in its document of National Policy of Education.

This has been necessitated by two important reasons. Firstly, the Ethiopian imperialistic education has successively destroyed and dismantled the education system, besides disintegrating its social, economic and cultural values, whatever little the early colonizers, the Italians and the Britishers had developed prior to 1950s. Secondly, the need to formulate a new system of Education in the changed context keeping in view the future aspirations of its young generations, who at the time of independence and as on today continue to be about 60 per cent of the nation's population, in tune with the country's requirements is an inescapable, concomitant and an indispensable eventuality.

The new formal system has refined the admission age for various levels, besides reorganizing the earlier levels in the school education. As a result, the admission age for the two years of pre-school is fixed as 4 and 5 years, while the age for Primary Education is 6-10 years, followed by the age for Middle School Education as 11-13 years. The admission age for four years Secondary School Education is fixed as 14 to 17 years. The formal school education offers a lot of versatility and plasticity for the students to have both the opportunities to go for both Vocational and Technical Education as also continue their education in the vertical line. Enough planning is done to provide education to dropouts and adults through non-formal and continuing life long education programmes, about which the present research is likely to be a state of the art one, as to make them join the mainstream at some point up or down, depending on the achievement level of the student.

The school system runs from mid-September to the end of June. In the highlands, the school year is 206 days while in the low lands it is 197 days. The Primary and the Middle School are considered in the new revised system as the Basic Education. As the Government proposes to introduce 12th grade, the revised system includes classes 1 to 5, as Primary, 6, 7 and 8 as Middle School, 9, 10, 11 and 12 and as Higher Secondary School.

Students in classes 1 and 2 would have 25 periods of instruction per week while classes 3, 4 and 5 receive 35 periods per week (620-868 hours per year). Schools in highlands receive 674 hours of instruction in classes 1 and 2 and 943 hours of instruction in classes 3, 4 and 5. For Secondary schools, the instruction classes are held about 868 hours per year. According to OECD, the average classroom instruction per year should be around 900-1000 hours for primary level and 1000-1200 per secondary level. It means increasing the workload of the teachers in a way.

But the present workload of the teachers is one force to reckon with that in decelerating the Government's efforts to implement new curriculum reforms. Today the weekly average teaching workload is 32.4 periods per week for elementary education, 32.1 for middle school and 30.1 for the secondary schools. Compared to the Primary, Middle and Secondary Schools teachers have a maximum workload with a necessity to handle more than 6 to 10 sections in the same school. This is in addition to preparing lesson plans and teaching notes. The double shift system has been one of the factors that affected the quality of education in an unprecedented manner.

The classroom size is a mind boggling perennial and perpetual problem in the last one decade of Eritrean Education System. Both repeaters and freshers together render the classroom size a prohibitive one beyond the teacher's control, besides affecting the homogeneous composition that the classroom required to be. The classroom size thus presently is as high as 50.5 at primary level, 60.9 at middle level and 62.2 at secondary level. In addition to this the student population in schools is ever increasing and sometimes touching the sky high with some schools registering students upto 6000 which means doubling, or trebling of enrollment than what the school capacity is originally intended to. In certain schools where a single teacher is present the situation is even worse with the teacher and students ratio being in the range of 1:90. These situations often lead to chaotic and riotous situation in the classroom causing serious obstruction to the classroom transactions.

Another terrible problem that the Government of Eritrea is seriously confronted with is the continuity of the repeaters. Around 18 per cent repeaters exist per each grade and 10 to 14 per cent dropouts are regular phenomenon per each grade. About 50 per cent of eligible primary children do not enter the middle school and probably fall back to functional illiteracy. More than half of the students in any given grade is over aged. For grade 1, the official entrance age till some time back was 7 (now in the revised policy it is 5 years). However, the majority of grade 1 students are over aged. In 1999 about 65 per cent students of grade 1 are over aged. In grade 5, 83 per cent of the enrolled students were overaged, in grade 9 about 56 per cent are over aged and in grade 11 about 70 per cent students are over aged. Even zoba, wise there are differences in the completion of cycles. For instance in some places like central high lands, on an average a primary cycle is completed in 9 years whereas in certain zobas of low lands the same primary cycle is completed in 16 years.

Further, the teacher support materials are few to none Science laboratories are almost non-existent in many schools. Where science laboratories exist there are no equipment, water, gas and electricity. School libraries found in some places are not having latest books and the urgent need for new books is not yet met with.

The present curriculum, as already described in the foreground, is not quite relevant to the contemporary needs of the Eritrea. It was one time of Ethiopian origin. After independence, but for the superficial changes, there was no major change in the curriculum keeping in mind the future needs of the country. Now that the Government of Eritrea has decided to revise and update the curriculum on par with international standards, preferably by adopting the syllabus of the US and other African countries based on the relevance, the curriculum is mainly divided into core content and enrich content which would together see to imparting both knowledge and skill related to the students' chosen area.

The teachers' efficiency and the teacher training are two important sides of the problem affecting the educational standards of the Eritrean Education system. Initially there was a dearth of trained teachers. Subsequently the Teacher Training Institutes used to train the students who could not make to Eritrean Secondary School Certificate Examination as Primary Teachers. However, this in practice could not prove to be very effective at the ground level. In short it could not generate the required motivation level to the students who as a result preferred to drop though this alone could not be described the sole reason for dropouts. But poor quality of training and teaching at Primary, Middle and Secondary levels is one compelling strong reason for high rate of dropout perceived. As a step in the right direction, the Ministry of Education, under the inspiring leadership of the Minister of the State, H.E. Mr. Osman Saleh, issued the guidelines to indicate the shift required in teaching from the teacher-centred method to student-centred method (Guidelines on learner centered and interactive pedagogy in the national curriculum, November 2003).

This apart the Government has embarked upon the project, under DANIDA aid, of revamping the existing curriculum as to make it more meaningful and relevant. A contingent of Indian Professors appointed as the committee members of the various curricular committee groups is engaged in the gigantic task of finalizing the curriculum of the school subjects on the lines the State has mandated them.

While the Government has to handle all these enormous problems, there are problems, which could be addressed by it by simple administrative mechanism. It is clear from the above, that the government has a major problem of finding enough finance to bring all the changes it intended to bring about. Secondly by evolving internal strategies, it would like to mobilize resources. These strategies include: *(i)* an increase in Government's expenditure on an average by 21 per cent by the end of next five years, *(ii)* introducing cost sharing and/or cost recovery/taxation schemes, *(iii)* create coordinated partnerships with development partners, *(iv)* strengthen decentralization, *(v)* encourage private sector investment on schools, *(vi)* establish an Educational Act, and *(vii)* empower the community to develop responsibility in financing education.

At the end of all, the Government has to plan for the plugging of the gap that would occur by 2005 from US 48 million dollars to US 74 million dollars by 2020. This implies an average annual gap of 37 million US dollars. An increase in the share of the government budge to education, as stated above, may cut down the gap to 19 million US dollars annually. It means the Government has to increase its spending on education as a share of its public expenditure of GDP from the current 3 per cent to 6, 7 and 8 respectively by 2005, 2008 and 2010. Further by 15 per cent by the end of 2015 to meet the objectives of EFA.

Administrative Constraints

There are many gray areas which the Government took cognizance in the process of coming to grips over the current situation of Education in the country. Firstly, it has not yet promulgated a comprehensive piece of Legislation to bring all the Educational Institutions, Private and Public, under one umbrella. Secondly, the participation of line Ministries and other Departments is not in order and coherent. Thirdly, the administration of the school system from the Ministry down to remote rural areas has become too wielding and large. As such the school administration all over the country has been running without proper inspection. This itself is one major cause of poor standards of education in many places of the State.

The school administration from the Centre to Zobas is to be properly streamlined with proper decentralization and accountability of standards and resources. The involvement of Private Sector at all levels must be enhanced with the government investing the funds in that sector to some other priority sector. This needs a comprehensive vision and planning for the next one decade when the Government is occupied with the idea of embracing the objectives of Education For All.

The TVET is also not having any independent Technical Directorate. It is also working under the operative control of the Ministry of Education. In other words, the Ministry is shouldering omnibus responsibilities, which some time fail it to devote the proper attention to any priority sector in the times of need. This may lead to sectorial failures with the want of proper communication, advice and strategies. It is also under the planning of the government to have a planned annual budget both for recurrent and non-recurrent heads contrary to the ad hoc system of finance planning. It means there would be transparency in the expenditure and total accountability to the approved budget heads. The Government of Eritrea and the Ministry of Education, both have taken note of this situation in the World Bank document. It also clearly understood the import of the World Bank observation with regard to lack of coordination between the donors and the funding priorities of the policy papers of the MOE. Further, the communication gap is accentuated by the improper articulation between the various Ministries especially the Ministry of Finance.

The options in the curriculum are to be enhanced if the Government intends to adopt the US curriculum pattern. The curricular subjects at the basic level should be optional if the government intends to bring the dropout rate to low level and also ensure to bring the dropouts back to the stream of education. Presently the option is available from the point of 9th grade itself and that too limited to two options only.

To make the students of basic education level to study all the subjects, irrespective of their attitudes and aptitudes, is not going to make it really a US system of education. Nor does it contribute to high motivation levels. Particularly options with regard to Maths, Science and Social subjects at basic level should be inevitable and these should be substituted by either vocation skills relevant to Eritrean conditions or for future prospects of the students in meeting their aesthetic and moral aspirations.

The decision of the government with regard to the detention system is very much awaited. The detention system has contributed to enormous wastage of time, money and human resources. Soon an administrative decision has to do away with it.

The urgent need to train thousands of teachers in the shortest possible term as to meet the ever-expanding sectorial demands is possible in part by the right administrative decision.

Apart from establishing a number of Teacher Training Institutions, there are alternative means by which the government can offer training to the teachers in various methods as to meet the country's requirements and enrich them further in their expertise and it is to this the present article is going to veer round in the subsequent chapters as a matter of one of the priorities.

The Government has made a number of policy decisions regarding all those mentioned earlier in all its three important documents, namely: *The Rapid Transformation of the Eritrean*

Educational System (July 2002), National Education Policy (February 2003), Interim-Poverty Reduction Strategy Paper (I-PRSP, June 2003). These decisions are being translated into action. Further, it has taken in to its view a full picture of the fact analyzed by the *World Bank* in its report on *Eritrea-Education and Training Sector Note* (24448-ERI).

The essence of all the three documents is to place emphasis on the equity and access in combination with the quality and relevance. The implementation of new vision of the Ministry of Education is invariably linked with the above 4 watchwords. The expansion programmes, whatever are going to be launched in the basic, higher secondary and TVET sectors in the next five years, are being planned keeping in mind the dropout and repetition rates in mind along with the low enrollment rates region-wise with respect to boys and girls (gender parity). Until unless this is achieved, the country cannot meet the objectives of Education for All and Millenium Development Goals. Hence, the Government of Eritrea and the Ministry of Education in the recent meeting held with the donor countries on December 15, 2003 have come up with a presentation of a model that offers equitable and balanced distribution of funding for all levels of education covering the whole gamut of population, boys, girls, adults--men and women (Education Sector Development Programme—ESDP).

Furthermore, in all these documents it would be clear that the Government wanted to achieve its objectives by giving priority to Adult Literacy and non-formal, continuing and lifelong education. To become a knowledge society and to bridge the growing gap between the world countries and Eritrea, the planning of Adult and non-formal Education is going to hold key and is likely to play a more pivotal role both as an independent institution and as a complementary to the efforts that the Government wants to make as outlined above.

Education For All—A Fast Track

The Education For All—is a commitment of all the nations in the world. It is a dream to be translated into action by Third World countries especially. It is linked to the economic prosperity of individual nations. It is by itself both a means and ends in providing sustainable alternative to eradicate poverty the majority of the third world nations are confronted with. Against this realization, about

164 countries have affirmed at Dakar in April 2000 their determination to fight out the illiteracy and poverty by 2015. This has been called the Dakar Framework of Action.

According to this, all countries must achieve and implement the following on a priority basis.

1. Expand early childhood care and education.
2. Free and compulsory education of good quality by 2015.
3. Promote the acquisition of life-skills by adolescents and youth.
4. Expand adult literacy to 50 per cent by 2015.
5. Eliminate gender disparity by 2005 and achieve gender equality in education by 2015.
6. Enhance educational quality.

It has set three major deadlines:

1. 2002: finalizing national action plan,
2. 2005: Ensuring equality for boys and girls, and
3. 2015: Achieving Education for All.

Though achieving these goals by themselves is not a simpler task for any country, a good number of African, Latin American and Caribbean countries, besides Asian nations, have approached this idea by almost all means at their disposal. However, some of the countries mentioned among the continents above are not basically rich enough to reach out to the people in such a measure as to meet the goals set by the Dakar Framework of Action. Their sources of income are not commensurate with the funding required to achieve these objectives. In view of this, the World Bank, to accelerate the process, has gone into the exercise of providing donor funding to those countries which would like to hasten the process of eradicating illiteracy from their countries.

Devised as a new development package for rapid spread of education, the World Bank has coined the word—the Fast Track Initiative and under the FTI, it (the World Bank) arranges the donor financing for the countries which wanted to embrace the above initiative.

The governments must qualify to this funding by ensuring a plan of action at their national level ensuring every child complete

Table–9
Educational Enrollment Trends 1980-96

		Primary		*Secondary*		*Tertiary*	
		M	*F*	*M*	*F*	*M*	*F*
All developing countries	1980	103.5	85.5	41.8	28.2	6.7	3.7
Gross enrollment ratio	1990	195.2	91.3	48.2	36.1	8.5	5.7
	1996	105.8	93.8	55.1	45.3	11.1	8.1
Growth over period %	1980-96	2.2	9.7	31.8	60.6	65.7	118.9
Sub-Saharan Africa							
Gross enrolment ratio	1980	87.4	68.9	21.8	12.5	2.6	0.7
	1990	79.5	65.9	24.7	18.6	4.1	1.9
	1996	81.3	67.2	27.9	22.4	4.7	1.5
Growth over period %	1980-96	-7.0	-2.5	28.0	79.2	80.8	257.1
South Asia							
Gross enrollment ratio	1980	90.4	60.0	36.3	18.2	6.2	2.3
	1990	102.4	76.8	49.4	29.9	7.4	3.7
	1996	105.8	83.0	53.4	36.0	8.6	4.9
Growth over period %	1980-96	17.0	38.3	47.1	97.8	38.7	113.0

Source: *UNESCO Statistical Yearbook/Annuaire Statistique/Annario estadistico 1998, Paris/Lanham, Mayland, UNESCO Publishing/Bernan Press.*

Courtesy: World Education Forum: Thematic Studies, UNESCO, 2000.

the primary education without fail. They also abide by the normative framework of reform developed by the World Bank. As part of the requirement the Government concerned must prepare an action plan as a National Policy of Education, a Poverty Reduction Strategy Paper (PRSP) or an Interim Poverty Reduction Strategy Paper (I-PRSP). These policy documents reflect the country's macroeconomic, structural and social policies and programmes to promote the growth and reduce poverty by indicating the external financing needs to meet the goals set by the EFA.

The Government of Eritrea, ever since it liberated in 1993, is continuously engaged in the exercise of achieving these goals even before Dakar Framework of Action and by coincidence when these objectives became part of EFA and Fast Track Initiative, it took active participation by formulating all the policies as conceived by the World Bank. In a conference held at Amsterdam in April 2002, Eritrea proposed to formally embrace the EFA-Fast Track Initiative. As a result of this the analysis that has been discussed hitherto has emerged lending a bird's eyeview of the whole scenario both in terms of the ground realities and their alleviating remedies in terms of long-term and short-term strategies which include infrastructural and capacity building too.

The Ministry of Education intends to organize its EFA efforts by a 3-phase strategy. The first phase is consolidation, second phase is developmental and third phase is qualitative. The consolidation phase is (2002-06) dedicated to the building up of the movement of EFA and accelerate the progress of Primary and Middle school education besides improving the efficiency and quality of teaching and learning environment. The developmental stage will focus on the consolidation of the required institutional capacity and provision mechanisms. By the end of this the EFA should automatically symbolize with the nation's prosperity and progress from the grassroots level of the country. The qualitative stage (2012-16) is the stage where the country achieves Universal Basic Education and a high level illiteracy. It gears up the nation by then to an international standard and the nation as a whole gets transformed into a knowledge society. All these phases or stages of transition of development call for a strong role of Lifelong Learning and Continuing Education and the Ministry of Education in all its policy papers has invariably linked the success of its programmes and plan of action to the pivotal role these programmes play.

As such the Government of Eritrea and the Ministry of Education plan to create a set of cultural institutions at local level with the purpose of expanding relevant and quality oriented informal learning. They want to rope in the modern technologies like Television and Radio, besides linking it up with the ICT.

As part of realizing the above ambitions on a multiple track of programme of action, the Ministry of Education has prepared an action plan for the next five years—*Adult Literacy and Post-literacy Programmes in Eritrea (2004-2008).* The report comprehensively presents the Government's eagerness to eradicate the illiteracy since 1998 when it first entered into a partnership programme on expanding literacy with SIDA (Swedish–IDA funding). Adult literacy and post literacy programmes as a national policy have been implemented since 1999 and more than 80 per cent literacy centres have been established as a consequence in the villages and remote areas. Similarly, the Continuing and Lifelong study has been accommodated through the evening classes and extension programmes, library reading rooms, radio listening centres and through recreational theatre arts.

However, the concept of Distance Education was not under consideration that time mostly due to lack of the expertise to handle such a programme on a national basis. Further, the idea of implementing Adult literacy, Continuing and Lifelong education by harnessing the Electronic and Print Media more effectively is a latest one and is in its genesis. If handled properly with adequate funding, the role of media proves itself to be a big booster to the existing sagging formal and non-formal school education. The subsequent chapters are going to revolve round on this in establishing the expediency involved in quickly going in for such a state of the art role of media in successfully articulating and complementing the many programmes and plans of action that the Government of Eritrea has presently embarked upon.

2

Media as Promoters of Educational Level and Awareness

Radio—A Pioneer and Ubiquitous Leader

The purpose of this chapter is to establish the importance and relevance of Radio Education in relation to the geographical and ethnic variations the State of Eritrea is beset with. Firstly, in the first chapter, an introduction of the geographical and demographic diversities of the country is presented and secondly, they have been correlated to the socio-economic and regional backwardness of the country owing to decades of armed struggle (1961-91) prior to independence and due to war from Ethiopia on a trivial border dispute (1998-2000) in the post independent era, besides a serial drought affecting the whole country for over three consecutive years. All this is presented along the sidelines of how the country's education has been linked primarily to country's prosperity and economy and how the concomitant remedies and strategies are adapted by the Government to salvage this situation part of which included Education through Radio and Television.

This chapter is an attempt thus to share with *what conditions are here for the Radio to play a key role in successfully promoting the education as a State Policy* and *to what extent the Radio could fulfill the expected objectives and bring about the desired outcomes*. It depends again *on the various ways* the Radio could be used for the educational broadcasting. For *the ways* depend on the conditions that exist and the conditions depend on the context for which the educational broadcasting is used. Further, the necessity to examine what are the ideal principles of educational broadcasting that a country or a government should choose to implement is an unavoidable and inevitable eventuality for there are many dimensions to it. *Firstly what roles can the Educational broadcasting play? What can it do better than anything else? How effective it is? What is needed to make it effective? Will the Educational broadcasting survive the onslaught of color television? What are the different strategies that can go for improving the education of the State by Educational Broadcasting?* The following is what an effort to an answer these questions in terms of the required software and production infrastructure.

At the outset the Radio has becom^ a friend of all internationally. It has been an advisor, a companion and a dependable source of information, enlightenment and communication over one and a half-century since it is first invented by an Italian Scientist Guglielmo Marconi in the early 19th century. It has brougl.t quite unexpectedly the World so closer to the Man that the concept of *Global Village* of Marshall McLuhan got translated to reality way back in the nineteenth century itself. There are many sides to the efficacy of the Radio which mankind kept on experimenting and realizing that each time a new discovery of hitherto unknown dimension of it has enriched the human knowledge and understanding of how to use it for different purposes. Indeed this has benefited the humanity in an unimaginable measure. The evolution of Radio from its early and first crystal sets of 1920s (with head phones) to the present VHF and FM transistors through valve wireless sets of 1950s (in built loud speakers) has an impressive association with a nation's history and its economic progress.

Firstly, it has been the fastest mode of communication and the messages on radio could be flashed instantaneously. This briskness of the communication is followed by the expediencies emerging on the several fronts. Information related to Health, Environment, Agriculture, Market trends and prices has found its way to Radio to facilitate the promotional and relief measures as may be required in different parts of the country from time to time. No sooner did Marconi company get the permission in Britain in 1920 by the Post Office to operate from the transmitter in Chelmsford, than people began to invent more and more ways to democratize the Radio and make it accessible to various walks of life. One of the major inventions of twentieth century that put Radio on a higher pedestal was its ability to revolutionize the country's economy, an economy that is linked to the eradication of illiteracy and poverty, and transformation of an unskilled manpower to a skilled and knowledge society which would in turn make it globally competitive.

For a long time, both in the developed countries and in the developing countries, Radio's role in galvanizing a nation's economy could hardly be overemphasized. Beginning with the Farmers to the Fishermen, Children to the Adults, Police and Military to Civil Servants, down to the Common people, the association of Radio with the cause of various socio-economic and political movements of a county or countries became almost integral and synonymous with, and even symbolized, a country's development and prosperity. The subsequent innovations on the principle of Radio are what we have seen as Transistors, HAM handsets, and walkie–talkies that allowed a two-way flow of communication etc.

In fact, the principle of Radio, what has begun originally as a simple effort of Marconi to send messages from a point to point preferably for a short distances, has become later a universal phenomenon. Today Computer to Television all services operating on Satellite or on Very High Frequency Transmitters are nothing but the extensions of the principle of Radio.

What makes Radio such an efficient instrument of communication lies in its suggestiveness and flexibility besides in its studios' jingle sounds and operational strategies. The entry of Transistors in 1947 made it portent enough of its potential to create a revolution that could sweep the world soon. In 1964 Frank Gillard of the BBC said, '*Transistor has made the radio into the truly Ubiquitous mass medium. Radio is no longer something to which necessarily have to go. Radio goes with you. So it becomes a personal service. You come to count on it.... to give you a certain service at a certain hours, wherever you might happen to be. Consequently the usefulness of the Medium is enormously enhanced and those in charge of sound in the years ahead must increasingly take this service function into account.... In planning their programme output.*

Notwithstanding the arrival of another innovation in the form of visual medium as Television, which has been pioneered by John Logie Baird and others in 1920, Radio continued its upsurge entire nineteenth century through twentieth century to twenty-first century, which led to establishment of various channels, within in different countries, each channel dedicated to a different purpose (Music, drama and poetry, conversation and dialogue, Educational, News etc.).

Though Television played a great role in attracting the viewers' time both as an audio-visual medium since 1939, the competitive role of Radio in producing the programmes (particularly mixed programming like BBC Radio 4 even today), that vied with the TV, has made a niche for itself for all the times to come. Thus, even today, in spite of having different TV channels both under the Public Sector and Private Sector, the Four Channels of the Radio of BBC continued to thrive on the licene revenue itself. It is enough to show that given the political will of the governments, the success of the Radio is undeterred and unmarred by any amount of TV channels and competition from other media agencies even today.

The success of Radio even into the modern age of TV color transmission is largely due to VHF, FM and Transistorization, which has made the sound, broadcasting easier and cheaper and relevant to the social needs. For the developments in Electronic Media in Britain have cascade effects all over the world, both in the developed and in the developing nations. Almost all the developing countries of the Third World have found the need of Radio for various reasons. One of the important reasons for any country, either developing or developed is to use the Radio for educational purposes. *What makes the Radio so advantageous than the other forms of Media is an important thing that is going to be dwelt upon here.*

To begin with, it is pertinent to present the advantages of the Radio both as a technology of transmission and as an instrument. It means, in other words presenting a holistic approach to Radio in relation to the country's educational requirements.

Characteristics of Radio as a Technology: The Magic of Radio

The messages that emerge from Radio, as a matter of an Educational Programme, or for that matter of any programme, to be elaborate a little bit more – a drama of a History, a Conversation on a Science or Agriculture or Health, a depiction of a Geography in relation to a nation's Economy, are not simple straight statements like what transpires in a classroom between a teacher and students. They are more than that in their effect and what is going to be discussed here veers rounds to this. The Radio messages are composed of Words,

Sounds, Music, Silence and Time which in varying permutations and combinations, depending upon the finesse and the creative potential of the producer who makes it, by themselves bring about a different ambience in the imagination and understanding of the listener – what the message is precisely about.

In other words, it takes away the disadvantages, if any, of its being a blind medium. In fact, the advantages arising out of the blindness of the medium of Radio redound compared to many tall claims of the different visual media. One of the greatest advantages that Radio has offered in educating the masses lies in its ability to boost the imagination power which in turn has led to establishing the high order of creative thinking among listeners. Therefore, it is necessary and relevant to understand here that the efficacy of Radio in using it as a medium of messages lies in how these basic characteristics or features are properly exploited for the benefit of the intended target group.

Words

Words are signs in the medium of Radio and do not resemble what they represent. They are essentially symbolic in character and the symbolism has straight appeal to the imaginative power of the listener. For instance a reference to any object, animal, person or an abstract body of thoughts could be done by resorting to many synonymous words or by adopting alternative ways of expression (include such as accent and stress – which are either semiotic or called as effects). They are as a matter of fact not there physically. Yet these words and the synonymous references bring them visually on our intellectual eye. More the synonymous references and alternative expressions are the greater the appeal to the imagination. Therefore the words on the medium of Radio constitute a double role – one related to the objects they represent and another the voice of the person who is characterizing and delivering the message. This is often referred to in the parlance of Radio technology as a – binary code. It is to be further understood here in the context of Radio that the voice of the announcer continuing the programme is not only an index of herself but also the index of the Radio she belongs to and often she refers to both to convey the uniformity of the network that is transmitting the programme. Thus, it is clear that the signification in Radio is not static or rigid but rather highly fluid or elastic which varies according to context and the pre-conceptions that the programmes are required to have.

Sounds

The sounds are natural part of the world and there is never silence reigning the world at any given time. There are hundreds thousands of sounds in a given environment but they are selectively heard by the living beings including humans. What concerns one is selectively heard and responded to. The Radio simply re-creates these sounds to bring in the natural and external environment into the ambience of the listener's imaginative frame. In a way they are symbolical like words but differ in their qualitative appeal to the imagination. They are iconic and represent the natural sounds outside in the world (the horse footsteps are created by slapping the two coconut shells against each other). The technique the Radio adopts is to choose the sounds, which are relevant and contextual for the slated programme of transmission and eliminate or fade out the rest or relegate the unnecessary to a background of din or noise. These are called "sound effects" in the terminology of Radio messages.

The elevation of the Sound effects lies in the precise determination of distinction between relevant sounds too. For instance an owl-hoot may convey a number of meanings to the listener. It may indicate a simple forest or garden environment or it may forebode an ominous event in the case of a melodrama or it may suggest a tragic or eerie ambience. So, what sort of elevation is to be imparted to the sound of an owl-hoot is again subject to the careful selection by the programmer in relation to the context. This is also referred to as an extended signification and seems to be established in the Radio transmissions, be them Drama or depiction of History, a narration of a short story or a fantasy, through a process of cultivated custom and habit. They became almost an acoustic short hand. They are otherwise known as non-literal signifiers too.

Music

Music is another powerful constituent of the radio messages. Its role in providing an entertainment to the audience could hardly be overemphasized. The very fact that BBC Radio 1 had shifted its responsibility to offer the light music on full time basis to Radio 2 suggests how entertaining the music, either light or pop is. But when it comes to making a programme the function of the music is completely contextual as in the case of words and sounds. There is also an argument that music does not have any special effect by itself on audience as do the words and sounds have.

But music has a very specific role ascribed to it in the sense it would enhance the mood of the setting or ambience or context so that the audiences get engrossed into it. For example the background music. It acts as a background in respect of a drama, often takes peak or low notes to tune the mood of the audiences to the context. It means it could be used very effectively to capture the mood of the audience from any diversion. More than visual mediums like Cinema and Television, the Radio's music is found to be more breathtaking one. On the other hand it acts as a complementary phenomenon for certain expressions like sorrow, and pleasure. It also offers a variety of notes for a feel of blowing air, dashing waves, pouring rain and thundering of the sky. One can find the simulations of storms or battles also in the Radio music. In this sense, it has both imitative function and iconic index.

For instance it is difficult to understand a documentary or a drama in Radio without the involvement of music. All Science and Social—be it historical or geographical, ecological or biological—music sets tone for a successful take off. Its role in pronouncing the words is as much effective and superb as its ability to convey the message of the same words. For a competent director, who produces the Radio programmes for achieving various objectives including educational objectives, the art of exploiting the music for enhancing the quality of the programme and capturing the mood of audience is an essential qualification. In short the educational programmes without proper background and effective music are bound to fail and do not show any impact either on the teachers or on the students. Therefore, music is a great player in enlivening the words and sounds used in the broadcasting of an educational programme or an entertainment programme or a general programme.

Above all the role of music as a signature song or title song, which is called in the parlance of Radio as 'framing' or 'boundary' conventions', is so impressive that the children and adults both alike cling at once onto the music and the programme that accompanies it immediately (Goffman (1980, 164-65). It is often considered a 'paradigm' or 'genre' of the programme (Fiske and Hartley, 1978,169). The music here is said to act as an abstract announcer or an announcer de facto. Its signification not only extends the mere announcement of the programme which commences shortly or which ended shortly but also goes to accredit the uniqueness and quality of the programme. Its signification at times it symbolizes the entire net- work or the station that it is being broadcast from too. In addition to music has significance in bringing the links of a story or a drama in succession to a continuity of thought and imagination by its intermittent notes and tunes. It is something similar to rise of the curtain or fall of the curtain in a theatre drama.

Further by Radio conventions, music, which offers a national anthem, when played, it is taken as a harbinger of an official programme of State Head or National Head – be the President or the Prime Minister or the Queen on the Radio. In such cases, it plays the role of an actuality and often appears as performing an indexical function. The song of National Anthem played by the music in the Radio falls under this category.

Silence

Though Radio is essentially a sound oriented medium, through which it symbolizes a number of expressions and typifies messages, it has another side of its function-namely-silence which is as affective as the former one. The silence in the Radio has both negative as well as positive connotations. The connotation stands established based on the duration of the silence. If the silence is for a long duration it only suggests that the Radio is 'off the air' or the 'dead air'. If the Radio is on air and suddenly the medium breaks into the silence, it is indicative of some significance of the event, which could not for obvious reasons be expressed in noise. Hence the imaginative sense of the listener is evoked at this point of time. Such enactment of silence often signifies various other things which include not only physical actions but abstract, dramatic qualities, generate pathos or irony by confirming or countering the words which surround them. The context alone offers the clue to the imaginative sense of the listener or audience.

Time

Time has extraordinary significance in the context of Radio. Among all the media of communications it is the Radio which has been prominently considered a watchdog of time. Why? The answer is very simple and straightforward as the Radio operates within the framework of the time and space. As the space in the print medium is a premium, so is the time for the Radio. Every passing second and every fraction of a second is a premium in the application of Radio technology (software programing).

This has brought the Radio a Commercial dimension and has thus been a singular cause of huge revenue through commercials. Right from the 'cue call' and the 'sign posting' the counting of time begins. Each programme is meticulously planned not only in terms of the content, form and style but also in the time sense. Each second is carefully exploited for effective culmination of the intended idea or expression. Every programme is planned and re-planned as to ensure that it finishes the intended task in the specific time slot and achieves the desired effect.

Further, time is used to enhance the dramatic effect of the content, expression, style and form of a given programme. It is here the talent of the producer and the director counts a lot. To achieve the desired effect of a comedy or a tragedy, the punching and clinching of the dialogues should occur in the shortest possible specified time failing which the dialogues, however effectively they might have been written would not meet the intended effect. It means that the words in the Radio context may not mean everything sometimes except in the narrative scripts about which a prior announcement, sign posting, would be made and the audiences are tuned before.

As an indication of passing time the monitoring agency or the Control Room or the Radio Engineering Division keeps sending the 'cue calls' from time to time to suggest the various stages of the on-going news reading or live conversation or phone-in conversation or recording of a talk. As for the recording and transmitting a programme such as dramas, conversations, discussions, songs and folk programmes, the greatest advantage in relation to binding the programme to a specific time slot stems from the technique of 'Editing'. However, this may be useful in respect of reducing the unnecessary consumption of time by the participants or by the artists. As for ensuring the effectiveness of the given programme the timeliness of the dialogue delivery, the pause and the connectivity between dialogues, there is a little that Editing could do.

Primary Code

The discussion about the various dimensions of software such as the significance of words, sounds, music, silence and time – in the foregoing – suggests that none of them in isolation can bring about the effect of – all applied together – in a concerted manner. Further without words, mere sound effects or music too cannot make the communication of the Radio complete and clear to the listener. Therefore, it is basically admitted by all the communicators of Radio that the Primary code or function of the Radio is 'lingual' and the all other software of the Radio are woven round this lingual function which remains central to any form of the programme.

Here comes the question whether the Radio programmes are impromptu or previously scripted. The answer is simple. The Radio programmes are always previously scripted. No programme usually goes on air directly without first being scripted, edited and rehearsed in view of the emphasis placed on the time slots of Radio. Even news reading which is considered a live one is not an impromptu programme. But for small improvisations during the reading of the News, such as inclusion of the latest news or flash, always the News reading has been of a previously scripted one and even experienced news readers would rehearse a number of times and check and cross check with the time slots allotted for various items of the news before they go on air after the 'cue call' is received.

Each item of the news is weighed in relation to its significance, timeliness and relevance and the specific time slot is allotted item wise by the producer after receiving the final edited copy of the news to be broadcast. The content of the news is always edited from time to time. Thus, it leaves no scope for a direct transmission even in the broadcasting of news. The main aspect related to the style of scripting is always a matter of technical significance.

The script of talks especially must be written assuming it as one individual talking to another individual or a group of individuals. This calls for a separate syntax and construction of sentences. In the ordinary speech there may not be specific syntax or rules of expression or grammar as the individuals are face to face and the gestures or sounds or other modified body language could compensate any shortcoming in the expression or syntax. But, Radio as is already mentioned before is as blind medium where the voice of the speaker is only heard but not seen by the listener and the speaker does not see the listener. In this situation the script calls for a very careful creative planning and execution. The scripts should deliver dialogues, speak the messages in the talks within the time-frame. It is a unique structure by itself. This is the Primary Code of the Radio.

Similarity between the Primary Code of Radio and the Classroom Situation

The Primary Code of the Radio is thus lingual, necessarily in a talk form based on a written script (paradoxical though it may seem) without tautology, and should be time bound. This is exactly exploited for the Educational and Developmental Communication programmes. The understanding of the above software of the Radio in relation to the complexities of the Education and promotion of Health, Hygiene, Agriculture, Science and Technology is an important condition leading to the establishment of Educational channels in many developed and developing countries.

It is therefore very pertinent here to examine in detail how the Primary Code of the Radio has many similarities to the classroom situation. Look at the classroom parameters – where there are teacher, a good number of students, a black-board, a topic of an ongoing lesson and a time-limit to complete the lesson. On the other side, in the studios of Radio, there is an artificially created class-room ambience for the audience (it does not really exist in the studio but in the mind of the listener), a speaker and a couple of students with a simulation of noise background of a classroom situation and a prepared script as a talk (that is more precise than the teacher's lecture on a given topic of the lesson). But for the blindness of the medium, the classroom situation could not have been to its fullness in the Radio.

The blindness of the medium therefore overtakes in effectiveness many other disadvantages of the classroom which teachers might face in the form of obstructions, discipline and interference etc. Further, the carefully prepared script without frequent repetitions and pin pointed un-ambivalent messages perfectly reach the listener than the messages delivered by the teacher in a classroom where a few out of fifty or sixty might receive the messages in the right genre. The feedback whatever is usually elicited by the teachers in the form of evaluation of the given classroom session according to their pre-written lesson plan could be rehashed in the studio also. As to the total reception of the programme and evaluation of the content and delivery of the messages, the Radio has better means of conducting the Summative Evaluation over a period of time. But this summative evaluation has no comparison with the quality of teaching that takes place in the classroom situation between the teacher and the students though in the general sense the results of a given class at the end of the academic year are shown as the outcomes of the classroom teaching or indices of the efficacy of the teacher or the quality of the teaching.

Two-way Communication Radio in Educational Channels – Extension of Jakobson's Model

The usual Radio programmes like Drama, Music, Talks and Conversations only deliver the messages but do not immediately get a feedback. As such most of the communication process of the Radio is referential, occasionally others too, in nature in the given context and represents a most familiar communication model of Roman Jakobson. Many other models are also put forward to depict the communication process of the Radio but, of all, the model of Jakobson offers a greater flexibility and simplicity.

Context and Message
Sender – Receiver
Context and Code

According to Jakobson one or the other of the six elements in the above communication model is always dominant in a single act of communication. If this holds true, then this model can be rearranged with the dominant element on the front. But if the dominance of the elements sustained over a series of acts of communication, then it is possible to develop an analogous theory of programmes or genres. For instance where an act of communication is entirely referential in nature and purely associated with linguistic exuberance, then one can guess the programme to be either a news or a documentary or a commentary of public events. On the other if the act of communication is emotive in language then the programme might be either an interview or a chat. Sometimes the process of communication involves conative function, then the obvious programme is either commercial or public service notices advising safety rules on the road or the dangers involved in the neglect of gas cylinders in the house etc.

But sometimes the act of communication address to the aesthetic sense of the audience due to the concerted action of several factors like the words, sounds and music and in such cases the programmes could be plays, story-telling and poetry-reading or reeling out a lesson of History or Social sciences. Though programmes are not developed strictly according to the above classification, most of the times the Educational programmes would be using either the referential language or the aesthetic language both of which include a variety of programmes having appeal to the imagination of the teachers and students. The phone-in programme combined with the educational channel has further edge on these acts of communication process in the sense it offers a promising feedback. It is using this as a basis Andrew Crisell has slightly modified Jakobson's model as follows:

Referential/aesthetic
Emotive– –Conative
Phatic/metalingual

In other words both the sender and the receiver are benefited in this two-way communication process and the receiver not only receives the codes transmitted by the programme but also sends back the messages. Thus sender becomes the receiver also. If the model is viewed from the broadcaster's angle, the sender has sent the message codes and the receiver has received and just responded, it is simply Phatic. It means that the given programme has audience present and are listening to it. If the communication process is viewed from the listener's side, the listener not only listened to it but also understood its meanings and responded to it—hence it is metalingual. Sometimes these listeners respond in an emotive or conative depending on the nature of the topic in the process of communication.

Distinction between Educational and Educative Programmes

Though it is difficult to draw the distinction between the Educational and Educative Programmes, according to Anthony Bates, (1984: 7-8) who prefers a more gradual classification from 'enrichment' (at the educative end) through 'learning resources', meeting 'special needs' to 'direct teaching' there needs to be a line of distinction based on a traditional perceptions at least.

According to BBC broadcasting the Educative programmes (such as news, current affairs, documentaries of contemporary socio, political situations across the world) do not impose any 'discipline of response' from the audience whereas the Educational programmes elicit a 'discipline of response.' Further, the Educative programmes are aimed at a wide range of audience and their contents are to be retained as general impressions rather than a systematic and classified body of knowledge (curricular topics and non-formal curricular educational topics). On the other the Educational programmes contain information topic specific and intend to contribute to the vertical growth of the knowledge of the listener or audience in the sense it would or should be useful to him/her in complementing the knowledge already acquired either from the books or from the classroom experience.

The efficient role of Radio in the context of classroom education through educational broadcasting is summed up by Andrew Crisell— *We ought to begin by acknowledging that the educational limitations of radio can be overestimated. Its oral mode is, after all, the same as that of the classroom lesson and of that other enduring teaching tool, the lecture – and like lessons and lectures it allows the student to carry out actions or to take notes. Moreover when it consists of direct instruction it differs from books and television in leaving her with the free use of her eyes and hands (a particular advantage when learning such skills as dancing or computer programming) and even in the case of the straight lecture or talk the freedom from such visual distractions as the cut of the teacher's suit may be a salutary one. Furthermore, since in educational broadcasting the listeners are likely to be better informed and more highly motivated than in educative broadcasting, problems of presentation and language are less insistent.'*

Ideally for the Radio broadcasts two types of formats are suited— though it does not bar the innovations: one format is a direct instruction method through which students are expected to perform specific actions and improve their psychomotor and affective domains. The other format is in the form of talks or lectures, which often appear like educative and not educational. But there are many innovations over these. There are many educational broadcasts, even in the developing countries like India, which almost recreated the classroom situation with the artists enacting the roles of the teachers and the students. History, Geography, Civics, Natural sciences other forms of classroom curriculum such as Literature could be dramatized as documentaries by the Radio artists themselves. Young generations of artists have been trained by the senior artists for making such programmes to achieve the sustainability of such programmes.

In respect of subjects dealing with formulae, equations and mathematical concepts, symbols the creative writers of Radio programmes have come up with 'ideal talks' which exclusively deal with the concepts written like talks with plenty of examples that the studios can simulate by the combination of sounds and music, besides words.

These 'ideal talks' have been found to be most effective in the sense they have been tested in the timeframe as messages with the limited main points which would reinforce them through repetition.

In view of this dynamic role of Radio in the educational broadcasting, the extension of Radio education in the form of 'Store and Retrieval' system has apparently manifested in the form of audio-cassettes through the Radio cum tape recorders and by the mini-tape recorders or walk-mans. This has enhanced the shelf value of the programmes, which were produced out of painstaking efforts. Further the BBC broadcasters enhanced the value of the educational broadcasting by supplementing the listeners with the contents of the broadcasts by publishing them in *The Listener*, a magazine brought out to complement the students or listeners' needs for reference and perusal over a period of time.

Further, the BBC School Broadcasts had brought out for many years along with its programmes a 35 mm film-strip known as *radiovisio* (Andrew Crisell, p. 31). *It consists of all important nuances about which certain additional information is necessary and is televised simultaneously to have an enhanced understanding of what is being heard from Radio supported by the music.* By using these the efficacy of Radio as a medium of instruction has become unlimited and it can be even used today to teach such harder concepts like Mathematics etc.

Finally, the capacity of Radio in imparting the educational programmes thrives on two important aspects; firstly it offers experiences which are more than mere sounds and words and secondly it compensates the other deficiencies by invoking the imagination of the listener. Thus radio's major contribution to education is its unique combination of two processes which are both regarded as important yet which the other media can provide separately. It is the only medium in which reality is in some sense directly presented yet must at the same be imagined. These two processes are pivotal to education in that they can increase the learning motivation and radio is capable of doing this even with respect to those disciplines in which it can offer little by way of direct instruction.

To appreciate fully under what specific conditions and for what specific purposes the broadcasting in education is eff 'tive, the foregoing discussion has been very essential (ref. p. 29). In the words of Anthony Bates... *'the reasons why educational broadcasting has been used in the way it has, (as is described above), it is necessary to understand the nature of broadcasting organizations. Educational broadcasting is only one, relatively small, parts of a much larger organizational output.*

Broadcasting is a complex technology, which has its own impetus and development, its own organization structures and technical requirements. Educational broadcasters are part of that complex structure, and are therefore very much influenced by the values and criteria of general broadcasting. Judging effectiveness means applying values. Broadcasters have their own criteria for judging effectiveness, based on a set of values or an ideology influenced by the nature of the organizations for which they work and by the professional demands of their occupation.

The Ways to Effectively Utilize Educational Broadcasting

Broadcasting has been used for a wide variety of educational purposes. It has been used to reduce illiteracy, poverty and disease for national recovery, to create a sense of national identity and to educate those who otherwise would have received no education at all.

There are three broad principles or objectives behind using the Educational broadcasting for the development of any country's education system. One is *to improve the quality of existing educational provision*. The focus in this approach is on the use of educational broadcasting *for improvement within the formal education system with the target groups being those in the full-time education at school or college.* The second one to utilize the educational broadcasting is to *equalize or spread more widely and quickly educational opportunities – what Mc Anany and Mayo (1979) have called the 'democratization of educational opportunity'(Anthony Bates 1984, p. 16)*. The focus here is on providing educational opportunities beyond the formal school and college system, through part-time, off-campus education, which is also often referred to *as non-formal education stream*, for those outside the normal age range or geographical reach of the basic school and college system.

The third objective, though it has political overtone, is related to utilizing the Educational broadcasting *for bringing about radical changes in the social structure and in the mobilization of the poor and oppressed and in achieving gender parity and liberating the women from the shackles of the traditions* (Anthony Bates p. 17).

Since the broadcasting began in early 1920s, so far *three important ages* passed in the history of the Radio. The *first age* belonged to 1920-1945 coinciding with the conclusion of the Second World War. The *second age* began in the 1950s and ended by 1980s. This has been quickly followed by the *third age*, which has begun in 1980s and is continuing presently. But whatever changes the Broadcasting has undergone over these three ages, they reflected on the educational broadcasting.

The first educational broadcasting, in the sense of the word has begun in 1926 by the British Broadcasting Corporation and soon it spread to Sweden and other Western European countries. Ever since the Educational broadcasting has been going on for over 75 years and various developed (the Western Europe and the US) and developing nations (China and India) quickly started implementing this solely to meet the objectives, which could sometimes be even political or sociological too, mentioned already above.

For instance an educational project launched in Nepal in 1970s had done an excellent work in resolving some of the burning problems of system there. Nepalese primary-school teachers were untrained and the then existing teacher education institutions were not in a position to train them in the next two or three years too. A radio-based distance education project had come up as the most sustainable alternative and it indeed resolved the crisis.

Similarly in El Salvador, in the late 1960s the government wanted to expand the enrollment of the students for classes seventh to ninth through eight. There was a heavy dropout problem too, in addition to the want of classrooms and additional teachers. Even if the teachers were hired their quality of instruction was not of the desirable standard and at best suited for the primary level. By launching an audio-visual project through instructional television the government could overcome the crisis and the students enrollment had gone up by 1970s by four times (20,000 at the start of the reform to 65000 after 5 years) of the 1960s.

Another example of Radio coming to the rescue of learners in a more complex subject like Mathematics is the Radio Mathematics of Nicaragua. It is an excellent programme very carefully developed and evaluated over a period of 10 years. The group providing technical assistance had put in painstaking efforts in constructing mathematics curricula for computer-assisted instruction to the creation of a radio-based curriculum. The project staff spent one year in developing each grade's programming such as designing curriculum, producing programmes with a complex and artful understanding of how mathematics is learned and gathering extensive feedback from classroom observation and testing. The programme directors were aware that each programme was to be used and reused and hence heavy investment on the software was justified. Programmes were produced or more precisely new curricula were developed that no master teacher was likely to duplicate. Subsequently the methods applied in this project are utilized in the teaching of Mathematics in Philippines and Thailand.

The ways the Educational broadcasting could cater to the many sides of the education system of a given country is shown in the form of a chart (see the Table 10). The strategic role of the entire broadcasting spectrum broadly covers two important branches of the education system namely–formal education and non-formal education. The formal education system covers educational institutions like schools and colleges on one hand and the In-service Teacher Training Institutions on the other.

As for the requirements of these institutions, the broadcasting evolves a two pronged strategy. It caters by indirect teaching and direct teaching methods which include enrichment and learning resources of the learners while simultaneously offering multiple windows like meeting specific needs, expanding formal systems and curriculum reform open.

In the Non-Formal Education it adapts a multi-pronged approach by attempting to equalize or enlarge the existing opportunities. The most important of them are: reducing inequalities prior to schooling, reducing inadequacies after schooling, by launching a social action, by politicizing the Masses to invoke in them the sense of awareness of their rights and responsibilities, especially of women and disadvantaged groups and by planning to open up a feeder line of education in the form of life-long and continuing education.

All the above strategies of the broadcasting services are construed as different forms of Development Communication and the various roles that these communication strategies assume from time to time are referred to variously depending on the emphasis that each strategy adapts under the political conditions that each polity sets out as priorities or targets. The prominent roles these communication strategies assume are: as a low cost loudspeaker, as an institutional catalyst, as a political lightening rod, as an organizer and maintainer, as an equalizer, as a quality assurance controller, as an accelerator of interaction, as a motivator or legitimator as feed forward, as a magnifier of dependency and integration and as a medium of creating supply and demand.

Formal Education

The broadcasting services of the Radio in the sector of formal education are of direct relevance to the learners of the schools and colleges as they are based on the curriculum and are specially designed not only to meet the deficiencies of the learning processes but also complement and enrich their learning experiences. Thus according to Anthony Bates, programmes aimed directly at students within the formal education system could be considered along a continuum from 'enrichment', through 'learning resources', 'meeting special needs' to direct teaching and curriculum reform (Anthony Bates, p. 18).

Enrichment

By the very word 'enrichment', it is clearly understood that it is not as essential one to enhance the learner's understanding in the context of the classroom. It means an addition of something to make it more effective and useful to the learner. It may mean an effort to reinforce the idea or the content or the skill of the given lesson too. Where the teachers fail to do these supplementary functions for reasons of lack of required expertise, creativity or other constraints like lack of good libraries, print materials and time, these enrichment broadcasts complement the classroom learning process of the learners. They also contribute to enhance the motivation of the learner besides help reinforcing the ideas of the content time and again.

The problem of enrichment is more complex in respect of the countries like Britain where there is no prescribed curriculum either at the Primary level or at the Higher Education level. Where each board or University or institution prescribes its own curriculum, the problem of enrichment of a classroom task becomes all the more difficult for the broadcasting services. In such cases mere claim of broadcasting an 'enriched' material or 'content' would not find any sense in terms of the defined learning objectives of the lessons for there is no specific frame of reference with which they can be justified and the learning outcomes could be evaluated.

However, this problem is overcome in the British broadcasting service by virtue of a meticulous coordination and planning with its own education officers and in liaison with the practising teachers of the schools.

As such a thorough study of each specific subject in relation to many combinations it assumes under the specifications of different educational institutions has enabled the British broadcasting educational councils to arrive at the more specific needs of the learners in each subject in terms of its additional content, skills, motivation and reinforcement. As such the lessons of broadcasting have become automatically quite relevant and useful to the learners and the teachers, the differences in the curriculum between the institutions notwithstanding.

Even in the developing countries where the curriculum is centralized and is not subject to frequent changes, the Radio broadcasts or the Television telecasts are used to enrich the content of the prescribed curriculum of a particular subject. The curriculum here is not designed keeping in mind the integration of Radio broadcasting design with the curriculum. It is almost planned independent of that. Therefore the Radio programme designers and the officials of the Ministry of Education together finalize the programme style and content around the curriculum which would more often than not be taking into consideration the additional inputs of content, skills, reinforcement and motivation required to enhance the learning process and the teaching process of the classrooms.

Table–10

Strategic Roles for Television and Radio

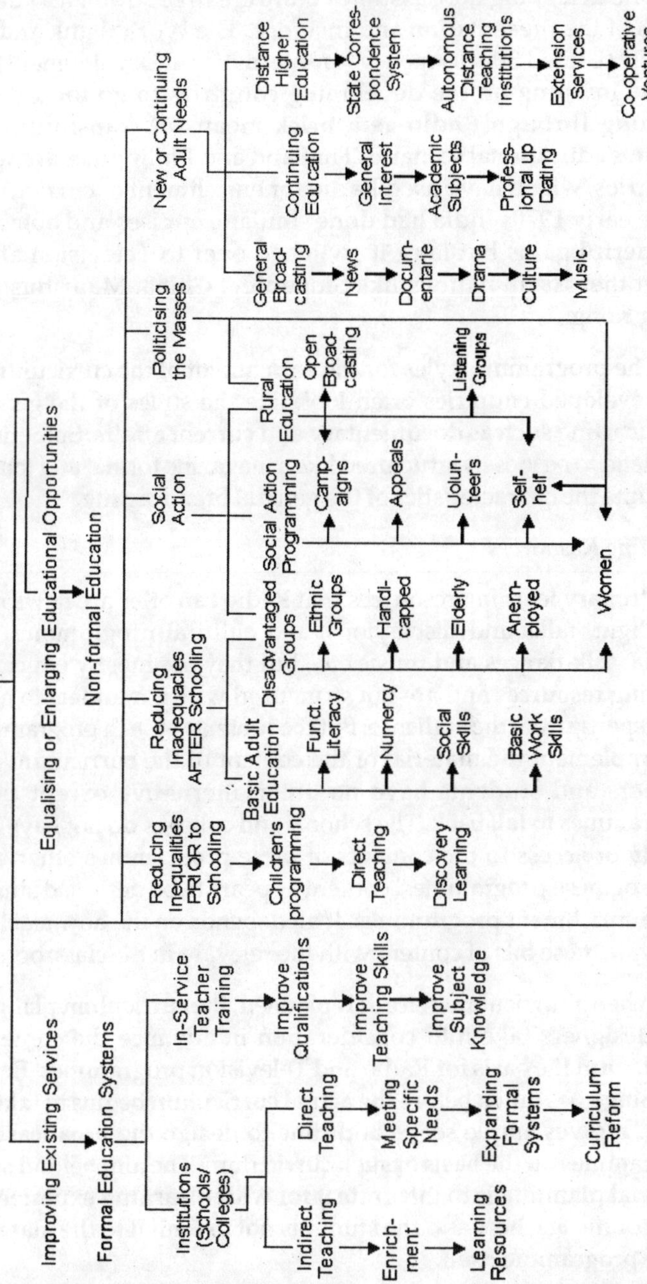

Courtesy: **Anthony, W. Bates: Broadcasting in Education.**

The designing here assumes more creative strategies both in terms of the presentation and imagery. The World Bank and the USAID (United States Agency for International Development) are of late insisting on the developing countries to go for a direct teaching through Radio as a brisk means of transforming a nation's educational scenario. Thailand and Philippines are some countries, which have used Radio for enrichment of curriculum. In the early 1970s India had done similar exercises and obtained wonderful gains but later it switched over to Television along with other Asian nations like Singapore, China, Mauritius and Hong Kong.

The programme styles for the enrichment of the curriculum in the developed countries often look like the styles of the general broadcasting such as documentary and current affairs. Sometimes they tend to be loosely structured like a magazine format and tend to subsume the characteristics of the general broadcasting.

Learning Resources

The Primary learning resources that Radio can offer are news reel, spot light, talks and discussions, and cultural programmes like drama, folk-dances and music etc., but they are mostly educative learning resources and are not structured with a mandate to elicit the response from the audience. But the contents of such programmes do supplement the material of the content of the curriculum and teachers and students have no other alternative except these programmes to fall back. The schools and colleges do not have any facility or access to the contents of these programmes otherwise. Some of these programmes' content appears to be designed similar to the enrichment programmes. It all depends on the how teachers integrate these bits of content with the relevant in the classroom.

When a curriculum reform is planned, the curriculum planners and designers take into consideration in advance the contents, which form the basis for Radio and Television programmes. Entire planning goes much before the actual curriculum begins to take its place. It gives ample scope and time to design the broadcasting programmes on the basis of such curriculum. The aim behind such material planning is to integrate it for wider learning experiences both for the teachers and the students not to limit it to the material in the programme itself.

Meeting Special Needs

This is a programming which is mainly meant to cater to those schools where there is no adequate staff for all the subjects or where there is no teacher for a specific subject due to non-recruitment or due to sudden illness or due to retirement or resignation of a teacher. Particularly in the current age of contract appointments in lieu of regular service recruitments, adapted by several developing and developed nations as a consequence of privatization of education, the scarcity of subject teachers for specific subjects is not hard to imagine. The only way out to provide reasonable education to students in such schools is by recoursing to the Radio or Television programmes which are carefully planned and shot as learning resources or enrichment materials. These programmes thus shot would enable the other subject teachers to handle these subjects for the benefit of the students. These teachers after going through these programmes, and by following the manuals would be in a position to offer guidance to the students in respect of the most difficult areas of those subjects too.

Further, these programmes are quite handy to the government to either broadcast or supply them in the form of recorded cassettes for the benefit of students through local study centers where the running of an independent school, primary or high school, is not possible due to geographical reasons, or due to low population densities.

The programme formats while preparing for such subjects which require specialist teacher appointments are to be carefully formulated taking into consideration the educational level and competencies of the other subject teachers available there. It should be borne in mind that the other subject teachers' educational background and competency level is going to be a major constraint when the actual relation of the content of the programme, produced or shot for such schools, to the students comes to play. Therefore, the planners must include specialist teachers as also non-specialist teachers while finalizing the format and style of the presentation.

Further a careful data collection and analyses of the scholastic performance of the students in each subject school wise and area wise throw the gleanings into what subjects such kind of specialized approach is required for. Based on this the shooting of educational programmes is to be planned. It is not enough to say that the programmes are planned by a mere random selection. For all the purposes of producing or shooting the educational programmes, be it learning resources or enrichment, it must be borne in mind whether they would meet the special needs of those schools or areas where there is an open deficiency for teachers in specific subjects. The content, style and presentation should be more directive, didactic and should preferably take into consideration the teaching notes and lesson plans also for providing sufficient leverage for the reinforcement, recall and acquiring skills – Blooms Taxonomy.

Direct Teaching and Curricular Reform

Though this is not a desirable way, many developing and developed nations of late resorted to this kind of Radio or Television broadcasting for their schools and colleges. The idea behind resorting to this kind of programme is to revolutionize the education to achieve the intended targets in a short span of 10 to 20 years compared to the long-term they take in the usual natural course (Wilbur Schramm, 1977).

In such programming the core content and the style or method of instruction are almost to substitute the teacher's role in the classroom. Hence they would incorporate all such gestures and movements of the concerned teacher who would use them to express these ideas in the classroom situation. However, these programmes are to be broadcast under the supervision of the class monitors, whose qualifications are of no consequence in the changed context. It is enough if the monitors see to the discipline of the classroom when the audiotape or videotape is on.

The monitor is thus performing a supplementary role as a supervisor, organizer and manager and nothing beyond that. He has nothing to add upon the content of the Radio programme or Television programme. He cannot interpret and interpolate to explain to the students in the case of doubt. Hence the programmes which are to be shot to meet these demands must be self-explanatory giving all the relevant information in the form of side references or insertions as box items etc., to avoid any possible scope to a doubt. It needs a careful scrutiny and planning before hand and it should be run on trial in certain pilot schools before being launched on a nationwide basis.

Table–11

Number of School Broadcast Series Nationally Networked in Britain (School Year 1981-82)

		No. of different series
Radio	BBC network[1]	76
Television	BBC	59
	ITV	39
	Total[2]	98

Notes: 1. Figures exclude local broadcasts. Commercial radio stations and BBC local radio stations occasionally offer programmes aimed at school children. For instance, Capital Radio broadcasts drama productions of plays in the General Certificate of Education examination syllabuses. However, local radio programmes are not generally networked, and are rarely intended for direct use in schools.

2. Figures exclude programmes broadcast in one region only.

Source: Educational Broadcasting Council, 1982.

Table–12

Utilization of Television and Radio for Different Secondary School Subject Areas

Subject	*Television*					*Radio*		
	No. of series			*% of schools using series*		*No. of series*	*% of schools using series*	
	Total	*BBC*	*ITV*	*Mean*	*Range*	*BBC*	*Mean*	*Range*
History	2	2	–	39.00	38-40	2	11.50	8-15
Careers/Guidance	7	4	3	32.14	10.47	2	8.50	7-10
Geography	11	8	3	31.18	21-42	2	18.50	15-22
Science	9	3	6	27.89	19.36	1	21.00	21
English	4	2	2	21.25	14-30	5	8.80	5-12
General Studies	1	–	1	20.00	20	5	4.80	2-9
Languages	11	9	2	14.45	6-26	9	9.76	4-15
Other	3	–	3	21.00	14-27	3	6.33	2-10
Total	48	28	20	24.63	6-47	29	9.41	2-22

Note: This table excludes those series, which span the primary and secondary age ranges.

Source: Educational Broadcasting Council, 1982.

Courtesy: Anthony W. Bates: Broadcasting in Education.

There are as of now three ways in which the developing countries are using the Direct Teaching in the formal school system. One is to extend and expand the cover of the formal education to those who, for reasons concerned to geographical, traditional and economical conditions, could not either prosecute their studies from the beginning or dropped out half-way and crossed the minimum classroom age for a particular induction level. The Radio and Television programmes produced on the lines above are broadcast in the schools, which are obviously different from the regular schools for formal system, where traditional teaching is still in vogue, under the supervision of the monitors. However, the broadcast programmes are strictly the same as that of the regular stream of formal system and are based on the same curriculum.

Programmes of this kind under the projects names—Radio Primaria and Tele Secundaria are implemented in Mexico. Project ETV (Educational Televison) Maranhao is implemented in Brazil. In some cases like in Australia, there is different project called Radio Schools of Australia. Under this project the students, who are not either literates or dropouts, would study in their homes using these programmes or their recorded cassettes under the supervision of their parents and they use two-way radio sets for communication with the teachers in the Radio station to redress their doubts if any.

The second one is to improve the quality of instruction. This is aimed at imparting better knowledge, skills and awareness to the teachers whose educational background, skill efficiency and training are not adequate to meet the required standards of the level of the school. There may be several reasons for the backwardness of the teachers. Some may be of historical and some may be political. Sometimes the economic constraints in generating the required resources may also greatly hinder the growth and educational level of the teachers. To offset these deficiencies which are not solely due to teachers' own personality and intellectual deficiencies, different countries launched different programmes.

For instance one important step forward in the right direction is the Project of Radio Nicaragua which created a wonderful but very meticulously planned programme called Radio Mathematics of Nicaragua. Subsequently this project has been adapted by many other developing nations including Thailand and Philippines.

Table–13
Evaluation and Progress Reports on Projects Using Broadcasting for Direct Teaching or Curriculum Reform

Project Medium	*Country*	*Type of Project*	*Evaluation or Progress Report*
Radio Taramuhara	Mexico	Direct teaching	Schmelkes de Sotelo, 1977
Radioprimaria	Mexico	Direct teaching	Spain, 1977
Telesecundaria	Mexico	Direct teaching	Mayo *et al.*, 1975
Radio Mathematics	Nicaragua	Direct teaching	Friend *et al.*, 1980
ETV Maranhao	Brazil	Direct teaching	Arena *et al.*, 1977
TV	American Samoa	Curriculum Reform	Schramm *et al.*, Masland & Masland, 1976; Schramm *et al.*, 1980
TV	El Salvador	Curriculum Reform	Mayo *et al.*, 1976; Igle, 1976
TV and Radio	Ivory Coast	Curriculum Reform	Kaye, 1976; Eicher and Orivel, 1980
TV	Niger	Curriculum Reform	Schramm, 1977
TV and Radio	South Korea	Curriculum Reform	Schramm, 1977; Jamison and Yoon Tai Kim, 1977; Hawkridge and Robinson, 1982.

Courtesy: Anthony W Bates: Broadcasting in Education.

The third one is to reform the school curriculum at the national level. It deals with the reform of both the subject matter and the teaching methodology. The syllabus reforms are taken up keeping in mind the content required for making suitable formats, sources, presentation, and styles for the production of the Radio or TV programmes for Educational broadcasting. It is not only an academic but also a creative planning which called for the concerted effort and joint action of both the teachers and the Radio and TV production officials. However, it must be noted that curriculum reform is generally combined with the TV formatting for a long time than with the Radio. However that does not diminish the importance of Radio in any measure.

Radio is a force and is central in giving effect to any such reforms. Especially in poorer countries where TV infrastructure is yet not firmly rooted and widely spread, the Radio's role in ushering in the reforms in the national curriculum and offering equitable access to all is immense and colossal. Countries like American Samoa, El Salvador, the Ivory Coast and Niger have mainly relied on the Television aided curriculum reform. Radio based distance education has also been used for direct teaching in basic education in countries like Mongolia. For smaller countries with less density of population the Radio has more advantages than the Television.

Mongolia like any other developing country faced similar challenges that many of its counterparts elsewhere in the world have confronted (World Education Forum, Thematic Studies, UNESCO, 2000, p. 23). The globalization of economy posed new challenges and threats of survival for the State of Mongolia. In order to meet the new demands of the basic education, retraining, continuing education and literacy training for both the young people and adults and to meet the educational requirements of people in general where over a third of its population live a nomadic life with an economy based on animal husbandry, radio-centered education seemed to be the only fastest alternative.

Learning for Life, a UNESCO and Mongolian government programme launched in 1977 has catered nearly to 37,000 marginalized youth. The programme was supported by the self-learning booklets, learning centers, and teacher training sessions to acquire competencies in micro-enterprises and marketing. Curriculum reform by conventional methods is possible for any country, be it developed or developing. The only question here is at what cost. The curriculum reform by conventional methods requires long-term planning, budgeting and employing huge manpower, teachers who have to come from different corners of the country and stay at some place to sift through the process of reforming the syllabus either by updating the old syllabus or totally dispensing with the old or by adding the new syllabus with a small part of the old syllabus being retained here and there. It calls for a thorough debate and discussion.

All these would take years of time and involve so much of expenditure besides disturbing the teachers from their regular chores. Even after reforming a national curriculum the problem of retraining the teachers as to make them capable of handling the new syllabus is an onerous task. Alternatively both the developed countries like

Table–14
Different Broadcasting Strategies for Children in School

Broadcasting Strategies	*Technology Use*	*Project Examples*
1. Interactive radio instruction	National and regional radio broadcasting (terrestrial and satellite) + radios receivers (mains, batteries, solar-powers or wind-up) + print materials	English in Action, OLSET, South Africa Portuguese, PALOP counties (Mozambique, Angola) Radio Math, CENEMC, Venezuela English in Action, BRAC, Bangladesh
2. Schools Broadcasting Radio	National and community radio broadcasting (terrestrial and satellite) + radios (including solar and wind-up) print materials	Al Manaahil, Jordan Drama Workshop, BBC Education Radio UK, Namibian Broadcasting Corporation Schools Broadcasting Unit, Gambia
3. Child-and teacher-initiated	Community radio broadcasts subjects and information requested by children or teachers, e.g. producers download information from internet to broadcast or create print information for learners in own languages.	Kathmale Radio, Sri Lanka
4. Television	National and regional TV broadcasting (terrestrial and satellite) + TV receivers + print materials	NHK School Broadcasts, Japan BBC Education TV, UK
5. Children's programming on national and international radio and television stations	Radio and TV cartoons about children's rights and conflict resolution	Children in conflict, BBC World Service Cartoons for Children's Right, UNICEF Common Ground Production, Macedonia
	TV series promoting literacy	Ricon del Cuento (Story telling corner), Colombia Seasame Street, USA
	TV Health campaigning + school health curricula (part of a wider multi-faceted strategy)	Soul City and Khululeka Series, South Africa Broadcasting Corporation

Courtesy: World Education Forum: Thematic Studies.

Britain and the US including Canada are resorting to reforming the syllabus by using the Television as an effective mode.

There are certain characteristics, which are common among those countries, which had a run for the Direct Teaching. Firstly, they had a high percentage of low enrollment in the formal schools, followed by high percentage of dropouts, unequitable access poorly qualified teachers; lack of adequate buildings, books and other basic educational resources, a rapidly increasing population and an uneven distribution of educational resources, education being the privilege of the affluent sections of the society and increasing need for the skilled and semi-skilled workers, low GDP per annum and dependence on the foreign aid.

To alleviate the nation from these problems the education has been the single most alternative. Hence Ivory Coast had not only gone for the construction of the full-fledged TV center but also got the training of the staff done for producing nearly 500 hours programme in a year's time. They had also distributed to all the schools nearly for 5000 classes, many located in isolated humid villages in the forests and bushes. Further Ivory Coast had undertaken a project for training the teachers with the help of these direct teaching programmes and nearly 200 tons of support print materials were distributed in one year's time. Similarly in American Samoa to cover entire formal school system in a year's time around 6000 Educational Television programmes were produced. In Nicaragua the schools were directly linked to the Radio project of Mathematics and it covered all the rural and the poor urban primary schools also. Of course they did not go for the printed material to support these programmes to save the costs.

The Educational Television of Maranhao provided the secondary education with Audio visual programmes of Education which run semi-autonomously through a system of group of activities to pupils living in the very poor homes in a remote part of the Amazon basin in Brazil. The programme is not funded by any foreign aid, which is notable feature of it.

This apart there are certain general similarities between all these programmes or projects. Firstly, they are all funded by the foreign aid. Secondly, they all had a centralized national curriculum. Thirdly, all the countries had a low educational base before the introduction of the Television or Radio for direct teaching. Finally most of countries are small and centralized as to enable the planners to cover the entire sector of education system with the signals of the TV.

Teacher Development and Training

Very few countries in the world have an all developed and well-qualified teaching force to teach in the formal school system. Most of the teaching faculty in many parts of the world is not either graduates or matriculates too. This has led to poor dispensation of education at all levels. The Radio and Television had thus come quite useful by way of conducting a number of distance education programmes which helped the teachers to acquire the qualifications upto the graduation level without having to give up their teaching profession.

Poland is the first country to go for such a programme on a large scale. It has not only gone for educational reform but also has taken up to upgrade the Teachers qualifications. Out of 3,60,000 teachers about 1,60,000 or 44 per cent were not graduates. Therefore, the Ministry of Education created "The National Radio-Television University for Teachers" (NURT) which provides a distance education of 4-year graduation course. No entry qualifications are required. By 1977 around 75,000 teachers were enrolled. Teachers received three television and two radio programmes a week. The broadcast timings were at the end of the schoolwork a day. The fortnightly teacher's journal, *Oswiata I Wychowanie* publishes the texts of the TV and Radio programmes. Recommendations for further reading, exercises and notes on the programmes are also provided. In addition, seminars and tutorials are arranged at local teachers' centres at weekends. The programmes are made and broadcast by the Polish national broadcasting system in consultation with the NURT. The curriculum for the regular students as also the distance mode students is same.

The British Open University system, which became a classic example and legend in the field of distance education for several developing countries also offers Direct Teaching through Television and Radio to the students enrolled on it.

Developing Professional Skills

The use of Radio and Television for the development of professional skills of the teachers is an important dimension of the Direct

Teaching. For instance France in 1977 while reforming the education system, has given high priority to teacher education. Television and Radio along with the print materials are used in a concerted and integrated manner to promote teacher's continuing education. The broadcasting programmes inform the teachers of the new teaching content, encourage them to accept changes and innovations and to help teachers overcome the difficulties, which may arise in their work. Between 76-77, there were about three TV and 4 Radio programmes a week dedicated for the development of the teachers.

Improving Subject Teaching

The advent of Radio and Television broadcasting has come quite handy in offering training programmes to teachers especially to improve their teaching skills and methods. Particularly subjects like Mathematics and Sciences require always new and innovative methods as to cater to the students of varying intellectual levels in a classroom situation. The 'Delta' project of Sweden attracted about 55000 teachers who had been trained by the Radio and TV broadcasts with the printed materials as support materials with regard to the innovative approaches to teaching of Mathematics. Teachers attended local centers for a period of 5 or 6 days during the school vacation. Each day was spent viewing and listening to broadcast television and radio programmes and discussing the programmes. The teachers again use the cassettes of the programmes as reference materials at home. Similarly Ivory Coast and Poland's NURT had utilized projects of Mathematics for the innovative and improved teaching methods of their teachers.

The Indian Government has also launched a similar programme through the Satellite Instructional Television Experiment to access nearly 96000 teachers in 2,400 villages located in far and remote areas. The programme was launched for the improvement in teaching methods in Natural Sciences and was supervised by the ISRO (Indian Space Research Organization). Each target village was provided with a Television set located in the community center of the village along with an aerial and dish.

The teaching method in Natural Sciences was a programme of 15 days duration for the elementary school teachers. It was supported by the printed material such as teacher manuals, practical handbooks and support materials like posters etc.

The National Center designed it for Educational Technology in Delhi. The material was produced in different languages. One of the unique features of these programmes is it offered a number of audio channels in almost all the state languages round the clock simultaneously allowing the villagers to choose the appropriate sound channel to accompany the programme according to the language of the area. The audio was thus synchronized by the local group with the programme telecast on T.V. (Natural Sciences – primary teachers).

The USA also used similar satellite ATS-6 for a year earlier to provide two courses for in-service teachers as part of the Appalachian Educational Satellite Project. The satellite was covering the mountainous ridge running across thirteen states of the US where there was no conventional mode of communications earlier. The other way of training the in-service teachers proved to be futile in view of the hard geographical realities.

As such Direct teaching through this had been chosen to educate and improve the teaching methods of the teachers. The satellite transmission has been done from the University of Kentucky at Lexington. The feedback was by a Radio link from these backward areas through another satellite ATS-3. Four courses were offered, two on careers education and two on teaching elementary reading. Each course consisted of sixteen television programmes and supporting printed material. More than 1000 teachers participated in this programme.

The Interactive Radio Instruction

The Interactive Radio Instruction projects were of unique kind though most of the countries which first resorted to these on pilot project level shelved them later on the pretexts of non-feasibility and non-sustainability solely for want of funds. These bring readymade broadcasts of 20-30 minutes in the form of direct teaching and offer learning exercises to the classroom on a daily basis. The radio lessons were developed in subjects like Mathematics, Sciences, Health and Languages in the State or National Curricula. They were planned with specific learning objectives and were intended to improve the quality of the classroom teaching, besides to supplement poorly trained teachers and under-resourced schools. There would be a two-way communication on the radio sets and the children interact with the presenter who would be usually a qualified teacher with regard to their doubts or the tasks they perform.

Interactive Radio Instruction is different from the school broadcasting, which we discussed in the foregoing. Though the direct teaching and direct response from the students—are its (IRI) significant features, the development of the curriculum has been a very costly input and has been identified as a major stumbling block by many developing countries. Further, the adaptations of these programmes for different countries would not be possible.

If one does so, they would look like straight-line implementation of what is prepared for one country being applied irrelevantly for another. The lack of adaptability and flexibility to the local needs and skills of learning would to some extent handicap the learning process. To overcome this disadvantage, one had to suitably amend or modify the materials prepared by another country for oneself. Certainly this is going to prove very costly.

Another important problem that seems to be hard to overcome is its role in usurping the role of the teacher in the classroom. Though subsequently efforts have been strategically made by decentralizing through the cassettes preparation and distribution to Local Radio the Interactive Radio Programme in respect of Health and Education including Early Childhood Care and Education, the plan of action for such decentralization proved to be very costly too.

Table–15
Interactive Radio Instruction
(*Courtesy:* World Education Forum: Thematic Studies)

Country and Project	*Dates*	*Subject, level, quantity*	*Scale*
1	2	3	4
Nicaragua: Radio Mathematics Project	1974-79	Mathematics in first four primary grades	Half-hour dialy broadcasts
Thailand: Radio mathematics	1980-at least 84	Mathematics in first three primary grades	Half-hour daily broadcasts
Kenya: Radio Language Arts	1980-85	English language in first three primary grades	Half-hour daily broadcosts
Dominican Republic:	1982-at	Reading and mathe-	One-hour daily

(Contd.)

Country and Project	*Dates*	*Subject, level,*	*Scale*
1	2	3	4
RADECO	least 1989	matics for first three primary grades	broadcast
Papua New Guinea: Radio Science	1987-at least 1994	Science for primary grades 4-6	60 20-minute lessons for each grade
Lesotho: English in action broadcasts for	1987-90	English for primary grade 1-3	391 half-daily 1-3 grades
Honduras: Honduran Radio Learning Project	1987-	Maths primary grades 1-3 English, Spanish	465 lessons produced
Bolivia: Radio Mathematics, Radio Health, Early Childhood development	1986-	Mathematics: primary grades 2-5	Daily
Ecuador	1988-91	Mathematics Early Childhood Education	n/a
Guatemala, Costa Rica, El Salvador, Dominican Republic	1988-92	Maths, Spanish	n/a
Costa Rica: Radio Environmental Education	1991-	Environmental Education for primary grades 4 and 5	n/a
South Africa: English in Action	1992-	English language, primary grades 1-2	130 30-minute cassettes; daily broadcasts
Lusophhone Africa	1992-	Maths grades 3-4	n/a
Venezuela	1996-	Maths	275 30-minute lessons

No. of students	*Cost*	*Comment*
5	6	7
10,000 maximum[b]	Average cost 1975 55.60@50,000 students[c]	Closed as result of revolution

(Contd.)

No. of students	*Cost*	*Comment*
5	6	7
n/a	n/a	Adaptation on Nicaragua materials, undertaken mainly by Thai staff
n/a	n/a	Project closed when USAID funding ended
57 schools, 80 class-rooms by 1989[d]	n/a	Project run for non-formal groups, with auxiliary on radiophonic school model
9,000 in 1990 40,000 in 1992 75,000 in 1994[e]	n/a	Project survive USAID cuts 1989 and funding withdrawal 1990
200,900 in 1990 (80,500 in standard 1,63,400 in s 2,57,000 in s3)	1990 $1.34 per student[f]	Materials adapted from Kenay and now part of regular curriculum, reported to be still operating 1997[g]
100,000 grade 1,50,000 grade 2,30,000 grade 3, in maths 1990[h]	1990 $2.94 per student @ 200,000 enrollment[i] ($3.67)	Run in partnership with commercial publisher, not institutionalized[g]
250,000 enrolled	1990 $2.80 per student @ enrollment of 70,000, falling to $ 1.28 @ 300,000[k] ($3.49 to $1.60)	Run in association with Church-based NGO
300	n/a	Pilot in 21 schools, completed by 1991[l]
n/a	n/a	Adaptation of Honduras materials Costa Rice closed down; El Salvador continued
36,000 students in 1200 schools 1991[l]	n/a	Two pilot schemes run but not then implemented
15,200 grade 1,9,600 grade 2 in 1995	Cost in range 1994 Rand 3.13-8.16 per student[m] ($0.97 to $2.53)	Project criticized for behaviorist origins but then remodeled and continues with NORAD funding
n/a	n/a	Developed in Cape Verde for use also in Angola, Mozambique, Sao Tome[g]

No. of students	*Cost*	*Comment*
5	6	7
300,000 students in 12,000 classes	n/a	Funded with World Bank loan with some recurrent costs from state budgets[g]

Source: Perraton 2000: 48-51.

Notes: Costs in italics are in constant 1998 US$$.

(a) Other projects, with less detail, are referred to in Bosch 1997 and Dock and Helwig 1999;
(b) Friend *et al.*, 1980: 30;
(c) Jamison *et al.*, 1978: 136;
(d) Radio Learning Project n.d.: 43;
(e) Olsson 1994: 16;
(f) Tilson 1991: 337 but including direct costs omitted from his figure;
(g) Bosch 1997: 9-10;
(h) Radio Learning Project n.d.:
(i) Tilson 1991: 326;
(j) Fryer 1995: 20;
(k) Tilson 1991: 307-8;
(l) Anzalone 1991: 48;
(m) Cobbe 1995: 21;
(n) Helwig *et al.*, 1999: 24-5.

As a matter of fact, the programme has been developed by the USAID (the United Sates Agency for International Development) in the early 1970s and has since been implemented in about 20 countries comprising Latin American, African and Asian countries.

There are some inter-country projects also, which operate combining a group of countries. For instance five African countries with Portuguese as an official language (PALOP) with the assistance from UNESCO, the Netherlands government and the USAID, are involved in the concerted effort of developing the *Interactive Radio Instruction* curriculum for *Mathematics* and *Portuguese as a Second language*.

The evaluation of these programmes have demonstrated a good outcome in terms of the consistence of the children performance, narrowing the gap in the scholastic achievement between the rural and urban, between the boys and the girls and in improving the teaching standards of the schools.

One survey of Flavell and Micallef (1995) on the exclusive role and the effectiveness of Radio and Radio plus in improving the

English Language Skills of the secondary students in Mozambique has shown the relative edge of Radio plus over plain Radio educational broadcasting. The study which was conducted on large scale longitudinal sampling over a nine-month period in seven Mozambican state schools concluded that the general exposure to radio is beneficial when radio is used in conjunction with good quality local print materials and with the local teachers being well trained how to use Radio and its recorded audio cassettes effectively for the benefit and enrichment of English language of the students.

Used in an integrated manner along with the printed materials and teacher awareness, besides creativity to effectively use these programmes, the Radio plus seems to be a better option than Radio alone. Most of the African nations which are now effectively using the Radio for the improvement in English through Radio English Direct are likely to benefit if they follow the integrated method. This required including an awareness programme for the teachers as to how to use the Radio along with other materials or resources in their teacher training failing which the Teacher's role gets reduced to that of simply monitoring the class for maintenance of discipline during the Radio programme or to run the Radio programme to take off from the routine monotony of teaching.

This year the British Council has conducted a workshop in collaboration with the Government of Nigeria on "Taking to Radio Waves" at Kaduna. The programme was related to encouraging the 8 countries in re-broadcasting of the BBC English Language Teaching programmes along with the indigenously produced English Language Programmes. The countries, which participated in the above workshop, were Nigeria, Sudan, Senegal, Cameroon, Eritrea, Benin, Mali and Ethiopia.

The Government of Eritrea has immediately followed it up and submitted the proposal to the British Council to launch this programme with its collaboration for the benefit of the English Language Learners and the Teachers.

Evaluation of the Outcomes of the Broadcasting of Educational Programmes

The evaluation of the outcomes of the Broadcasting of the educational programmes particularly by Radio has not been done much in the developed countries. But a lot of intensive research on the outcomes of these broadcasts has come from the developing countries. Wilbur Schramm (1977) has carried out the most comprehensive review of the research into the relative success of the different strategies for the Educational Television and Radio. The study was done on the efficacy of the Radio and the Television in offering the learning resources and enrichment. His analysis on the effectiveness of these two broad categories drew on studies of Television projects in the USA, Japan, Colombia and India and of Radio in Thailand. In each of these studies there were control groups i.e. Schools or classes which did not watch the educational programmes and which watched as carefully as possible. The results of these studies indicated that those who used these programmes to supplement their classroom learning had better scores over the control groups which did not use these programmes.

Another study of Japanese Broadcasting Authority (NHK, 1969) on Japanese schools where Radio programmes for the School children were implemented between 1960-68 concluded that over a period of time of constantly listening to the Radio lessons, the students started showing a better performance in the tests conducted over the control groups who have not at all heard those programmes.

They have thus found that the sustainability of the programmes are based on long-term application of these to the learning process of the children exposed to the Radio school broadcasts. At the same time, the study was cautious to add that these results are subject to the standard of the quality of the programmes produced, ability of the teachers to effectively relate them to the students, students' abilities and interests and the length of the period of utilization. As such both Schramm and NHK concluded that there would be substantial gains by the implementation of these educational broadcasts in general.

Non-Formal Education

Non-formal education, in so far media is concerned, is strictly related to helping an individual to solve his or her own problems independent of a particular curricular content. It concerns with the improving of the personal, social and work life of individuals. However in the extended signification, the non-formal education has acquired some of the characteristics of the formal education.

Today non-formal education tends to have structured and organized mode of instruction, with a systematic content of curriculum and with the objectives to achieve specific outcomes after a period of instruction. In many aspects, it assumed the form of distance education. In not having a specific qualification requirement as a background to qualify for a study through non-formal mode, it really met the definition of *non-formal education*. But in the sense of getting merged at the end (as an outcome) with the mainstream of formal education at a later date or in the sense of offering a graded or structured education, it met the definition of a *formal education*.

The idea of providing non-formal stream of education to the under-privileged or drop outs or aged adults by any government is to bringback those most of the deprived to the mainstream of education. Thus distance education programmes are in a sense part of non-formal education (Anthony Bates). At the same time, by virtue of their having a prescribed curriculum, syllabus, term examinations on par with the regular stream of formal education, it is formal education (Wilbur Schramm, 1977).

Generally speaking the Media has a double role in the non-formal education. One is providing educative programmes to those enthusiastic learners through news reels and documentaries on current affairs to increase the general level of awareness and the other is to broadcast programmes on a structured curricular content on the same lines and goals that of formal educational programmes offered which were already discussed at length in the foregoing.

This apart there are other objectives for which the non-formal education is considered a main alternative by any government. Firstly to reduce the *inequalities in access* and *inequalities in educational qualifications* prior to entry to the formal education system, to reduce *inadequacies arising from within the formal school education* after joining it, to meet the new needs that crop up while passing through the prime age. All these broadly cover the goals of any government, which aspire to achieve Universalization of Basic Education before 2010. Further they would automatically become part of any project or programme labelled variously as adult education, non-formal education, or continuing education or life-long education.

Basic Adult Education, as mentioned already, is a controversial term both in the sense of the objectives to be achieved or the needs of the target groups. In some countries, the governments tend to define the basic adult education as a programme mainly intended to achieve simple literacy, numeracy and social coping skills. They also include general awareness of health and hygiene, agriculture, environment, safety and civic sense under the term Adult Education. Both the Radio and Televison have been used to achieve these goals.

Broadcasting for adult literacy has begun first in Italy way back in 1960. The Telescuola in Southern Italy first offered a course entitled, *None Mai troppotardi* (It is never too late) had attracted the masses in an unpredictable measure. Ever since there were a number countries which have been implementing the programmes for adult literacy in one way or the other. In Britain the BBC initiated a major literacy campaign between 1974-79 which proved to be very successful programme though it was the first of its kind. The programmes for the numeracy have not been as many as for the other activities of the Adult Education, the demand for such programmes not-withstanding. The Yorkshire Television series 'Make it Count' was the first of its kind in imparting basic arithmetic skills to those who had no minimum skills of making simple additions and subtractions.

Most of the emphasis in Adult Education is always on the coping skills (or life skills) which included awareness of their rights and responsibilities, employment opportunities, awareness of protecting their rights against commercialism and from excess consumerism. In some countries, the Adult Literacy included both coping skills and skills of numeracy. But in some countries it is not only a matter of offering the above skills to the adults of the age range of 30 to 45, but also it included a systematic planned instruction to attract them back to the mainstream of education. Hence the curriculum forming for the Adult Education is of an important dimension to the whole gamut of the problem. There cannot be or should not be one common curriculum for all the age groups.

There needs to be a lot of planning and understanding of the problem on a holistic basis. There should be planning of the curriculum for various grades and age groups. Those who are in the age group of likely return as a target group to the fold of mainstream of education or formal education, the curriculum should be planned almost on similar lines with decreased level difficulty and with a few subjects as optionals. Those who have crossed the age of possible return to the mainstream above 16+, should be offered a different curriculum to make them fit for a direct admission to the Open University system. Those who crossed the age group of those who are likely to join the University level too through the distance mode and more or less likely to remain as illiterates for ever should be given a different curriculum. It is here the coping skills, functional literacy and numeracy coupled with documentaries and news reels on current affairs and contemporary developments that could build a desired level of awareness to the adults.

Hence curriculum planning for Adults Education is pivotal to any possibility of success. Many countries had a good number of intentions and plans to make the programmes of Adult literacy successful. But the failures stare into these programmes chiefly because of lack of development of a suitable curriculum for different target groups. Again this problem is more accentuated by lack of suitable strategy, manpower beside infrastructure.

Countries like India offered all the above categories of curriculum to the Adults and have been much successful in lowering the Adult illiteracy in the last one and half a decade. On the other there were projects like 'Danish for Adults' (a multi-media project) which used Radio as a sole means of transmitting the messages and the value of the programme got enhanced by the supplementary printed material as also the group work of the Adult educators. The Dutch Open School project, like 'Danish for Adults' is another example of a complex project but part of it was built around themes like interior decoration or obtaining a playground etc.

One aim is for each group to determine its own themes and priorities for study, which posed of course a lot of problem to the Radio and Television in choosing the appropriate, content and material. Yet the project went ahead under the aegis of Dutch Educational Television Company—TELEAC which took sole responsibility to produce the programmes. There were programmes, which dealt with a common spelling problem each week, information on the different kinds of available adult education, items on politics and justice and some English Language Teaching. Dutch Radio was responsible to offer the broadcasting services for the Adult Literacy programmes.

In Britain there were broadcasting programmes like *Living Decisions in Family and Community* offered by the BBC Radio series way back in 1973. This was followed by another series *What Right have you Got?* – Both the programme series were aimed at offering the awareness of making decisions, importance of decision making in day to day life and realizing the opportunities through such decisions. All these are woven round the coping skills required for the adults.

However in Northern Europe and North America the Adult literacy programmes tended to be different and are woven round specific contents and learning objectives. In fact there were series, which were offering a structured, and highly learner centered education to the Adults to bring them to the fold of the formal educational qualifications. Even BBC Radio in early 1960s offered in collaboration with the National Extension College programmes related to the Adults who were inclined to take 'O' level or 'A' level English examinations.

Though Britain has crossed that stage now, there are many countries like Spain, Latin American countries, Brazil, Malawi, the Dominion Republic and African countries, which are following the same pattern of course with a slightly modified versions. For instance, in Brazil, a special examination, the 'Madureza' is available for adults seeking the equivalent of the secondary school leaving certificate. Further, the 'Minerva' project was set up in Brazil to produce radio-based programme of studies leading up to the 'Madureza'. Of course, all these programmes are supported by the enormous print materials, booklets and pamphlets which enhanced the listening value of the programmes.

The complexities of the Adult Education, as could be gauged from the preceding discussion on various facets and dimensions of it, are much higher than the formal or traditional education. The number of alternative ways to offer the adult education coupled with the flexibility in the definitions makes the task even difficult and worse confounded than what one could conceive as a wide range of choice open for a given government.

Lifelong education and continuing education are two such important definitions or dimensions where it is very difficult to draw distinction between programmes which meant for the Adult

Education and General Education. Both the definitions or dimensions offer the programmes which are not based on any structured syllabus but are self-contained in unleashing a lot of information that would go to enhance the awareness level of the individuals who could not pursue the education to a desired level in their lives. McCron (1981) raises a number of questions in bringing these programmes under the fold of education.

The programmes related to health, hygiene, environment, agriculture, market economy, climate, promotion of native skills, small scale industries, government welfare measures, fast changing global trends in tourism and travel, indigenous and overseas employment for the skilled and semi-skilled workers, art and sculpture etc., would enhance the level of the awareness of the individuals enormously undoubtedly but they are more educative and unstructured and do not form the part of any curriculum of the non-formal or distance education. Yet the programmes offer immense information both as enrichment material or learning resource which, if effectively utilized by the teachers, students and adult educators, would go a long way in igniting the imagination of individuals.

The broadcasters have variously categorized these programmes. Some called these programmes as social action programmes. For instance the BBC Radio programmes of 1934 on 'Unemployment clubs', 'Werwinkel' project of Holland. Similarly some called these programmes as Rural programmes. An example is 'The Archers' a fifteen minute daily BBC programme of 1953s dealing with the country folk to inculcate in them the modern methods of farming practices in the post second world war. This programme was continued to its third generation artists, the grandchildren of the first generation artists still enacting the roles with 1.5 million listeners even today holding on to these programmes.

The Radio farms of India started in Gujarat in 1954 also come under this category. The Radio farms had done miracle in Indian agricultural economy ever since and they are taken both for their practical and realistic value by the Indian farmers even today. Some called these as programmes for the disadvantaged and minority groups. Whatsoever may be the title of these programmes, they are generally believed to be highly educative and reaching wide range of audiences.

However practical experience and theory together suggest that the combination of broadcasting with group study could be an effective way providing non-formal education for adults (World Education Forum: Dakar, Senegal, 26-28 April, 2000, p. 6). To be very successful in adult education programmes, there should be a multi-media approach. One is to press the media in to service in support of state literacy campaigns. Kenyan example is though variant deserves a mention here. Kenya government used distance-teaching methods to train literacy educators. Second one is to offer a wide range of mass communication methods equivalent to conventional schooling both for the adults and the disadvantaged children. Third is the involvement of extension agencies and public education programmes especially in agriculture and health.

Most of the countries in the world which embarked upon a new and a variety of eradication of illiteracy programmes have ended up abruptly without having to know the reasons – where and why they ended up in such a grand failure. The failures of these countries are obvious for they followed the examples of developed counties very blindly. All the strategies of communication applicable to the developed countries are not straight away applicable and relevant to the third world countries. Secondly, there should be a strong political will to translate the objectives and goals of these programmes into a reality. It is therefore imperative to know where and why a particular action plan and programme of adult literacy failed.

The failures could be at the making of message level or at the lack of properly discussed and formulated strategy. On the other the failure could be due to the lack of proper administrative hierarchy involving the motivated voluntary agencies etc. Hence Hornick classified the Development Communication into two categories; Communication for political organization and Communication as complement. This has aptly explained the failure of communication in the developing countries and the reasons how the initial euphoria around the adult literacy programmes evaporated soon.

A careful analysis of the failures of Adult literacy programmes in developing countries has suggested two possible wayouts: One is to press into service the Radio than rely upon the Television, which is a very costly exercise that many developing and nascent counties may not be able to run on a sustainable pace and plane and the second is to bring in a participatory methodology. Projects run by the British Charity – Action Aid – for example are founded on a carefully constructed methodology known as REFLECT (Regenerated Freirean Literacy through Empowering Community Techniques). These two possible alternative strategies in conjunction with the Community Radio Programmes would offer several out-reach educational programmes for the benefit of the rural illiterate, deprived and under privileged.

The Television-Visual and Complementary Medium

The mere mention of the word Television brings to our mind many things, which are of great interest and intrigue. There cannot be a single soul, which would not be influenced by the electrifying and captivating presence of a TV in a home or in a school or in a shop. What is not cynosure of Television? From a kid to an elderly person everything and anything beamed on the little screen of TV is of immense interest. The variety of channels the cable operators provide, the infinite variety of programmes each channel would plan and broadcast – the special pay channels of sports, music, fashion, and what not – all together, individually and collectively, make the time of the individual very precious and entertaining. Which precedes the other – information, education and entertainment – among the three appears to be a real challenge for an academician to brood over and conclude.

There are so many controversies as to the utility and efficacy of the TV as a medium of education or information (UNESCO, Media Education: Mass Media and the school: Descartes or McLuhan? Pierre Schaeffer, p. 44). Marshal McLuhan argues that by leaving TV for school, a child's progress in his mind takes a regressive path. His emphasis on the role of TV, irrespective of its evil effects on the impressionable age, in education has no parallel. Many conventional educationists have not accepted his argument. They argued that by watching TV, the listener, especially the child becomes very passive and passive reception is not going to contribute to the vertical intellectual growth of the child (UNESCO, *Ibid.*, p. 58). Nor does TV watching enable the child to condition the mind and discriminate between the relevant and irrelevant.

Parallel School

But to many this argument does not cut the ice with. Firstly there are many similarities between the Television and the classroom. By virtue of the aggressive role of the teacher in a conventional environment, the students are more passive audience than before the TV. On the other many a classroom conditioning situations do not apply to learning through TV. This is in a way an additional point that TV scores over the classroom monotony. Adverting to the role of TV in Education, in an attempt to resolve the conflict between its role as a medium of information and its role as a medium of messages, the UNESCO tried to strike a balance between two paradoxical views of Descartes and McLuhan. Neither media could be a source of information alone, where it becomes subservient to the classroom conventional teaching, nor Media itself could be the complete and comprehensive message. The UNESCO had taken the view that the schools should be situated within the world of Radio and Television.

The UNESCO has thus observed that *As far as the mass media were concerned, information was contemporary, while the schools' area of interest lay in the records of the past. Education in the true sense, which the schools appeared to have neglected for some time, was taken up again in the more immediate context of the current scene by way of 'exposure to the world' (through TV). With regard to entertainment, as we have repeatedly been told, this could serve a 'cultural' function provided it was of suitably high quality; indeed, it might be more effective in this sense than many an earnest lecture. The human community thus found itself attended by the schools on one hand and the media on the other, in the role of a father and a mother, as it were, with the former assuming the masculine function of providing training, while the latter undertook the feminine role of gathering to its bosom information from the entire universe* (*Ibid*, p. 49).

Therefore, the Educational broadcasting has become a *parallel school* in the context of modern education. The disparateness and predominance of images, visuals, messages, content, the lack of balance between fiction and reality, quality and the mediocrity – all warrant a supplementary role of teachers in the school. The images whatever are remembered by the students even after months, notwithstanding, the images that are likely to be forgotten should be stored in an information storage and retrieval system. Thus the 'parallel school' included in its definition three important components – the mass communication production machinery, the produced and finished product comprising messages and visuals and the storage and retrieval system in the form of audio and video cassettes and their players. Against this backdrop the conventional school performs it supplementary or complementary role as a paternal structure.

It is then a meaningful coherence between what is learnt in school and what is apparently flashed on the screen, as a jungle of messages and visuals could be established. The *cultural mosaic* of information, defined by Abraham Moles, apparently heaped on the TV screen by the abundance of the programmes, either meant for children or for adults, could not escape without influencing the minds of the people. There cannot be a selective transmission at any time. The schools of Africa, Papua, India, from the Wild West to Mowgli's jungle were thus not concerned with programmemed instruction and education. They offer the general knowledge and know-how to live in the world with intelligence and realistic values. The schools of course in their complementary role are expected of to impart the critique values rather than teach the *conceptual order*.

Pierre Schaeffer has called this 'the sharing out of the cheap cuts'. Any effort to integrate both the schools call upon both re-conversion of the existing teaching staff to new tasks and a real awareness on the part of the communicators of the problems involved in education. Since the school is a 'communication society', it is very selective in its acceptance of the new forms of 'parallel school'.

Communication programmes related to family education, functional literacy teaching, health and hygiene etc., are considered of educational value. Similarly systems like Radio, Television, films are gradually adopted by the school to allow the communication programmes for the benefit of the students in the formal system of education. Owing to different types of media, different types of levels of work related to education, owing to the different target groups and different formats that are required for the production of the programmes, myriads of combinations arise in the effective utilization of communication technology. At the same time, the planners at the top level must be aware that the production of these programmes in their original splendor and grandeur call for a lot of hard work at the ground level. Otherwise, the simplest way is to resort to projects like Rural Radio.

The social, cultural and economic development of a country depends to a great extent upon its way of responding to and utilizing mass communication. (UNESCO-Mass Communication Education: Ana Maria Sandi, p. 86). Soedjatmoko defines the learning capacity of a nation as the 'collective capacity' to generate, to ingest, to reach out for and to utilize a vast amount of new and relevant information. (UNESCO, *Ibid.*, p. 86).

It is therefore no wonder if one calls Television as an 'early window' to the world (R.M. Liebert, J.M. Neale, E.S. Davidson, 1973). It is an *alternative school.* Programmes like 'Success in Reading' dealing with system of teaching reading and writing by using newspapers and magazines instead of classical first-grade hand writing book proved to be very successful in many schools. In Romania a successful television programme that has been maintained for many years is a scientific programme—the Tele Encyclopaedia. Pupils, parents and teachers alike watched it. But the unfortunate side of this programme is that there is no reference, in the least, or discussion about or to it in the school during the regular hours. The successful science serial conceived by the J. Bronowski has sent the ripples across the young all over the world. Another scientific Television serial, 'Connections' produced in a lively manner by the British Journalist James Burke has generated unprecedented interest among the children and the adults as it could successfully portray how the science and the society went forward together in a progressive society of information and communication.

The Classroom—A Teacher's Kingdom

Even in the modern 21st century there is no alternative to the conventional school and classroom system despite the tall claim of tremendous technological development and innovations in the field of education and communication. Ninety per cent of the countries in the UN even today depend on the chalk and talk method of teaching in a classroom. Only ten per cent of the countries, mostly UK, USSR and France etc. could provide the classrooms fitted with modern electronic gadgetry such as Televisions, Computers for using the Power point demonstrations and teleconferencing facilities.

As such the role of the teacher in the classroom reigns supreme. The didactics of the teacher have no parallel. The teacher plays the aggressive and lead role. Mostly lecture mode dominates the teaching methodology occasionally dotted by the demonstration method if the school, and the country in which the school is situated, is fortunate enough to have one laboratory. The low cost teaching aids as a means of accessing the students to the abstract concepts are the products of a few genuine efforts of teachers committed to the cause of education. Yet the teachers assume the role of kings and wish that no one interfered in their domain of work. They cannot tolerate the idea of Television usurping their role in a classroom situation. They feel it as an affront to their so far princely role, which they unleashed without being questioned even once.

Of all the dominant roles that teachers tend to unleash in the classroom context, Hovan refers to two important variants: one relates to teacher's unquestionable role in teaching-testing-grading-rewarding-punishing and the other relates to his lively interaction with students with or without the contextual situations. The advent of Television in its new robes as a teacher directly teaching the students naturally pricks the sub-conscious of the teachers as the latter feel presumably being replaced with technology. It instantaneously arouses hostility towards such innovations. It makes them feel situated out of the context or alienated from the advancing innovations in education. The very people who have to play a very pivotal role would tend to remain outside the domain of Television programmes or educational broadcasting. This is one reason often attributed to the failures of the Media role in the Education. Any person who has to allow a parallel innovation must be part and parcel of the innovation process and help giving full effect to it by his active participation.

Even if the teachers wish to do away with these advances, it is impossible to achieve any success in this regard. For the present day student has full exposure to the Media in one way or the other. Even if educational broadcasting is not in the reach of the student, other forms of Media, such as Cinema or Cable films, Videocassettes are accessible to him. He has the full-blown impact of all the visual images on his mind. Therefore, the today's learner is gradually drifting away from the conventional and traditional controls of the classroom. In fact with a dramatic change in the minds of the learners against this backdrop there is no point in teachers' hanging on to their traditional classroom dominance. They have to don the new garbs of awareness in the context of changing scenario. They must acquaint themselves as to how to draw a maximum of benefit from the programmes of the Media broadcasting and how to correlate them with the textbook ideas. They must, in other words, strike a balance between the examples of the outside situations and the experiences of the classroom teaching.

It is in day-to-day teaching efforts and long range curriculum planning that teachers can incorporate ideas, examples and personalities from outside the classroom into concerns inside the learning environment (UNESCO—The two worlds of today's learners: Donald P Ely, p. 102).

The New Literacy Movement

The fast changing scenario on the information and communication front at the global level calls for a modification in the definition of literacy. Mere lack of knowledge of three Rs does no longer constitute the broad definition of illiteracy. Today illiteracy is viewed by many countries, particularly of Third World, as an inability to read and write. But the so-called illiteracy is not at all illiteracy in the sense the illiterates are able to fully comprehend the socio, economic and political developments happening around. The influence of the Media as Cinema and Television, and Communication network including phones and cellular phones, computers and electronic business and commerce has been obvious on the illiterate too. Most of them who could not read and write could yet do some mechanical operations with all these in the modern age. Therefore, the illiteracy as conceived by the educationists in the past has to undergo a modification in the definition. Today illiteracy includes lack of knowledge of computer and visual illiteracy. The education offered through the adult education programmes or through non-formal education centres, or through lifelong or continuing education must include the ability to not only read and write but the ability to interpret the phenomenon around in terms of pictures, paintings, posters and visual images. It is in this context that the adult education through the Television becomes an important policy matter for any developing nation.

The Visual Literacy Movement has taken roots in the early 1970s in the US and the National Conference on Visual Literacy suggested the essence of the definition of the Visual Literacy as follows:

When a person has developed a set of visual abilities through seeing and sensory experiences, and when they are able to discriminate and interpret visual actions, objects, patterns and symbols in the environment, then they are becoming visually literate. It is through the creative use of these abilities that a visually literate person is able to comprehend and communicate. An appreciation of the visual skills of others will lead to greater enjoyment of visual communication.

In many North American Primary and Secondary schools the programmes related to visual literacy have already been implemented. In Australia, the educators are planning and experimenting to introduce this education through the programmes like 'Media studies' and 'mental imagery'. A major training programme for adults in the US is the Television Awareness Training. The most important facet of this programme is to impart a 24-hour instruction on how to use Television and what the teaching messages are and how can make changes that seem appropriate. The curriculum forms the study of Television from the viewpoint of human values. Another example is the five-session in service course for teachers on *Visual Learning* – a course structure prepared by the New York State Education Department.

Interest in the visual symbols as a means of communication is not a latest phenomenon. Stalwarts like Adelbert Ames, Rudolf Arnheim, Ernst Cassirer, Charles Morris have explored the relationships of signs and symbols to human communication. Marshall McLuhan, MD Vernon and Jerome Bruner are some social scientists and communocologists who are working on this topic of interest of late.

Curriculum and Its Relationship to Television

The curriculum and the teaching are two important components of the classroom experience. It is how the curriculum is related to the student that plays a crucial role in bringing the concepts closer to the understanding. In fact over half-a-century there has been a tremendous output of variety of subjects besides an enormous output of content in each subject. The new findings kept on either confirming the old facts or modifying the facts of the past or dismissing the old facts. But the classroom teaching did not undergo the proportionate change. As the textbook facts became more and more complex with increasing logical propositions and mathematical symbols, there should have been accompanying changes in the teaching. But, the teaching remained more or less static and traditional. It presented a lot of difficulty to the understanding levels of the students in a classroom, which especially consists of a number of heterogeneous groups of students with a range of intellectual quotients.

The consequence of above situation often raises a number of doubts whether the learning experience of classroom is meaningful at all. The way many scientific facts are taught in the classroom does not allow the relation of abstract ideas in the proper perspective to the students as they are originally conceived by the scientists. Secondly, the treatment of the abstract ideas off the context under which the scientists have come to arrive at those ideas or findings is going to leave the students with no option but to remember it by rote memory and/or by simply mugging up the symbols and formulae. This deprives the students of the originality of the findings.

The classroom experience thus offers a meaningless learning. The students are not in a position to independently judge and make an idea of the abstract knowledge they gained in the classroom. It does not allow them to develop the skill of decision making. Nor does it permit the student to attach any value to the possible outcomes, if at all any decision is made and implemented. Thus the meaningful learning in terms of the participation and anticipation is missing or lost in the modern conventional education.

Further, the cognitive learning of Ausubel organizers in terms of symbols and images in subjects like Mathematics, Sciences and Social studies is totally glossed over in the present conventional teaching methodology. Ausubel identifies three types of meaningful learning: Representational learning which consists of learning isolated symbols, Propositional learning which concerns the assimilation of propositions along with their logical sense and the Concept learning a more advanced type in which the terms become mere notions which constitute generalizations of a number of anterior meanings and experiences. Ausubel thus advocated the idea of 'progressive differentiation' and 'integrative reconciliation' as ways of integrating the concepts at a lower level into concepts at a higher level through which teacher must wade through. He called it as effective utilization of 'advanced organizers' in facilitating the relation of abstract ideas to the learners. He described it as follows:

The function of the organizer is to provide ideational scaffolding for the stable incorporation and retention of the more detailed and differentiated material.

With this method, according to Ausubel, each lesson or learning sequence should be preceded by the presentation of an *organizer* (symbols or images or visuals) introducing the student to the context in to which will integrate the new 'curriculum content'. Ausubel has limited his research to verbal and written communication but research has shown that *organizers* can consist of sounds and images. Therefore in terms of Media, the Ausubel *image* and the *concept* both are two sides of the same coin. Thus in the extended signification of Ausubel organizers, the Media can relate the subject curriculum to the Television as follows:

1. The subject matter is presented not in a sequential or analytical manner but as a whole, seen from a general point of view.
2. A maximum of detail can be presented and any number of 'cues' provided to facilitate meaningful learning.
3. The use of moving images permits diachronic presentation.
4. The presentation of the subject directly, without any intermediary, gives an effective component to the new content, involving not only the individual's cognitive structure but also his socio-affective experiences, interests and motivation.
5. Organizers are suitable for learners of all ages and all types of subject matter (UNESCO; Yuri Babansky, p. 128).

The *image* is *an analogue or representational symbol*, while the *word* is a *digital symbol*. The image is direct, unique, and specific the word is abstract, conceptual and translatable.

The Curricular Planning for Formal and Non-Formal Broadcasting

The most important problem concerning the educational broadcasting through Television or Radio, more particularly for Television, is the planning of curriculum for the formal and non-formal broadcasting. What should be the basis of production of TV programmes? Should a formal education curriculum be planned first to produce the TV Educational programmes a prior consideration must be given to the requirements of TV production from the content point of view before finalizing the curriculum. It calls for a new orientation of training for the teachers involved in curriculum planning. In the case of direct teaching through Educational broadcasting the Television would have to have an independent research cell with its own education officers who can sift through the prescribed syllabus and content on their own and collect the materials for the production of programmes lesson wise and subject-wise. In such cases there is no requirement for a curricular reform, which often many countries found burdensome. Whatever is done by the research and development unit of the broadcasting service on the front of the curriculum for its production automatically results in the curriculum reform for such an effort calls for a lot of reference work of the given content and a wide coverage of a range of standard study materials.

This apart, there should be enough space in the curriculum of formal education for the active involvement of Television broadcasting as an important and indispensable teacher-student activity. More often than not, for the reasons of lack of infrastructure or due to the availability of a single TV for the entire institution, the educational broadcasting takes a secondary or tertiary significance in the school or college situation.

Since 1964, the educational broadcasting has been on the Television screen in Britain. However, their importance and influence on the education of the children is a much less researched one in Britain. The first ever research was that of Hayter (1974) who found that the Television has greatly enhanced the educational experience of the students in the schools where it had been implemented with a missionary zeal. Subsequently Wade and Poole (1983) proved that the educational television is an important aid to the teacher to perfect one's own skills and understanding of the subject he is concerned with. The Bullock Committee Report (1975: pp. 322-27) clearly emphasized the vital role the Television plays in the language teaching and learning with regard to reading and writing skills.

Although educational television has been largely neglected within curriculum considerations, its existence and possible contribution to young children's education has been acknowledged by many otherwise. Lesser (1972), Bryant, Alexander and Brown

(1983), Home (1983) and Fowles & Horner (1974) unanimously insist that an American series '*Sesame Street*' has proved that children not only learn from television but that active interaction is not always necessary (Teachers and Television: Ernest Choat, Harry Griffin and Dorothy Hobart, 1987, p. 4).

Lesser (1972) contended that Television is a vehicle for direct teaching by telling and showing what is intended children should learn, then teaching them by telling and showing it to them, and finally by telling and showing them again what they have been taught. This contention is reiterated by the findings of Fowles and Voyat (1974) who maintained that television facilitates rote verbal learning and it is not mere passive reception as some educationists opposed to the Television invading the educational arena. (Teachers and Television: Ernest Choat, Harry Griffin and Dorothy Hobart: Croom Helm, 1987, p. 4.) Most of these findings are based on the American series 'Sesame street' and 'The Electric Company'. However, these findings suggested that the Television can teach and there is a lot of unexploited scope in this part of education which the educational administering authorities must utilize. It also called for the involvement of teachers as part of curriculum planning and classroom experience since the students of younger age group would try to relate the abstractions and visuals more with their past knowledge and it sometimes need for a formal guidance and corrections. Otherwise they are likely to end up in a maze of images and in a labyrinth of confusion of ideas.

Most of the young children will not have the mental development to reason the barrage of images flying before on the Television screen. They do not know the significance of some images and some visuals in relation to the sounds and music that accompany them. They may not have full intellectual development and maturity to grasp the meaning of many that they see in the classroom. Hence, the teachers are expected to organize a small session or group of students and relate them to the students in a way that leaves very less scope for the children to go astray from the intended outcomes or learning objectives. Mere watching therefore does not make the children rich in their awareness and understanding as is sought to be projected by the Marshall McLuhan (UNESCO Media Education, p. 58).

This apart, the long exposure to Television does not create understanding either. The children need to have real life situations or classroom experiences to supplement what they have seen or heard in the educational broadcasting. Noble (1975 : 83-84) brought out another dimension of the student's psyche to the understanding of what one sees on the Television screen. Noble referred to it as 'ego-centrism'. He has proved that there are five ways that a child can interpret or understand the visual images shown to him on the Television. Firstly, he would assume that all the images shown are either good or bad. Secondly, he would look at all the images from his personal past experience stand point of view, which is in fact very limited. This will make them believe everything shown on the television screen is real. The distinction between the fiction created on the screen and the reality shown on the screen would not be in the grasp of the child. For example, the child takes the puppets and the animation characters for reality.

Thirdly, he would try to search for the similar characters on the Television screen from his personal family circle and friends. Fourthly they tend to give their own classification to the images on the screen. Fifthly, the children cannot understand forward and backward sequences or reverse operations of the television serial and as such they cannot recall them or recapitulate them too. In other words they will not be able to perceive the beginning, middle and the end of the sequence.

These examples suggest that the television production of programmes for the formal or non-formal education, for certain age groups, cannot by itself automatically ensure better learning experiences to the learners and/ or audience. Against this backdrop it is natural to conclude that the Television programmes are to be age specific and the programmes meant for the children, especially of 3 to 7 years age, must take into count the Piaget's theory of intellectual and cognitive development. Likewise, the planning and production of educational broadcasting must consider the age requirements besides the curriculum constraints. As the children grow in their age, their attention gets focused on the theme of the serial or plot of the story. But children in the age of adolescence would have variously assumed the images from the Noble's egocentrism theory point of view. Therefore, the crux of the issue is how to involve teacher as an intermediary to facilitate proper awareness and understanding of what visuals offer on the Television screen. It is here a planned curriculum that incorporated a regular schedule of involvement of Educational Television became much relevant as much as planning of curriculum keeping the production parameters of the Television in mind.

The educational broadcasting in respect of English Language Teaching and Mathematics proved to be very successful both in Britain and the US. The teachers responses to a limited survey of research have confirmed that the curriculum planning used in the broadcasting was done with the involvement of teachers and as such the programmes elicited a fair response from the students of below 8 years age group as much as above the 8 years age group. The children below 8 years age group developed very good language skills and mathematical skills whereas students above the 8 years age group expanded their awareness and understanding of these subjects. Similarly the series produced on the topics of the curriculum such as sciences and social had come quite as an enrichment resource or learning resources both for the teachers and the students (Teachers and Television: Ernets Choat, Harry Griffin and Dorothy Hobart, 1987, pp. 100-18).

The Complexities of Education Complicate the Broadcasting Programmes

The West based educational methodology has become an ideal compelling force for the developing countries to emulate. Further, the desire to compete with western educational patterns often leaves very little scope for the developing countries and the nascent countries to take some liberty and freedom in their country's educational planning and development.

Since times immemorial the curriculum is always subjects based and content dominated. The advancements in technology and science had contributed voluminous information to the curriculum apart from multiplying the number of subjects. It has lent credence to the belief that a child must acquire all roundness right from the age of kindergarten. Though this opinion does not stand for any experimental validity, without including a number of subjects at the kindergarten level, the Ministry of Education in the developing countries and the people of these nations are not willing to accept the education as a progressive and advanced education. Thus there

Table–16
Complexities of Present Education Systems
(*a*) Comte's Linear Classification, (*b*) Ampere's Branching Classification and (*c*) A Knowledge Network

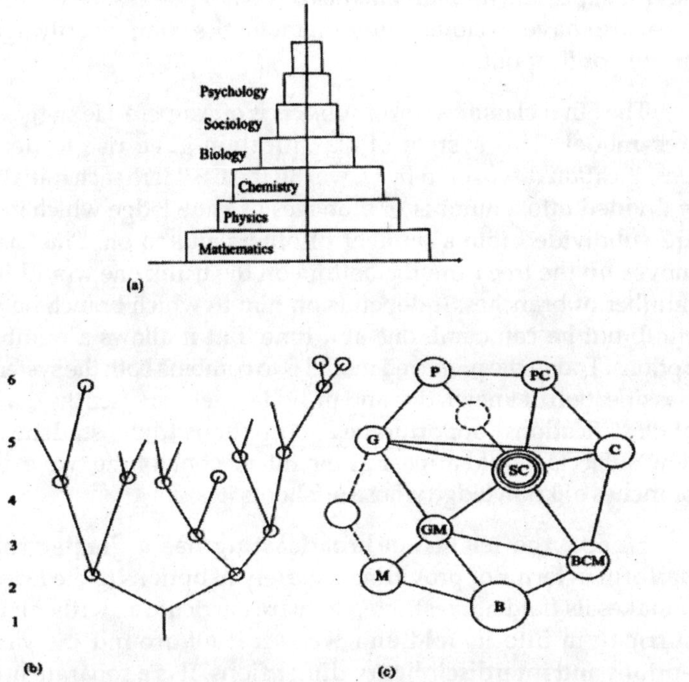

Courtesy: UNESCO – Media Education.

is an overcrowding of subjects creating a maze of information to the utmost confusion of the child.

The planning of subjects for each level has created such a complication, it becomes very difficult to prepare any additional planning for a slow learner for whom any one subject or all subjects may appear a Hercules' task. For instance Auguste Comte's classification of subjects is a liner classification obeying the principle of the subordination of one discipline to another. As such if one subject is introduced, the subordinate subject must follow suit. This is the basis of Comte's well-known model according to which if one has to study physics or chemistry, he must perforce study mathematics. Thus every scientist or founder of a subject created an impression that Mathematics is indispensable for the learning of anything in the world. As such Mathematics has become a compulsory subject whether one likes it or not. Those who do not have an aptitude for mathematics or do not possess the desired IQ level also have to either study mathematics compulsorily against his will or dropout.

The other classification of subjects is of Ampere. He suggested a tree model. This system of classification gave rise to decimal classification discovered by Dewey in the US. Here each initial field is divided into a number of branches of knowledge which in turn are subdivided into a number of others and so on. Thus as one moves up the tree from the bottom on the trunk one would find a number of branches. It depends on him to which branch he must climb but he can climb one at a time. But it allows a number of options. Today the preferred model is to combine both the systems of classification of knowledge and provide a network (see the diagram of classifications) opportunities and options to the students. The new subjects would appear at the intersection of the two existing branches of knowledge whose offshoots it is.

Hence, the television broadcasting has a greater role to perform in terms of providing a variety of options to the learners. It makes its field not restricted to mere curriculum. Rather it takes curriculum into its fold and weaves itself around the various options and interdisciplinary dimensions. It is a separate branch of planning by itself that calls for a well-defined research division with the educational officers and teachers sharing equal responsibility.

This makes the television broadcasting a very expensive proposal. It involves production centres with well-equipped infrastructure. It needs an R & D Unit. Its production must involve a careful curriculum planning against the backdrop discussed in the preceding pages. The produced or finished programmes must be put on cassettes and CDs for the distribution. The educational institutions must have a reasonable infrastructure to avail a maximum benefit of these programmes for its students. The infrastructure includes Video players and Television sets. In a way the countries which cannot afford such high investment and capital on infrastructure would prefer to transmit the messages on Radio.

The tables included in the pages show clearly the expenses involved and the gains obtained in various countries by implementing a number of Television and Radio broadcasting programmes. They included the direct teaching programmes, besides the programmes of enrichment and learning resources. Their efficacy in the adult education and non-formal education has also been illustrated by the data shown in the tables.

Print Media—Leaflets, Pamphlets, Newsletters and Support Materials

Whatever may be the efficacy of the broadcasting programmes of the Radio and the Television, the print media sustains its credibility even in this modern age, the criticism of 'Geutenberg galaxy' notwithstanding. Though the students no longer can totally rely upon the textbooks as sole sources of information, textbooks in the printed form play a very critical and crucial role in the education. They are indispensable.

Similarly with all the availability of electronic equipment like the Transistors, Walkmans, and tape-recorders, VCRs and VCPs there is something which need to be in the print to reinforce or supplement what is broadcast on the Radio or Television. Though some countries have preferred to go for educational broadcasting without these support materials, it is always found in the research that the programmes offered in conjunction with the printed materials proved to be very successful in offering the desired results.

Many broadcasting agencies including BBC offered most of its programmes in the form of Leaflets, Pamphlets, Newsletters and Posters as support materials. Though these materials enhance the cost value of the total programmes they are to stay as such. This would enable both the target groups—teachers and students or adult educators and adults—to keep up their interests in the pursuit of knowledge.

3
Establishing Electronic Network for Educational Programmes

FM Band Radio Stations

The two chapters that preceded dealt with the magnitude of the tasks related to the complexities of education and the possible role the Media, both Radio and Television, could play in achieving the intended objectives and goals of "Education For All" of the Government of Eritrea as envisaged by the World Bank in its Dakar Resolution.

In the present chapter, the question of meeting this colossal task by establishing an electronic network within the economic constraints is going to be examined in detail. The State of Eritrea has an independent Radio Station, called "Dimtsi Hafash" which means the "Voice of Masses". It started way back in 1979 during the struggle for freedom and celebrated its Silver Jubilee recently. The Radio Eritrea has both Medium Wave and Short Wave stations, besides an FM (Frequency Modulation) station called "Radio Zara". The Medium Wave station is installed with a 100kW capacity and operates on 837kHz and 945kHz whereas the Short Wave station is also of a 100 kW capacity and operates on 7100 and 7175kHz. The FM station is installed with the capacity of 2 kW and operates on 95 MHz. There is a 50kW MW Radio transmitter also as a standby in addition to another standby with a capacity of 10kW SW Radio transmitter.

The Department of Adult and Media education has a separate Medium Wave Radio station of 10kW with a frequency band of 1089 kHz, which broadcasts the programmes, related to the Adult Education. Though there was a proposal to create two or three simultaneous channels of transmission through which programmes in different languages could be broadcast, the proposal did not materialize for the reasons beyond the control of the Department. All the MW, SW, FM and Eri TV stations except the Adult Education Radio, are linked to 'Arab Sat' for effective transmission.

Both the MW and SW stations broadcast the programmes simultaneously to ensure 100 per cent audience. Those who could not access to MW would immediately switch over to SW. The MW 945kHz and the SW 7100kHz constitute Channel I and the MW 837 kHz and the SW 7175kHz constitute Channel II. Channel I beams the programmes in 5 Eritrean Languages—Tigrigna, Tigre, Kunama, Nara and Hidarab. Channel II constitutes an international division and deals with external services. Channel II broadcasts programmes in foreign languages such as Amharic and Eritrean languages like Afar, Saho and Bilen.

Fortunately the entire State of Eritrea receives these transmissions of Radio. The satellite transmissions are meant for the foreign countries and border countries where Eriteans lived in large numbers. The villagers in all the villages of Eritrea can access to these programmes by purchasing simple receivers the cost of which do not exceed more than 150 to 200 nakfa. However, the satellite transmissions could be received only with the installation of very costly receivers with a dish and an antenna, which may cost each household to the extent of 4000 to 5000 nakfa.

The FM transmissions however, due to the complexity posed by the hilly terrain with varying altitudes (ranging from 7000 ft. to 1000 ft) contrasting with the low lands on either side of the State of Eritrea, do not reach all places though they are linked to satellite. The reason for this is that the FM transmissions begin in the same slot of MW channel after the MW channel ceases its transmission in the morning or in the evening in the day. It means there is no separate channel of transmission for FM through Satellite.

The FM band Radio station therefore covers only a radius of 60 to 120 kms depending again upon the altitudes of the places of reception. However the usual complications of interference and noise associated with the MW continue to dog the Eri Radio MW too. The disturbance in the reception during the night transmissions is much higher than during the daytime. The reception during early morning hours is somewhat better than at any other time. Compared to MW transmissions the FM transmissions are found to be very clear.

To ensure better reception of FM transmissions at many places of the Western Lowlands the Government of Eritrea installed a booster station at Barentu of Gash Barka. Similarly 4 more booster stations are required to ensure a uniform and better reception. But seemingly this involves a lot of financial commitment on the part of the State of Eritrea, which, at this time of severe financial crunch, could hardly foresee any possibility for such a set up. Thus the problem of ensuring hundred per cent reception of FM transmissions over entire State of Eritrea remains unresolved. However the key role of FM in reshaping the country's economy in the next one decade could hardly be overlooked.

Considering the far reaching benefits of the FM Radio transmissions in future, the absence of booster stations, or other technological alternatives at the required places on the either side of the Western low lands, would result in the isolation and poor development of those areas, and would go obviously counter to the interests, objectives and goals— the Government has been struggling to achieve over the last one decade. If the satellite transmission of FM should reach all the villages of Eritrea the only alternative appears for now is to install the costly receivers, dish and antenna in all the houses of each village. But the poor villagers can ill afford these costly receivers at the present time. This leaves the problem of reception as complicated as ever as no acceptable and a uniform solution is in the sight with regard to ensuring 100 per cent reception of FM Radio transmissions of the State of Eritrea.

The Programmes

The Medium Wave and Short Wave stations beam the programmes for over 15 hours a day. About 40 per cent of these programmes are educational programmes exclusively. These programmes are in the formats of—drama, discussion, dialogues and interviews.

During the week ends, the children educational and entertainment programmes are broadcast in the local languages. To organize these programmes for the children, the staff of the Radio would visit the interior rural schools, pick them up from those schools, bring them over to the studios and record the programmes with them. The other programmes, broadcast by these Radio Stations, include programmes for farmers, youth and women. Programmes on health, environment and culture are also included in the day's transmission.

The FM station on the other hand broadcasts the programmes for 14 hours a day. The programmes include music and educational programmes related to HIV, traffic and health. Over 70 per cent of the FM transmissions are exclusively meant for music. Around 30 per cent are Educational broadcasts dealing with the above mentioned subjects, besides English Language Teaching Programmes of BBC (rebroadcasting) and Arabic entertainment programmes.

The Adult Education Radio of the Department of Adult and Media Education also offers programmes for over 21 hours a week, which include educational broadcasts, besides entertainment. The AER offers daily 3 hours programmes, which for 3 days would be in Tigrigna and for 3 days in Tigre. On the whole there will be 9 hours programmes in Tigrigna and 9 hours programmes in Tigre language. This apart on Sunday there will be two hours, one hour in the morning and one hour in the afternoon, entertainment programme in Tigrigna and one hour programme in the morning in Tigre. Thus the total hours of programmes would come to 21 per week in both the languages. Most of these programmes are in the formats of talks, dialogues, discussion and drama and they deal with the subjects like HIV, Malaria, Health and Nutrition, Hygiene, Environment and women's and children's welfare.

Now the Department of Adult Media Education is going to launch an English Language Teaching programme, which includes re-launching of the ELT programmes of the BBC, besides indigenously produced programmes in the English Language Teaching. The formats of the indigenous programmes included poetry, short story, and drama in addition to talks, discussion and dialogues. These programmes would soon be on the air to the delight of the listeners of Eritrea.

But the problem of poor reception of 10kW MW transmissions of the Radio of Adult and Media Education continues to stare into the face of the efforts done by it. Due to the earth line consumption and other interferences, the MW programmes could not be broadcast to its full capacity for the present. Only 6 kW out of its 10kW capacity could only be utilized. In fact, the Department of Adult and Media Education has even sought for a grant from the World Bank to erect a 10 kW Short wave transmitter with Omni directional antenna to make itself accessible to all the areas of the State. The proposal is in its final stage of consideration as the information last came in is any indication to that effect. If the proposal comes through there is nothing better than that.

Alternatively, the solution to the above complex problems seems to lie apparently in establishing a number of 2kW or 1 kW FM (relay stations) stations with Omni directional antennae all over the country to ensure that the programmes launched for formal and non- formal streams by the Adult and Media education reach the intended target audience. The Indian experience in establishing a number of FM stations all over the country is a good example to quote here.

For instance the Ministry of Information and Broadcasting in India has even allowed individual schools and colleges, both the State run and Privately owned, to apply for an independent and separate FM station for each institution. The institution can run its own radio with regard to its own educational requirements and is free to produce the educational broadcasts using its own teachers and the students, besides the syllabus and the curriculum. These FM stations however are established and provided expertise under the aegis of the Regional Broadcasting Radio Stations. Each such FM station would be able to cover a radius of 80 kms within which each school or college students would be located usually.

The Portable FM Localized Radio Stations in Hilly Areas

There is another example of portable FM radio stations playing a very crucial role in the broadcast of educational programmes in many developing countries across the globe. These low cost FM Radio Stations and digital radio systems operate either by the satellite and/or cellular technology. Internet backup of audio software technology has created conditions to listen to news from a far off place. This has been much more accentuated with the production of wind up and solar radio, which freed Radio from the consumption of excess power.

The Commonwealth of Learning Media and Empowerment (COLME) has developed the concept of using the portable FM Radio Stations in the last few years. The configuration of the FM Radio stations could be reset keeping in view of the local conditions. The station configurations range from three to five thousand US dollars including all elements, antenna, transmitter, console, mixer, microphones and CD and tape decks. The success of the FM portable Radio Stations depends by and large on the proper identification of the technological conditions conducive for their smooth operations to reach the intended target audience.

Firstly, it must be borne in mind that if the land were a mountainous or hilly terrain, the operational radius of the FM portable Radio Stations would be limited. Secondly the targeted audience must have transistors or radios at their home or there should be an organized community radio centre where the villagers can gather and listen to the programmes of their choice.

The FM transmissions would be sustainable and would have greater audience coverage if the local interests were taken into consideration apart from their local languages.

It includes the local school and college students' academic and curricular needs. The local expertise after sufficient training could be utilized for the production of the programmes related to formal and non-formal education. There is enough scope for upgrading these FM portable stations to the national network, besides to allow such technological innovations like phone-in programmes, interfacing and teleconferencing etc.

This would enable the local marketing and agricultural cooperative sectors to transact their business in a profitable manner. The same FM portable Radio stations could be utilized for the weather and climatic warnings, besides for programmes of entertainment and cultural value.

Solar FM Portable Radios: Apac-Uganda

This kind of FM portable Radio system is in the operation in many African nations including Niger and Uganda. In Uganda, it is implemented in the northern region of Apac (Pronounced as 'apatch'). In Uganda the Apac region is poorly developed and there are many problems associated with the smooth run of the FM portable

Radio stations. Firstly, the power shedding has a terrible impact on the smooth conduct of this Radio station. Even if power is supplied, there are terrible fluctuations. As such the power is not suitable for the running of electronic equipment. Thus, the necessity to find an alternative has come into question. At last 'Solar Power' driven portable FM broadcasting Radio Stations came into existence.

To run a solar driven portable FM radio station, eleven solar panels and ten deep cycle batteries would be required to provide lighting and to meet other station requirements for daily broadcasting. A solar system also drives a VHF radio system, and a computer network. The VHF radio system provides a live to air device that can be used for interviews and events in the local community. A second small solar station which powers the retransmission is to be installed 45 kms away from the place on a high elevation. This would pick up the main station's signal on 92.2MHz FM retransmitting it on 106.5 MHz FM. The station signal now covers a radius of over 100 kms. A 64Kbps down link via Worldspace on to the station's computer provides health and educational information. Also the service provides meteorological information for farmers in the local community that can be read on the radio after it is received via the down link. It can be used for rebroadcasting of the BBC Science and English Language Teaching programmes etc.

This system is being in use in several projects throughout Africa. Though in future Analogue systems supplanted with Digital systems are likely to enter the field, the Digital systems have certain drawbacks such as high cost of the receivers, which the poor villagers may not afford, besides difficulties in renewing the licence of the broadcasting.

Therefore, the better option seems to lie in choosing the analogue systems like the portable FM radio stations for the effective implementation of formal and non-formal education systems, besides community programmes. The above-described solar portable FM Radio station is also called Wantok Transmitter. It is so compact that it could be accommodated into a suitcase of 28 kgs weight. The people of Bankilare of Western Niger could reap the excellent benefits of this portable FM Radio first time.

Compared to the Ranet System, a latest innovation known as a drought monitoring system that could be used for educational

Table–17
Technology Choice and Costs

Project	*Pre-requisites*	*Running costs*	*Location of expenditure*
Radio	Broadcasting station with available airtime FM station offering new opportunities	Typically 1/10 of television	Mainly central Reception costs for receivers and batteries
Television	National television service audience big enough to justify production costs		
Cassettes	Modest studio facilities only	Distribution costs likely to make cost un-competitive with radio when audience > 500	Mainly central
DBS	Access to transponder, uplinks and down link or specialist receiver	As for broadcasting apart from receiver cost	Mainly central
Distance education for teacher training	Organizational structure for materials development and student support	Typically below cost of conventional education	Central for materials. May be local for student support
Teleconference	High technology at center, specia-lized equipment at satellites	Likely to exceed conventional teaching where tutors are employed at each site	Expenditure needed both centrally and at each satellite
Computers in schools	Provision of hardware and software to schools; maintenance; staff training	Probably exceeds cost of television	Cot may fall mainly on school
Computers in school with Internet access	As above, together with access to ISP and telephone lines	As above, but with line charges added	As above but communication costs likely to be met locally

Courtesy: World Education Forum – Thematic Studies.

purposes, which required a lot of service and maintenance support at the remote places, the portable solar FM radio stations have offered better service and delivery systems with least maintenance and service support.

Community Radio Centres and Libraries on par with the British Council Libraries

The Community Radio Centre is an important institution in the dissemination of knowledge and information at the rural level. It is organized in different countries in different ways. In purely democratic countries, like India, the local community people themselves organize these Community Radio Centres. They are primarily called as the Community Centres. People of particular community or people of a particular place (both kinds of community centres exist in the wider connotation) elect a representative body to run the Community Centre. The funds are raised for the running of the centre through donations from the affluent society such as landlords, businessmen and industrialists. Part of the funds are being given in the form of matching grants from the Government bodies like local self-governing bodies etc. Elections to these bodies are held at regular intervals under the supervision of an independent body and the elected members work in a spirit of voluntary service. In other countries, where democracy is not as deep rooted as in India, the Community Centres are run by the State itself. The funding thus becomes entirely a state expenditure. But the Community Centres, whatsoever may be the nature of their administrative set-up and funding, have a critical role in carrying the messages of the government closer to the people.

Organs of Community Centre

Each Community Centre, if has to deliver the messages of the government bodies and the voluntary agencies, engaged in the social service and upliftment, must comprise a *full-time library* rich in all kinds of books which included multiple sets of School and Colleges texts, formal and non-formal education books, support literature such as suggested references, standard reference books, Encyclopaedia, Dictionaries, Atlases and Maps, and general literature related to the local languages and international languages. There will be a general reading room consisting of newspapers of national and regional levels besides political and cultural magazines.

It also will have an **Audio-visual unit** where the screen for showing films of 16 mm and 35 mm is set-up. The unit must have sound proofing and stereo boxes for the audience to have clear audibility inside the unit theatre. The Theatre may not be a large one but it is enough if it reasonably accommodates around 250 people or children at a time. It must be having a **Wega Theatre Size TV (large flat screen)** for exhibiting the Video cassettes on different subjects and themes including some films of patriotic fervor, science and fiction. Therefore, the TV must have a **Video Cassette Player** attachment.

It is in the same room/hall or in another hall, **the Radio** must be fitted to broadcast all the programmes related to the educational needs of the students and the adults of the village. The Radio could be **Radio cum tape recorder** or **simple electric radio** or **radio transistor**. Further, the community centre may as well be furnished with at least **10 computers** with all the latest software, including **scanner and printer**. This unit must be linked to the **Cable and Internet.** A **photocopy unit** facility is going to be an added advantage. Thus each Community Centre looks like a **mini British Library or a multi-media centre.** Provision must be made to accommodate separate shelves for keeping the recorded audiocassettes and video cassettes.

Cost Effectiveness

From the above it appears that a Community Centre of the above description with as many as two spacious halls and provision for demarcation of different rooms for different purposes would cost the State or the voluntary body not below 10,000 US dollars at the present time. But the funds can be raised for this from the Christian Missionaries or the Christian Voluntary Agencies or the NGOs or from the Donor Funds given for the Adult Education Programmes to be implemented through the Community Centres. Similarly local landlords or construction engineering companies could be involved in providing either financial resources or manpower or technical expertise at low cost. The construction of such centres need not be done for each village. Depending upon geographical conditions, for the villages, which have transport and connecting road links between themselves, one Community Radio Centre could be located at the crossroads for the convenience of a cluster of villages.

Countries which used the Community Centres of Villages for Reforms in Education

The initial experience in using the ETV channel through the community stations has first come from the US. The American ETV has followed a national educational pattern with the operation and control left to the local community stations. The ETV channel of the US in fact was the most unplanned one in the sense of the word 'logistics'. The ETV channel has been connected to more than one hundred local community stations that made up the National Educational Television network.

The US educational Television is thus a collection of hundreds of individual ETV systems, operating at all levels, each state and local community seeking its own answers to its problems through it. However, the word 'local community' here does not connote the same meaning as 'community' in the Asian or Indian context connotes. The radical revolution in the adult and the non-formal education using these community centres is recently achieved in Sri Lanka. Radio Dwensa in Mali, Radio Sagarmatha in Nepal and Radio Bobo in Burkina Faso are some more shining examples of using these Community Centres in the sense of the word. In Philippines, eleven community radio stations have been established under the auspices of Tambuli Community Radio Project in isolated and economically depressed areas of the country. The project, which started in 1991, was funded by DANIDA until 1999. These low powered Radio stations using 20 to 100 watt transmitters are collectively operated with the help of the Community Volunteers. The programmes are transmitted as per the local requirements.

Way back in 1975 India has offered the Television Educational programmes under the SITE (Satellite Instructional Television Experiment) to the needy target groups in about 2,330 villages which are part of backward districts of 6 states of Indian Union. The programmes are offered in four languages—Oriya, Hindi, Telugu and Kannada. The unique feature of this programme is that it has utilized 550 Community Centres of the villages in Srinagar, the capital of Kashmir. In rest of the villages the Government of India established full-fledged television centres in the villages as described above.

Between 1979-83, during the period of Cultural Revolution, China has done similar exercise in its country though the quality of the programmes is purely within the regimen of the Communist Party ideology and not much innovative. In Niger around 1050 television sets, of which 800 operate on solar cells, are set up in the village community centres in the recent years. An additional 9000 sets are to follow in the coming years. The Ivory Coast has already installed a total of 20,000 public television sets in 70 per cent of its villages. Zimbabwe has just commenced setting up public receivers with the intention of installing at least one television set for every 10 to 15 families in rural areas.

In Egypt, Libya, Tunesia, Algeria and Morocco (that have a population exceeding 100 million) there is a relatively high and even distribution of TV sets with an average of 10 TV sets per 100 inhabitants. This varies between 5 TV sets per 100 inhabitants in Morocco and 15 per 100 in Egypt. If one perceives at the family size of these countries, one can say confidently that 50 per cent of the population of this area could gain access to Television viewing in the extended meaning of the family or of the Village Community Centre.

Supply of FM Transistors

In so far generating the messages for Educational broadcasting is concerned, the above discussion highlighted various alternatives before the government with regard to low cost production technology to the meet the geographical as well as sociological conditions of Eritrea. But the messages generated after all must reach the audience, the target groups.

Who are basically students, teachers and parents. To ensure the reception of these among the target groups who in a way are not even in a position to purchase their prescribed textbooks, the alternatives are to be considered prior to launching of these programmes through FM operated solarradio. The advanced developments in the Radio Technology in the last two decades resulted in the production low cost, mobile and pocket size radios, which run on pencil batteries which, are also very cheap to purchase.

Compared to TV technology, this has a lot of edge and effect in the developing countries as such radios—called as Transistors—are easily accessible at low price to poor and rich alike. Once the FM radio stations would come into existence in the developing countries the use of these FM Radio Transistors would become more effective for the broadcasting of educational programmes. It would ensure hundred per cent reception to the target groups.

The students too can carry this pocket size transistors along with them to school and listen to these educational broadcasts during the free hours in the school or during journey. In terms of the effectiveness, either in the hundred per cent reception or in the effectiveness, Anthony Bates argues in favour of Radio for Educational Broadcasting (*Ibid.*, p. 60) than Television. Especially for poor and developing countries, with widespread geographical variations, FM Radio Stations and Radio Transistors are precious and efficient instruments of carrying messages of Educational broadcasting.Yet, all the problems may not have been overcome. There may be many that may not yet prefer to purchase the FM Radio, Transistors. Hence, the Government must ensure that these FM transistors are provided to students along with the prescribed textbooks in the school itself. Or alternatively the schools or colleges, in a manner similar to lending the library books, may supply them. The funding for this may be either obtained from the Donor Agencies or met from the donations of the voluntary bodies engaged in the promotion of literacy and Adult Education. It is important to remember here that lack of proper attention to the distribution of required instruments in dissemination of educational broadcasting is one of the causes ascribed to the failure of these programmes in many developing countries.

Towers for Rural Transmission: Eri TV

To begin with it is proper to mention that the State of Eritrea has a full-fledged TV station working along with the Dimtsi Hafash (the Voice of Masses). The Eri TV is set-up with a capacity of 5 kW, and is linked to the satellite. It beams the programmes at 175 MHz in the PAL format. It has five relay towers to cover a maximum area of the State. The relay stations operate on 3 GHz. They are located at Keren, Afabet, Berentu, Tassene and Asab. They are all installed with a capacity of 1kW. The Eri TV completely covers the highland area of

Eritrea. The ERI TV does not cover the Denkel area however. If people located afar in lowlands on either side of the plateau could afford to purchase the receivers at the cost of 4000 nakfa then probably the entire State of Eritrea could have got the benefit of the transmission of the Eri TV.

But unfortunately, the poor farmer community and the nomadic or pastoral populations could ill afford such costly receivers. Further the maintainability and repair services of these receivers are very inadequate due to lack of expert personnel. Against this background the satellite linking of Eri TV has only enabled to offer coverage for the Eritreans located abroad and for the international viewers. The relay stations stated above could cover only a radius of 60 to 80 kms depending upon the geographical part the TV transmitter has to cover. Therefore, the educational broadcasting programmes, whatever are being contemplated by the State, must have alternative arrangements to come in the reach of every village area located in the far low lands on both the Eastern and Western side.

It is very pertinent to mention that the spread of Television in Third World countries for developmental purposes is possible if the cost of the TV sets and receivers is in the access of the poor people of these countries. Further, the successful utilization of TV becomes possible if the transmission of the TV programmes overcomes the geographical barriers. Towards achieving this, the 'electronic colonialism' of the developed countries has to undergo radical changes in the Technology.

Portable TV Receivers: 12 Volts Inbuilt Transformers

A portable 12 volts Television receiver with an inbuilt transformer, which converts the high voltage received from the mains supply to 12 volts, is quite handy for the poor people of the Third World countries. These receivers can be run with the rechargeable batteries such as car batteries as well. Since the development of power supply and the power grid in developing nations are a matter of either refining the existing technological expertise or acquiring the new ones, the expansion of Television network now should be made independent of the power supply. It is in this context the portable 12 volts inbuilt transformer TV receiver sets proved very successful in the Third World countries for availability of car or truck batteries in the latter is not a problem at all.

Alternatively solar cells with storage batteries are also found very useful in supplying power to Radios and Televisions. Many versions of this are also being tested whereas some are already under implementation in some developing countries. For instance in Niger, 800 of 1050 Community Television sets are using such solar cells with storage batteries. On a yearly basis, Niger is planning to add every year 450 such community village sets, until every village of 10000 villages has one community television set.

In India the Central Electronics Ltd., also developed a 'Solar TV set' consisting of a Television set, either colour or monochrome, with solar cells backed by storage batteries. The price including installation is somewhere around 1500 US dollars.

Solar Cells

Today solar cells are produced on a commercial scale. They are used for supplying power to small transposers and gap filling station transmitters that supply radio and television coverage to inaccessible regions. Very low-power, unattended, solar-powered television transmitters have been built in India for terrestrial broadcasting of satellite transmissions. Parabolic antennae with a six-metre radius receive the signals and re-broadcast then via two 10-watt transmitters. The batteries are designed in such a way that the stations can do without direct sunlight for four days consecutively.

The above technological excellence is applicable to Radio transmissions as much as Television. It is in this context worthy of reminding that in the absence of availability of Short Wave transmitters, to access the entire country, with wide geographical variations as reflected both in the living styles and in the altitudes, such as Eritrea, either FM Radio Stations of 1 kW operating with omnidirectional antenna or the Radio Stations running on Solar cells with storage batteries would reduce the costs on the state exchequer to a great extent and make the programmes successful too.

Indonesia Archipelago: Another Low Cost Model TV

Indonesia is one Asian nation which implemented a low cost television technology while ensuring a nation wide coverage. It has done this both on the fonts of production as well as on the Transmission. That is the reason, it occupied a special place in the history of evolution of Television Technology. Indonesia is mainly a country with as many as 6000 islands inhabited by the people. To access all these islands, by virtue of conventional technology of Television, is nothing but draining all its available resources for a single cause. Therefore, Indonesia developed an 'archipelago approach' in 1981.

The plan envisaged no regional studios or transmission towers. But the plan at the same time ensured that transmission is nationwide. It is rendered possible through Small mobile Production Units (SPU). These units are provided with a mini Outside Broadcasting (OB) van with two EFP (Electronic Field Production) cameras and an ENG (Electronic newsgathering) camera complete with video and audio controls and editing facilities. A power generator and a second minibus complete the equipment. 12 people, quite a large team, man the unit. It can however work for a long time without back-up support from the home station for it has all the technical and administrative manpower including a Director. This project initially started with four OB vans in 1979 on the occasion of Southeast Asian Games. Based on the experience gained over this, the Government of Indonesia went ahead to purchase ten more vans by 1982. All these stations are located now in various provinces. These mini OB vans can easily enter small roads in villages and can be airlifted in emergencies by Hercules Planes to access the remote islands also.

The television programmes are made on locations in the pretty villages, fields, and beaches or on riverbanks. The artists are not brought to studios. Studios themselves went to artists. The artists sang, danced and performed drams and conversations against the natural settings.

This experiment has led many island nations to simply follow the same. This is applicable to hilly terrains as much as island nations without an exception. This is one of the possible low cost methods through which a Government can access the TV programmes to entire country irrespective of geographical hurdles.

Provision of Production of Audio and Video Educational Materials (Cassettes, CDs etc.)

Any serious effort to implement an educational programme either through Radio or Television calls for a certain state of infrastructure which inevitably and invariably includes the raw materials. Let it be a Radio broadcasting or Television broadcasting, both will have a little effect on the memory of the audience. The part of the vast sounds, music, words and images that vanish into thin air compared to what had been effectively absorbed into by the audience, students and adults, is immense and colossal. If the audience had to only hear or listen to once, and learn from the experience, then it would never be able to discharge the intended supplementary role of enhancing the learning experience of the targeted audience. The cause of reinforcement would go unespoused. Further, the convenience of listening to or watching at one's own convenience again and again during one's leisure timings would be missing. Therefore, the educational broadcasts whatever are produced should be retained for further listening or watching on a permanent basis.

This calls for the production of Audio-Video materials such as audio cassettes and video cassettes besides CDs (Compact Discs). If these are not indigenously manufactured and are to be imported in bulk from foreign countries, the budget of the educational programmes would shoot up making it formidable. Whatever programmes are produced by the concerned educational technology station, be it Radio or ETV channel, they must be multiplied into thousands of copies and distributed to all the target groups such as schools and community centers and other interested audience in a short time. Therefore, a shortage of this important raw material can pose a serious hindrance to the very cause for which the educational programme is launched. This inturn may frustrate the planners and makers, besides the target groups too, from having any interest in this scheme itself.

Establishing Audio and Video Units in Educational Institutions, Community Centres or FM Radio Centres – Time-table Planning and Teacher Involvement

The launching of Educational television or Radio broadcasting channel is one side of the coin. It does not mean that the education in the State automatically gets the benefit of it. The fact is that there are many players who play a crucial role in making them a success. Of all the key players including bureaucrats, the most important are the School Teachers or College Lecturers or the Adult educators or the Community Centre organizers. If these educational programmes are not exhibited in a systematic manner that would benefit the intended targeted group in the schools, colleges and the community centres, it would defeat the very purpose for which they were produced. It is one important cause that is often ascribed to the failure of these programmes in many developing countries. Further provision for Audio-Visual equipment such as Radios (a minimum of two sets), Television Sets (a minimum of two sets), Tape Recorders and video cassette recorders in each school is very basic and crucial for the successful implementation of the Educational broadcasting in any developing country.

It needs a good bit involvement of teaching community in the form of prior training. It also makes it mandatory to design a timetable, which integrates the timings of the broadcasts with the curriculum being taught in the school or college or adult education Community Centre. A more difficult problem is that of training local school administrators and teachers in the proper use of Television or Radio as a supplementary teaching institution. For instance the broadcast materials must always be made available to children to listen or watch in keeping with the curricular lessons being taught in the school. If the broadcasts precede the lessons whatever are yet to be taught, there would not be any net gain out of such broadcasts. Further the precious time of the students would be wasted. Therefore, there must be proper framework of understanding between the academicians and the broadcast planners.

The curriculum taught in the school, college or adult education centre must correlate the programmes whatever are being planned for production by the broadcasting agencies. If these two important players fail to harmonize and integrate the production curriculum with the school or college curriculum, then the resulting educational experience does not give any meaningful learning experience. It leads to a chaotic and incoherent experience, which often may lead to disastrous impressions on the minds of the learners. Therefore, the teachers who offer the conventional educational training tq the students play a very critical role. Hence a proper timetable planning correlating the transmissions is most important player in seeing to the success of the educational television or radio broadcasts. But to achieve this the teachers must be suitably trained and motivated. These players sitting together and putting minds together in the common interest of the education must first finalize the school, college and adult education curriculum for the educational broadcasting. It should be finalized keeping in mind the school monthly and annual calendar in mind. They should also formulate the guidelines for the distribution of printed materials, which would be supplied along with the Radio broadcasts, or Television telecasts.

Not only this planning must be done, it should be strictly followed in all these institutions including the community centres. If there are local FM radio stations, they should plan the broadcasting and rebroadcasting these produced programmes in keeping with the time-table of the institutions and from time to time check with the school administrators and teachers' committees established for these liaisoning work.

In respect of the Community Centres where the adult educators monitor the Radio or Television educational broadcasts, they must be given a full understanding of the broadcasting programmes in line with the curriculum and time-table meant for the adult education, besides planning to arrange the reinforcement sessions or rebroadcasting sessions for all category of learners as it is a community centre.

There should be proper display of the broadcasts schedule on a notice board outside the Community Centre for all category learners to come and watch the programmes in turns or on a rotation as there is always a limited space in the Community Centre.

Establishing Audio-Visual Educational Research Centre and Educational Materials Research Centres

From the times of the first BBC Radio broadcasts for the Schools to the American ETV programmes, the programme production has faced a number of constraints and hurdles with regard to their style, format and content. Many doubted whether these programmes fall under the category of pedagogy at all. Some argued that though they do not strictly come under the definition of pedagogy, they still go a long way in educating the children. But gradually these educational broadcasts or ETV programmes spread entire Europe and then Asia. Japan was the first Asian nation, which has taken up these on a scientific basis and attempted on a full scale to give an alternative school form and shape to it. It was a success story in the Asian region. But subsequently many developing countries in the Latin America, Africa and Asia scrambled for the implementation of these programmes for different reasons. However, most of the developing nations either aped their programmes directly on the lines of the Britain or US or tried to implement them for direct teaching.

A few nations tried to have an innovation and/or adaptation of these programmes to their countries' needs. The detailed discussion of these could be found in the foregoing chapters. Now the time has come, due to the accumulated experiences of both developing and developed nations being open for research and scrutiny, to choose carefully and meticulously the kind of educational broadcasting that a country requires in keeping with its economic and topographical conditions.

The critical study of these experiences suggests that it is not right or correct to involve the Radio or TV for direct teaching purposes without proper research on the curriculum, content, format and materials. There are many steps that should be taken care of before going into the production of the programmes. First of all, whether the educational broadcasting must have the basis of a curriculum, be it in respect of school, college or adult education, or lifelong and continuing non-formal education, must be thoroughly debated by the educational and media experts. Secondly, the kind of software training such as developing cognitive kits and modules, dividing the curricular units into broadcasting units, creative writing of these units, planning for a comprehensive script and developing the script into a format—dialogue, background voice over (commentary), reporting, discussion, dramatization, should be done. It is after accomplishing all these, then the role of collecting materials, site selections and art direction would come into scene. The next phase follows the production or shooting.

The above process today calls for establishing a separate production unit called Audio Visual Research Centre or Educational Material Research Centre. It is no longer possible to shoot the TV programmes showing a teacher in a classroom with the back drop of a black board and recording whatever he speaks on a subject as a direct teaching material. Today the motivation is one important factor in the colourful production world. Similarly Radio broadcasts cannot be produced by simply reading out the lessons of the textbook before Radio microphone.

Today the quality, quantity, duration of the programmes and programme schedules, formats, content, style and presentation – all matter a lot to motivate a listener or audience. Therefore, the job before the educational Radio or Television channel is more complex and serious one. The ordinary staff of Radio or Television staff cannot do it. It needs a good bit of research, painful collation of all the available materials, thorough debate and discussion before arriving at the suitable format of production and transmission.

The establishment of Audio-Visual Research Centre or Educational Materials Research Centre is a precondition in one's own country's national interest. It would look into all the aspects of curricular reforming, enriching the content, and providing learning materials and direct teaching. It would bring in variety of formats of production that would meet international standards. Many developing nations of Asia including India had today well developed Audio-Visual Research Centres or Educational Materials Research Centres. Most of these are located in the states under the University jurisdiction with regard to their funding but are autonomous in administrative character.

They would consist of Software which has been discussed in the preceding paragraphs and hardware – which is also called the 'technology cocktail'.

Technology Cocktail – AVRC or EMRC

Production and operations Technology in Television covers all technical facilities and equipment necessary for Studio production as well as outside location shots. Today as the old Technology phases out, latest technology replaces it. In fact for a quality production, film technology has no substitute. But many Third World countries are not in a position to meet the Film Technology Costs and the quality. For reasons beyond control, these countries pursue a quicker means of finishing the job. This has allowed the Video Technology to replace the Film Technology though the quality fades out in the course of time. But most of these countries implement the educational programmes to meet the short-term needs and hence do not take much interest in the quality and shelf value. Thus very briefly the following hardware would meet the minimum requirements for the establishment of an AVRC or EMRC.

- Digital video processing
- Portable compact video cameras
- Portable compact magnetic recorders
- Camera recorders for Electronic News Gathering (ENG)
- New magnetic recording formats (B, C, U, Betacam and MAC (Multiplexed Analogue Components) formats)
- Digital sound recording PCM (Pulse Code Modulation)
- Computer assisted videotape editing
- Chroma key technique
- Next channel A/B mixer
- Digital time base corrector
- Digital frame memory (frame store, slow motion, stop motion, quad split)
- CCD (charge coupled device) scanner
- Electronic Field Production Units (EFP)
- Autocorrective studio systems
- High definition television (for production work)

This equipment would enable the AVRC or EMRC to produce the programmes effectively at low cost. Further, these equipment are easier to operate and therefore less training time is needed. The technicians easily perform most of the jobs. Therefore, the software and hardware together contribute in producing the high quality educational programmes.

The latter two are latest additions for further reduction in the costs.

4

Satellite Experiences of Some Asian Countries: Electronic Media

Advent of Satellite Transmission: A Scenario of Developed and Developing Countries

Use of satellites for transmission of Radio and Television programmes both in the developed and developing countries is seen as a measure of circumventing the hurdles posed by the terrestrial transmission technology. Initially the satellite technology has been used for Telecommunications in almost all the countries across the world. The developed and industrialized Europe, the USSR and the US are the first to put the satellite technology to use for telecommunications and then on to uplinking and downlinking of the earth stations of Radio and TV transmission to the regional stations. In the early 1960s the satellite services across the globe were limited to a couple of global satellites launched by the US and the USSR. As a result the services were very expensive which the developing countries could ill afford. Therefore, the developing countries were complacent with the services available for telecommunications to their countries. Some of the developing countries sought to have a tie-up with either the US or the USSR under an international aid or grant to mark a beginning of TV or Radio transmission in those countries.

It was the US, which launched its first satellite INTELESAT in to orbit in 1964. About 154 countries availed themselves of its services for telecommunications that time. In 1971, the USSR launched INTERSPUTNIK into orbit. It had about 14-member countries of former Soviet Block seeking the services of this satellite for telecommunications. This apart a few non-member countries of the

Third World also subscribed for the services of INTERSPUTNIK. Afghanistan, Cuba, North Korea, Laos, Vietnam and Southern Yemen are a few member countries who hired the services of INTERSPUTNIK as members of former Soviet block. At the same time some non-member countries like Algeria, Iraq, Libya, Nicaragua and Syria also hired the services of INTERSPUTNIK.

Countries with larger area surface have found the satellite technology quite cheaper to overcome the obstacles posed by the terrestrial transmission technology, especially either on hilly terrains or on islands unevenly placed. They also found the terrestrial transmission technology too capital intensive to afford. Against this backdrop, some of the Third World nations of Asia such as India, China and Indonesia have gone a step ahead in planning and developing their own indigenous satellites. Similarly some Latin American nations like Brazil, Argentina and Mexico pioneered the research in developing their own satellites. As far as Middle East was concerned, it had banked heavily on international agencies for developing a satellite, ARABSAT, at a whopping cost of 134 million US dollars, for all the Arab nations who could not find a common ground to have an indigenous research of their own.

As more and more nations came forward to launch their own satellites, the dependence on the foreign satellites had gradually come down resulting in the reduction of high costs of leasing. Further the competition from the contemporary technology in the form of development of Optical Fibre Cables which are cheaper and superior in transmission quality and can carry heavy traffic on themselves in the telecommunication sector impelled a deep slash in the leasing costs of the satellites. In addition to this, the high transmitting power of Direct Broadcasting Satellites (DBS) has rendered it even more possible to erect smaller and cheaper earth stations for Television and Radio transmissions.

The introduction of MAC (Multiplexed Analog Components – for Satellite and Terrestrial directional transmitting and receiving links) had resulted in the greater flexibility and exchange by reduction in the greater variety of different standard formats of TV transmission, which was earlier found to be very difficult. The advent of PCM (Pulse Code Modulation) technique has improved transmission power and quality while lowering power consumption and consequently operation costs. Direct Broadcasting Satellites opened up new avenues in high technical performance of transmission in effect along the sidelines of the introduction of High Definition Television (HDTV). The earlier version of TV sets of 8-12 inches with 405 lines transmission gradually evolved today to 1250 lines transmission with the size of the TV set enlarging to 36 inches with a flat screen.

UNESCO Minimum

In the last few decades the advent of satellite transmissions world over changed the scenario of the communication systems of many countries. Most of the developing countries could meet the minimum prescribed standards of the UNESCO – two television sets per 100 inhabitants. The UNESCO minimum is defined in 1961 in its first report – 'Mass Media in Developing Countries' which is given below for the general awareness and information.

10 Newspaper Copies, 5 Radio Sets, 2 Cinema Seats, 2 Television Sets – 100 inhabitants.

By 1984 most of the developing countries reached this goal and even exceeded this except a fewer small countries in Asia including Bangladesh, which was liberated in 1971. On the other hand, some of the Asian Nations such as Singapore, Taiwan, Malaysia and Korea have developed the Television Transmission on par with the industrialized Europe and the West such as US and Canada.

The experiences of these Asian nations in transforming into highly developed communication societies are totally different and present an interesting history of background.

Experiences of Asian Countries: Japan, 1939

Among all the nations of Asia it is Japan that deserves the credit of being a pioneer in introducing the TV broadcasting way back in 1939. The development of TV in Japan was almost parallel with that of Britain and other European countries in the West. The Japanese TV also came to work under the same broadcasting corporation established for the Radio in August 1926 called Japan Broadcasting Corporation or Nippon Hoso Kyokai (NHK). It was in May 1939, an experimental telecast of a domestic drama was successfully telecast from Tokyo. Ever since the Japanese Television broadcasting (NHK) system and network has grown from the strength to strength. Though the Radio and TV broadcasting system of Japan got trapped in the turmoil of the First and Second World Wars and also got embroiled in the heated debate as to what should be the constitutional status of the Broadcasting network and how should it operate within the definition of the freedom of speech, it came to be regarded as the most advanced system in Asia by 1958. It was in 1950 a comprehensive regulatory law of NHK broadcasting was passed that allowed the private enterprise in the Broadcasting sector at par.

It bestowed Japan with a leadership to play a leading role in the Far Eastern Radio and Television. It formed an Asian Broadcasters Conference in 1957. In 1962, Japan took the lead to form an Asian Broadcasting Union on the lines of the European Broadcasting Union. It came to function with effect from July 1964 with its headquarters in Tokyo. Its membership included Far East, South Asia and the Middle East. In 1961 a group of Japanese electronic equipment manufacturers and broadcasters established a corporation called as *Asia Vision* which would serve as a network in the Asia and the Far East. It became a wholly owned subsidiary of Fuji-TV a private TV network in Japan.

There is no monopoly in the Japanese broadcasting system. Around 59-60 broadcasting companies compete with NHK in Japan. A total of 13 Radio, 13 Television and 33 radio-television broadcasting companies with 138 Radio stations and 167 television stations are operating the TV network of Japan. A new dimension in ETV was ushered in when Japan announced to the world broadcasters, at the Second International Conference on School Broadcasting held in Tokyo in April 1964, that it had fully integrated television into its educational structure right from kindergarten to University level, besides adult education. After several years of initial experimenting with the educational programmes, the NHK inaugurated the first ETV station of separate ETV national network in 1958. By 1965, there were 46 ETV (25 of NHK and the rest are of other commercial companies) stations covering the entire country. The delegates at the conference were taken by the surprise when Japanese Broadcasters revealed these data to them.

The NHK stations retransmit their educational programmes over 238 smaller relay stations designed to reach schools and home receivers in isolated areas of the country. The commercial ETV stations have about 40 such satellite transmitters for their own stations.

These facilities all together rendered the Japanese ETV broadcasting most extensive and comprehensive in the world. By 1965 all Japanese schools were equipped withTV receivers and the audience feedback survey conducted by the NHK confirmed that about 90 per cent of the schools are using the broadcasting programmes as regular supplementation to the classroom teaching. The Japanese ETV programming has a wide range as much as the regular school curriculum. Almost every subject taught in the classroom has its counterpart in the ETV programme. Further, the Japanese TV would produce a number of programmes that would take care of life-long and continuing education.

Teachers and school administrators have formed a federation, which would keep studying the programmes beamed by the NHK ETV and advise them suitably from time to time. At the same time NHK also has its own advisory committee of the Ministry of Education officials and other experts who keep giving proper guidance and advice on how to integrate the broadcasting programmes with the school curricula in terms of content and format. Almost all the Japanese Educational programmes are related to enrichment category alone. It was Japan which first introduced correspondence courses for formal and non-formal streams on NHK Radio and TV in the East.

Indonesia, 1959-60

With a population of over 160 million (based on 1980 census data) spread over 6000 islands (which are widely scattered over an area of 5.1 million square kilometers). Indonesia presents an interesting and exemplary model of fast development in TV technology and transmission. The TV was introduced in Indonesia in 1960s. But developing a transmission network with directional links looked a formidable task as the islands are located far and wide rendering the nationwide coverage for a long time extremely difficult and even impossible, if it were to go by simple terrestrial transmission programme alone. When it researched for an alternative, a new concept emerged that made 'Archipelago' – a 'low cost transmission model' for the entire world. It is a story of grand success at low cost (a description of the operation of studio is already given in p. 83).

The system is established on nationwide transmission signals from satellite along the lines of distribution via terrestrial transmitters as well as mobile production units for covering news. The country launched its first satellite PALAPA into operation in July 1976. It was a multipurpose satellite. It was not only used for telecommunication but also for transmitting television signals to regional transmitter. Simultaneously the government has increased the number of earth stations (relay stations) from 40 to 200, which covered 65 per cent of Indonesian territory by 1980s. Now a couple of decades since the entire country is under the full coverage of TV and Radio transmission. Even the number of TV sets has gone up in leaps and bounds touching multiples 10 millions. It means that the television reaches entire population of this giant and topographically complicated island nation.

India, 1959

The Television was introduced in India in the early 1959. It was first established in Delhi, the capital of India with coverage not extending beyond 80 kms. It remained static until 1960s with a limited number of programmes. The lack of economic resources coupled with lack of technological know-how was said to be the root cause of stagnancy in this field. It was around this time the Ford Foundation, the largest US Philanthropic trust, in the US was interested in promoting both internal as well as external development of Educational Television. As part of its efforts to modernize the developing nations in the education sector through ETV, the Ford Foundation's first choice was India. In January 1960, a team from Ford Foundation surveyed the ETV prospects at the invitation of All India Radio (AIR). The team recommended that a foundation grant be made available to support the ETV instruction in Science and languages at the Ninth Class level in the Delhi State School System.

As a sequel to the recommendation the Ford Foundation had given a grant of whopping 470,000 dollars to the AIR for the implementation of the above project for 4 years. The Indian Government on its part has given a matching grant increasing it every year in the decreasing order of the Ford Foundation Grant. As a result of all these efforts, about 600 TV receivers could be distributed to all the State run schools in and around Delhi. Further a studio and test equipment were built up including a 500 kW amplifier to strengthen AIR–TV signal. This followed an intensive in-service training for the AIR and TV personnel in the smooth implementation of the programme.

In the following October 1960, the AIR sent seven of its programme and technical personnel for training in ETV to the US. In 1961 June the Delhi Directorate of Education and the AIR organized jointly an in-service workshop for 3 weeks for all ninth-class teachers of Physics, Chemistry, Hindi and English. More than 650 teachers underwent training in this workshop. They commenced implementing teaching through TV by September, 1961. In a short time about 152 schools in Delhi and around 12000 boys and girls got the benefit of the programme. Over 30000 students got the benefit of receiving the curricular instruction in Physics and Chemistry through ETV.

For a long time after 1964, when the Ford Foundation phased out its ETV programme, there was a period of lull as there was no other TV center or no other project. In the early 1967 a pilot agricultural television project called Krishi Darshan began in the area of Delhi with 80 Community Village sets installed around the countryside as a follow up the Radio forums conducted by the AIR.

It was in 1969, another breakthrough came in the establishment of terrestrial Television centers. The Government of India entered into an agreement with the National Aeronautics and Space Administration (NASA), US for implementing a pilot project called SITE (Satellite Instructional Television Experiment). By 1972, the Government could establish 6 more Television Centers in a quick succession: Amritsar, Bombay, Calcutta, Lucknow, Madras and Srinagar. Further, the Government planned to open a few more new centers at Ahmedabad, Bangalore and Trivandrum during the 6th Five-Year Plan commencing from 1978-83.

The SITE programme, in line with the spirit of the agreement with NASA, commenced under the technical and operational supervision of ISRO in August 1975. It was the first ever introduction of rural interests in the TV programmes with the value of wide social consumption. Direct reception sets with 24 inch screens had been installed in about 2, 330 villages of the backward districts of the 6 states with programmes in four languages: Oriya for Orissa, Hindi for Bihar, Rajasthan and Madhya Pradesh, Telugu for Andhra Pradesh and Kannada for Karnataka. The Community Television sets were provided with specially designed, locally erected, low-cost dish aerials and convertors. The other details in so far their relevance to the education are mentioned already in the earlier chapter. According to Anthony Bates – *SITE was clearly a major achievement, technologically, organizationally and, to a lesser extent, educationally. It reached extremely large numbers of isolated and poor villagers and had clear educational and social benefits. Many valuable lessons were learnt from this experiment.* Yet this remained a pilot project for a long time till India stepped into the age of its own satellite communication age.

In 1982, India had made a leap forward by launching its first ever indigenously made communication satellite INSAT 1 which made all the difference subsequently for the country's economic prosperity, growth and progress. Simultaneously the government decided to give a new impetus to TV transmission by launching new terrestrial transmitter network. In the following years, between 1981 and 1985 the number of terrestrial transmitting stations had gone up from 16 to 160. All the new transmitter stations were being installed by the Indian companies with indigenously manufactured components. The expansion resulted in the enhancement of nationwide coverage from 17 to 85 per cent by 1985. By the turn of 2000 the coverage of national premier channel DD (Door Darshan I & II) has not only exceeded the previously planned targets but the Government channels came in for neck to neck competition from the private channels as also international channels such as BBC, Alzazeera, HSBO, CBN, CNN etc., Cable TV operations and Direct to Home channel operations have come to vie with each other due to the DBS services becoming available to all Indians across the country. This resulted in unprecedented increase in the number of TV sets, which are today as many as Indian population. They are almost present like transistors in multiple sets in thousands of households across the country. Today both the government owned and the private TV. Channels are beaming the educational programmes of CSIR-UGC, IGNOU to capture the audience during the morning hours and on holidays.

Sri Lanka, 1978-79

It was the last of larger countries in Asia to introduce Television though it has the highest literacy rate next to Japan in Asia. Srilanka, formerly known as Ceylon, was a British Colony for a long time. It was allowed as a self-governing state since 1931 and was given full independence in 1948. The country was reluctant to go for Television for a long time though many foreign countries offered financial support since, as a state policy, it believed that it did not require it in view of scarce foreign resources. However in 1978 it agreed in principle to allow the establishment of TV station under a private ownership. Thus TV made its debut as a small private operator's low power transmitting station in 1978-79.

Within a short period of time, the private operator incurred heavy losses for the reasons beyond anyone's comprehension, the State had to take over it as a national television station in 1982. "Rupavahini" began the transmission of programmes to the entire country. Though there was an air of initial scepticism about the purchasing power of people to watch these programmes, by 1986 this has vanished into thin air. About 300,000 TV sets could find their way into the households of Sri Lanka to the surprise of the Government towards the end of 1986. Countries like Japan offered the required equipment and technical training while Canada and Germany gave programme training. The US offered technical help by lending one of its helicopters to hoist the main antenna to the top of its tower on Mount Pidurutalagala.

Experiences of Latin American Nations

Compared to Africa and Asia, it was Latin America, which first achieved the distinction of having the highest density of Television sets, exceeding the definition of UNESCO Minimum. In the highly populous countries of Latin America also there are TV sets between 10 to 20 per 100 inhabitants (based on 1980 survey). It is not an exaggeration by any reckoning to say that 90 per cent of the city dwellers of all Latin American cities have direct access to TV and this average slightly falls to 70 per cent when it comes to rural areas. Compared to African and Asian nations, the urbanization is very high in the Latin American nations and it is one reason, which explains the pace of expansion of TV technology. However the expansion of TV is hindered by the topography of the Andes region as also due to the vast expanses of the countries like Brazil, Mexico and Argentina which have a very larger surface areas.

Brazil

Brazil was the first Latin American nation to go for satellite transmission using the transponders of INTELESAT way back in 1974. Slightly smaller than the US, Brazil has the distinction of being the second in the world in the number of radio stations. Most of these radio companies are in the private sector. About 4 of 5 Brazil's Television stations are in the private sector. One of them, *Rede Globo* is considered the fifth largest TV network in the world. Even so, many parts of the Brazil's 23 states and 4 territories for a long remained poorly accessed by all the networks. Initially in 1967 the Brazilian Government planned to establish a national microwave grid to access the distant settlements of the State. Nearly 7 years later it got the access to INTELESAT, which fulfilled its unaccomplished mission of spreading the network over the entire country. But Brazil is not satisfied with this. The Brazilian National Telecommunications Agency Embratel erected 21 earth stations in addition to 65 earth stations set up by local Television stations. In 1982 Brazil opted for a nation's own satellite system. By February, 1985 BRAZILSAT 1 and by March, 1986 BRAZILSAT 2 were placed in the orbit. These two satellites accessed not only the entire country with the TV transmission but also linked the entire continent including the remotest areas. As a consequence 70 more earth stations are added.

Frankly speaking, today the capacity of the two satellites of Brazil far exceed the requirements of the country, thus giving an edge to its government to make a business with their transponders for the neighboring nations. The Joao Baptista do Amaral Foundation sponsored a literacy programme modeled on the Italian networks. "It is Never Too Late." The Brazil ETV Maranhao launched a programme for its secondary school students who achieved higher pass rates in public examinations than students from conventional private schools. In fact the ETV Maranhao project was intended for the students coming from poor families and remote areas such as Amazon basin. The programme was structured in such a way that it involved a great deal of social interaction, peer-group dynamics and pupil leadership. It was the first ETV channel outside Europe and the US being launched independent of any foreign aid.

Mexico

Like Brazil, Mexico too had taken the satellite coverage of INTELESAT initially. Later it proceeded for its own national satellite. During the INTELESAT services of 1982, the Mexican Government had established around 160 earth stations within two years. These acted to support the terrestrial transmission network. The national satellites MORELOS 1 and 2 replaced the services rendered by INTELESAT by 1986. Now the Mexican Government began using the national satellites for educational purposes. The launching of its own satellites enabled Mexican Government to access the entire country on network. The Mexican Government way back in 1964 planned Radio Primaria and Telesecundaria projects and proposed to construct 5 terrestrial stations in the central part of the country to meet these projects' needs in the next 7 years.

These projects were hooked on to the satellite services once satellite services became available. As a result of this, costs on these projects came down by 25 per cent. Further, Monterry Institute of Technology in Mexico received a Ford Foundation grant for a small ETV project also.

Cuba

It is a classic example of a radical shift in the policy of the State where the earlier freedom and autonomy enjoyed for a long by the Electronic Media has been usurped by the decree of an autocratic polity. Prior to 1959 the Cuban broadcasting has been a free wheeling commercial private system. Goar Mestre, a private owner with great innovation and creativity established a TV network in the early 1950s, which extended the entire country. It was the first country in the world where the TV transmission was made available to the entire population at once. Cuban broadcasting system during the period of Mestre made such innovations in commercial advertising as to become a model to continue even after Castro took over the reins of administration in a revolution and Mestre fleeing to Argentina. Mestre's innovation is called 'radio clock', a 24 hours sequence of 1 minute programmes, each minute containing 30 seconds of news, 25 seconds of commercials with a time check being played against a background of clock like 'ticks' one per second. This programming is still in use under Castro ruling even today and it enabled the scheduling of more than 1000 commercials a day.

Castro took over the broadcasting system in 1959 and converted it into a government system on the lines of the then USSR. Castro turned one of the TV networks into an educational channel and the other for the news and another as Government's voice. Since 1959 the Radio and the Television had been used to offer the classes, known as 'Radio Classes' and 'Tele Classes'. These have been used to train the teachers until the country became self-sufficient in the requirement of the teaching community. Primary, Secondary and Adult Education sectors of the country's education have availed themselves of these classes. The Radio and the Television also provided guidance to those who opted for vocational education through 'circles' of interest. The televised lessons were published as texts of the lessons in the local newspapers.

These 'circles' are formed at the end of each rung of education sector, such as primary and secondary and so on. Those with common interests at the end of each system of education are brought together to know their aptitude in various branches science, technology, arts and other fields. Towards meeting these interests, the Radio classes and Tele classes are synchronized. In 1977, the Cuban Radio and Television Institute backed the establishment of an educational service, called, Radio Victoria de Giron, exclusively to meet the educational needs of the over 40,000 students studying in the Victoria de Giron Citrus Cultivation Plan area. This area consisted of over 56 schools and includes in addition to basic secondary schools, a large number of pre-university and technical and vocational establishments. It is a very beautiful area known for many popular events during 1959 revolution located in the Matanzas province adjoining Jaguey Grande.

Experiences of African Nations

Around 1960 over a dozen African nations who became independent either from French or from British just then had shown a lot of interest in implementing the educational programmes through Radio and Television. These countries consisted of nearly half of the entire African population and about 80-90 per cent of them were illiterates. Of all those nations, which showed tremendous interest, Nigeria is the most prominent one.

Nigeria

Even before Nigeria became independent in 1960, the ETV's capabilities were tested in Nigeria on experimental basis. The WN-TV, the country's first Television station, under the grant of the regional Ministry of Education in Western Nigeria, conducted the trials of ETV for which 120 schools in the Lagos Ibadan area were selected. After independence in 1960, the central government with the aid coming from the Ford Foundation organized a National School Broadcasting service for Radio and Television. This permitted Nigerian stations to develop a modest inventory of classroom telecasts most of which dealt with the enrichment programmes rather than direct teaching. In 1963, the US had come forward to bear the expenses of a 5-year programme meant for ETV expansion to more number of schools.

This has led to the joint working of US-Nigerian academic groups for developing the curriculum for the Primary and the Secondary school levels for transmission during the school hours. This placed Nigeria far ahead of other African nations liberated that time in the ETV.

Ghana

Ghana is one African State that stands as an ideal example of a country, which inherited much of the British legacy and evolved, from its colonial traditions. Ghana is the first country, which became independent on the Western Coast of Africa in 1957. During the British period (1940) the radio was introduced in this Gold Coast (the then name of Ghana). Later the circumstances arising out of World War II compelled the British to Africanize the Radio and communicate with the African people in their mother tongues. By the time the British left the country, the native Africans occupied about 62 per cent of the positions of Radio Ghana though top administrative jobs were still occupied by the British.

Independence came to Ghana under the leadership of Kwame Nkrumah who had a Pan African mind and admiration for the role of Radio in promoting the same culture among African masses. In 1961 Kawme Nkrumah inaugurated the external broadcasting services which could access to both the native Africans as well as the foreigners abroad such as Europe and US. In 1965 a Television station was installed with the assistance from the Canadian Government.

Nkrumah was inspired by the rapid gains made by the then Communist Russia. He wanted therefore to use the Media, both Radio and Television to usher in a socialistic pattern of society. But these policies bankrupted the country. Nkrumah was overthrown in 1966. A swift change in the economic policy followed which preferred commercialization of the Mass Media. In 1968 a new law was introduced to bring all the broadcasting under the Ghana Broadcasting Corporation. It was modeled on the lines of the BBC and considered autonomous. Ghana today has two radio services: GBC-1 that feeds the domestic subscribers and GBC-2 which allows the commercial services transmitted mostly in English. GBC TV consists of 5 TV stations supplemented by four low power repeaters, all of which relay the same programmes nearly for 6 hours a day.

Algeria

It is a French Colony since 1830 and became independent in 1962. However, it had introduced the Radio in 1937 and Television in 1957. Initially the Government aimed at broadcasting exclusively at French Colonists who were about 10 per cent of the population. Television programmes came directly from France. Though French left, after 7 years of bitter independence struggle aided by the Egyptian sympathizers, the country still followed a number of French colonial policies and patterns including French language and culture. Algeria initially planned to be a socialist state with modifications of Islamic principles conducive to its establishment. The Broadcasting service is under the State control and about 70 per cent of the budget is met with the Government funds. The rest is collected as licence fees from the audience. Both the Radio and Television are accessible to entire nation. To interconnect the TV stations, it has erected on priority the microwave repeaters. In 1975 it took the transponders of INTELESAT on lease for its national coverage through satellite. It has also set up terrestrial micro wave links to establish a two-way TV communication with France TV. Today its Arabic radio network operates 24 hours a day. Television is on air 8 hours for four days and 11 hours for three days.

South Africa

It is a country where the minority Whites ruled over majority Blacks for a long time, observing apartheid even in its Radio and TV transmissions. Thus, it has the dubious fortune of having an advanced technology in respect of Media, thanks to the British imperialistic interests in it. Way back in 1920s itself South Africa pioneered the Radio services later switched over to FM stations to provide nation wide segregated services. However, Television entered South Africa in 1976. But it maintained a VHF and UHF network due to apartheid. VHF was meant for Whites and UHF was for blacks, which are mostly either 'tribal homelands' or 'black towns'. This continued till minority Whites handed over the reins of the country to the Blacks after decades of freedom struggle under the leadership of Nelson Mandela. A decade after independence, there are no latest data as to the progress achieved in this sector and in the sector of education though apartheid ceased now.

The Table 15, pp. 72-75 in the give the details of various ongoing educational programmes through electronic media in many of the African and Latin American countries. For many projects the costs are also given to show how effective these strategies are over the conventional programmes. The data suggest that most of the projects launched way back in 1970-80s in the countries cited above (e.g. Telesecundaria of Mexico, Teacher Training Education of Nigeria, SITE of India) are still being pursued under various funds of donor agencies as also with the internal matching grants from the Ministries of Education.

From the foregoing brief descriptions of the broadcasting histories of Asian, Latin American and African nations, it is possible to make out many interesting features technical significance that constitute a genre of knowledge and depth of analysis for comparative purposes. Firstly, these brief histories give us gleanings and insights into the actual circumstances that led to the establishment of Radio and TV network in those countries. Secondly, deep similarities and wide disparities that could be found comparatively between each of those with Eritrea would offer a constructive course of planning as to what actually suits the Eritrean context especially in terms of cost effectiveness both in acquiring the technical knowhow and meticulous planning.

Thirdly, the manner these countries extended their networks from terrestrial to satellite and how they met the financial requirements to effect the transition would throw light as to how to achieve these targets. Some countries entered into technical collaborations (e.g. India with the US, Srilanka with the Japan and Canada, Nigeria with the US) whereas some countries received grants and aid from the foreign agencies (e.g. India, Nigeria and Mexico—all from the US). Some countries like Brazil, without any foreign aid on their own embarked on to educational programmes successfully. Fourthly, the priorities that each country had kept before as a matter of promoting the educational needs of their people through media become apparent.

For instance the approach of Cuba in the post-1959 scenario has much similarity with Eritrea in establishing a separate Radio for the educational purposes. Similarly, the technical collaboration that Algeria retained with France after independence also in having a two-way link of TV with France is thought provoking. At the same time, the programmes of Brazil, Mexico and the achievements of India in the sector of Education act as torchbearers for much better planning of education through low cost technology coupled less man power resources. Of course, Japan continues to be the leader in Asia, as much as BBC and the US in the Europe and West, in developing the first Educational broadcasting fully integrated with the Education system of the country and continuing it as on today.

However, it should be borne in mind that each country's educational planning through electronic media is a condition upon its own state priorities and policies. The comparisons could be made only in respect of the conditions under what circumstances they became free and what planning went into establishing the Radio and TV network and how these countries overcame their geographical and economic barriers to reach the poorest of the remotest of their countries. For instance the example of Indonesia, Sri Lanka as islands stands in stark contrast with hilly countries like India (of course, India has plains and coastal side also).

Similarly the historical and economic backgrounds of Ghana, Nigeria have some similarities with that of Eritrea prior to their liberation. So any attempt to find suitable technological alternatives and answers to some of the plaguing problems of Eritrean Education system could be found after a careful weighing of the different alternatives and experiences these countries have come up with for solving them. The whole description in the foregoing would make a meaningful reading only if it is read and analyzed from against these broad aspects.

Yes, it is true that there is yet a lot to go to change the scenario of African nations. Especially the differences and disparities between the countries above Sahara and below Sahara are very thought-provoking and are posing a formidable challenge to the entire humanity. Poverty, underdevelopment and illiteracy have become the bane of these countries.

5

Learning Strategies of Some Third World Countries

The Need to Look for the Experiences of Others

In the two preceding chapters, information related to establishing electronic network in relation to the educational needs of developing countries on the lines of latest innovations and research that offer both cost effective and efficient alternative strategies have been dealt with. Whether a country is developed or developing, an educational strategy is of extreme consequence for it holds the key to the development and modernization. Even a developed country cannot rest for a while being indifferent to the country's educational strategy as any such apathy may lead the country to relapse into medieval period. Sometimes such indifference may prove to be catastrophic to the very existence of the country itself due to internal unrest among the youth that sometimes may become rebellious and revolt against the State by taking to extreme forms of violence. Hence a strategy and a policy of education, in keeping with the changing needs of the country and to the contemporary global developments, must always keep a vigil and guard on the psyche of the country, especially represented by its youth.

The educational strategy of developed countries has been a model for several underdeveloped countries in the Third World for a long time. But soon the Third World countries realized that this kind of simple aping may not lead to any consequence for the educational planning is something basically related to one's own economic background needs and the local culture. It must emerge from its own indigenous cultural background, requirements and constraints. Each country's topography and environmental conditions place on it an onus to have an educational model and strategy that suits to the country's people attitudes and aptitudes. A country's culture, traditions and the impact of the foreign invasions and the colonial rule—all together develop into a condition, by themselves, which delimits and delineates the strategy or model of education required for the country.

Most of the Third World countries were subject to the invasions of the aliens from the Europe and Arab world. Further most of them were subjected to colonial rule of the British, the French or the Portuguese or the Dutch. Migrations of the people from one place to another place due to geographical and environmental adversities besides calamities caused by the wars and internal strives have changed the texture and composition of each country in their own right. Most of the developing nations thus are confronted with the multi-ethnic, linguistic and religious groups—all of who place their own demands rendering the social structure much more complex to administer, in terms of a sociological framework.

Therefore, when it comes to an educational strategy or a model of a developing country or a country in the making, it becomes imperative to look at the experiences of other developing countries with similar topographic, economic and sociological genre of problems for a quick reference. It does not mean that the experiences of those countries could be directly imported of copied. But they hold a number of answers to some of the problems, which are presently faced.

For instance to speed up an educational programme to change the literacy scenario of a newly born country, a survey of similar exercises done by other Third World countries and their experiences would be of immense help as to plan an educational strategy with a mathematical and scientific precision. It would help cut down the unnecessary surveys, feasibility studies and expenses, and conserve time and efforts of the manpower.

One of the main differences that one could perceive today in the educational strategy between the developed and the developing countries is the urgency with which the latter have to hasten through the integration of modern scientific and technological advancement with that of education at every level. The developed countries had given a lot of time span for their children in conventional education where the latest scientific and technological outcomes were not textbook facts. Nor did they force their children to learn these as part of lifelong education or continuing education. But the developing countries could hardly afford this lengthy time span to its present generation of students. This kind of immediacy in integrating the latest scientific and technological advancements with each level of education supplemented by vocational or technical education has begun with the USSR in the early 1970s.

The Former Russia or the Soviet Union

It was Lenin who recognized first the importance of this strategy. He wanted to turn Russia from a country of bast sandals into a country of electricity. "To achieve such an abrupt shift from backwardness to what, for those times, were modern techniques and technology, the overcoming of general illiteracy was merely the beginning. It was also necessary to produce very large numbers of scientists, engineers and workers who could both create and make use of modern technology. This requirement of Soviet society, in the earliest period of its history, for a qualified and intellectually mature labour force coincided with the natural ambition of each individual to acquire knowledge; it was on the basis of this harmonious combination of State and individual interest that the multi-tiered educational system in Soviet Russia began to take shape."

The economic efficiency of this system was immediately subject to assessment. Accordingly the assessment revealed that the benefit resulting from the above system of education, which integrated the latest scientific and technological advancements, led to the enhanced productivity 27.6 times greater than the State expenditure on education. This practice continued in the erstwhile USSR for a long time till it broke down due to entirely different reasons, which are beyond the scope of this chapter. During the heydays, it has been shown that each year of secondary schooling raises a worker's labour productivity on an average by 30 per cent and workers with the secondary education learn to master complicated tasks and work operations 2.5 times faster and take only half as long to reach the next higher qualification category.

In the early 1960s the economists assessed that due to this strategy, every rouble spent on the State education resulted in about four roubles growth in the national income.

The Principle of Mental and Physical Work: The USSR Model

The principle of Mental and Physical work emerged in the Russian model of educational system where the educational system at every level integrated the latest advancements in science and technology with the curriculum. This has resulted in the increase of mental work of the students who could as a result perform the given tasks with great ease. The more and more the advanced information passed on, the greater the reduction in the physical work. To promote this the former Soviet Russia brought in teachers and professors in specialized areas on hire system to impart the advanced skills at their future work spots. As a result the young specialists will move from education to industry fully equipped with up to date knowledge and ability to use it. It means the education of a specialist does not cease but continues. A person who learns a lot of knowledge inside the four walls of the classroom but cannot put it to use would become a liability on the State. Such kind of education decelerates the national economy and turns unproductive.

As such the Russian model envisaged a continuing effort on the part of the learner to improve his qualifications. Improvement of qualification does not mean mere acquisition of a higher qualification though in the eyes of society it may look as an improvement. The acquisition of qualification must relate to translating the expertise to the national productivity. It means—not acquiring a higher qualification makes an individual fall behind the pace of ever expanding knowledge base of Science and Technology. Now if one looks at the both concepts—one acquiring higher qualification and one not acquiring the higher qualification, the possible interpretation that one can give to the acquiring of higher qualification is maintaining the knowledge level base in a dynamic state and at a maintenance level required for the nation. It means the increase in the proportion of mental and creative work in the production process and it has led to the emergence of a specific social group called, "worker-intellectuals." These are the specialists with secondary or higher educational background and are integrated into the work process.

This places two important conditions on the nation's education system. One is to offer specialist educational training at every level and to keep the learner aware that it needs to be continually kept up. It means that every student must be an 'eternal learner'. The second is that the education system must offer a constructive course of planning to help the learner wade through the maze of "information explosion." Since the learning is linked to nation's production and economy, the learner is exposed to the danger of confronting an enormous volume of information, in the form of textbooks, periodicals, magazines, websites, online research journals and publications. It makes the learner feel the task before very difficult as he hardly could find time to go through all this and separate bran from chaff. Therefore the education system itself must find out the relevant literature and help the learner quickly benefit from it. This has led to the concept of self-education or lifelong education in the Russian context.

Conventional Education Coupled to Vocational Education

The Russian system too has both conventional education of the West. But they did not believe the conventional system as a productive system. Firstly, the conventional system takes too long a time to make a learner productive and useful to the country's economy and to himself. As such they evolved a model in which every tier of education system is followed by a parallel vocational training. It means that a vocational training immediately follows the primary level of education. A learner can get into the vocational training immediately after the primary education and later pursue his education while working as an artisan or a factory worker. Alternatively he can pursue his education in Middle School and then to Secondary School. This is determined by the Government run by the Proletariat. As stated earlier, for those who joined the vocational stream, the further education or acquiring next higher qualification takes place right in the precincts of the place of work. This happens with every level of education such as middle and secondary level too.

There is a Government monitoring of the requirement of skilled category from time-to-time and accordingly it is determined how many should be turned to each professional area and what should be the minimum level of education required for the particular profession. According to the general statistical data on the educational level of the population of the USSR, the percentage of people with Secondary (incomplete or complete) and higher education among those employed primarily on physical work rose from 32.5 per cent in 1959 to 81.5 per cent in 1984—i.e., almost two and a half times. Similarly, the 1979 census data of the USSR revealed that the percentage of workers and farmers rose to 8.7 and 5.9 per cent from the 3.7 per cent of workers and 2.8 per cent of farmers of 1970s. In keeping with this the USSR State Committee passed a decree prescribing the higher qualifications as the basic requirements in about 380 jobs. Creative activity and other elements of intellectual work have thus become crucial to the productive work of the people engaged in physical labour. This development is complimented by the decision of the government to free high intellectual work force from the routine manual labour, which could be taken up by the automation available due to advancement of Science and Technology in their place. The spare time thus made available to the workforce as a result of these changes has been utilized for self-education or lifelong or continuing education.

If one takes a close look at the Russian model of Educational Strategy as a mechanism to transform the backward nation into a modern and advanced nation, there are many striking similarities between the Russia of 1960-70s and the State of Eritrea liberated to freedom in 1991. The Eritrean Government also came up lately with a mechanism similar to that of Russia of 1960-70s called the Rapid Transformation of Eritrean Education System (RTEES). The details of the system and the strategies adapted by the Government in implementing the above system are discussed in the first chapter in detail.

As a matter of taking the experiences of the Russian model are concerned, the above information gives an insight into how the USSR had raised to such a high level industrially as to become a super power in a very short time.

Self-Education and Lifelong Education

The concept of Self-Education and Lifelong Education in the Russian context had been very productive and effective than in the context of any country in the world in the past during 1960s-80s. The Russians indeed have taken a pragmatic view of the Self-Education or Life long Education and achieved wonderful results in a short time compared to the much-advanced West and the Europe in those days.

The concept of self-education or lifelong education originally stemmed from the ancient scripts of India and China. India pioneered the concept both in its cultural ethos as also by practically implementing it through the establishment of the universities first ever in the world. Even before the Greeks and ancient Egyptians had any systematic look at the education, the Nalanda University at Nalanda, near Patna of present Bihar came up under the Gupta kings of 6th century AD. It was the epicenter of the Buddhist Education with a defined curriculum. The education is offered not only in the Buddhist subjects but also in other subjects like Astronomy, Mathematics, Physics, Alchemy (rasavadam), Yoga, Ayurvedic Medicine and Surgery. Most of these are taught as subjects of science for human excellence. The educational excellence of Nalanda University had been well portrayed by the then Chinese traveller Huensang in his travelogue in which he furnished the cultural glory and richness of India in vivid details.

Inspired by these the Chinese also came-up with the similar strategies of Education as China was under the influence of same Buddhism that time. These two Asian giants unfortunately came under the powerful rule of invaders and colonialists from the West in the course of history and in the process nearly a few centuries later have to revert to the concept of self-education now in a different garb and paradigm.

According to Jack London, "the purpose of the University is to provide a preparation for subsequent learning for continuous study throughout life" and Goethe had put the same as, "our predecessors could be satisfied with the level of education they had received in their youth. But we must take up our studies again every five years if we do not want life to leave us behind." Whereas in the past life-long education was general only among the members of a cultural elite, representing an extremely small part of society, today it has become necessary for practically everybody, regardless of one's social position. The modern advancement of science and technology binds us to combine the education and the work. Thus Lenin once stated, "neither education and instruction without productive work, nor productive work without education and instruction in parallel, could be placed at the high point required by the present day level of technology and the state of scientific knowledge."

The first Soviet People's Commissar for Education, A.V. Lunacharsky, once asserted that, "a cultural state can be so only insofar as it is a profoundly educational one, in which each generation is more educated and cultured and more fully developed than the previous one, and that this can happen only if there is continuous instruction, if there is learning at all stages of life." The policy of Russian education in those days itself was, "to make the schools mandated with the task of imparting the children a certain quantum of knowledge and skills that later make self-education possible."

The concept of lifelong education or self-education thus in the Russian context was a logical outcome of two important factors. One is the extensive growth being witnessed in the adult education that virtually embraces every educated and employed in the national economy. The other is the unseen abstract continuous link that lies between the child education and the adult education. In other words, the terminology—child education and the adult education are in fact not two separate entities of education. They are part of one continuous chain of education.

But, to cater to seemingly different age groups falling into various levels of learning, the terms are conceptualized so. This is a matter of academic and administrative convenience for the planners to execute the programmes. But self-education and continuing lifelong education are the other side of the coin of regular education. This elaboration and definition clearly spells out a fact that learning to be a normal and necessary human activity at all periods of a man's life. It therefore gives an opportunity and necessity for the people at any age, "to use, refresh and update their earlier acquired knowledge and abilities, continually to broaden their outlook, to raise their cultural level and develop their capacities to acquire and advance in a speciality and even acquire a new speciality."

The above conceptualization followed by a vigorous planning by the State rendered the former Russia to eradicate illiteracy from its soil. But for the other lapses of the rulers of the Supreme Soviet (CPSU) which led to Glasnost and Perestroika and subsequent collapse of this giant power block in the Europe, there was little wrong in the educational strategy and implementation of the Russian education system. In fact, it was the first system of education, which was developed, indigenously independent of the influences of the West and the Europe and was equally successful too.

As the State of Eritrea and the Ministry of Education in several of their official policy papers reiterated the Government's strong commitment to the concept of self-education and lifelong continuing education by ascribing an effective role to the Media, the Russian experience narrated above would certainly yield a number of strategies of far reaching importance.

China

China is another important Asian giant beset with surging problems of population, agriculture and illiteracy. But, it seems very odd, that a comprehensive glance at its educational policy and strategies would only reveal that it had little to offer to any developing country. Firstly it has modeled its education system more or less on the same lines of the Soviet Russia. But for one conspicuous absence of Media role in the entire education system of the Soviet model, which, however, China had preferred to deviate from obviously due to the realization of the importance of Mass Media, there are many similarities between Chinese model of education and Russian model of education. Though the Soviet Russia was formed much earlier to the liberation of China and though both of them began transforming their poorer and backward economies into progressive and rich ones, the problem of explosion of population did not affect the Russia as much as it had impinged on the psyche of China. Topographically, however, both Russia and China had shared similar geographical conditions. In fact, Russia has been China's global neighbour on the West. But it is pertinent to note that Russia could overcome virtually every possible hurdle, topographical and environmental by virtue of its strong political will and collective conscience.

China too has a conventional education system along the sidelines of which it established vocational education and adult education. There are primary schools for children as also adults. In adults' primary schools literacy and basic skills are imparted. Secondary education is provided by the formal full-time middle schools, the secondary professional schools, the vocational schools, the technical schools, the secondary agricultural schools and the adults' secondary general and technical schools. Higher education is provided at the full-time universities and colleges, the colleges for professional training, the graduate schools and by institutes of higher learning for workers and peasants operating by means of radio and television broadcasts and correspondence courses. This is a very important strategy of China that deviated from the Soviet model. In the case of the latter, without the involvement of Media, the Soviet Russia could successfully eradicate illiteracy from its boundaries purely out of a collective and concerted effort. But this success eluded many communist countries of the Soviet block itself, let alone the other countries of Asia and Latin America, subsequently without the involvement of Media. For instance the former Yugoslavia, though it was a very small nation compared to the Soviet Russia, had to depend upon the Media role for eradication and elimination of illiteracy and to support the formal and non-formal education in schools and colleges.

The general principles of running the schools in China include:

- Combining learning and education with production at all levels.
- Taking special measures to suit local conditions.
- Teaching the students in accordance with their aptitudes.
- Finally, maintaining the flexibility as and when required.

Though literacy programmes of the past and the present include three important phases of the Chinese history, the most turbulent period that hindered all the activities of literacy and post literacy was the period of "upheaval". It was a second stage in the nation's history and covered 10 years period. The efforts of the Government in the first phase of 17 years and in the third stage commencing from October, 1976 to till date, could do a lot to change the scenario of literacy.

The State Council issued in 1978 its "Instructions on Anti-Illiteracy Education", and the Central Committee of the Party and the State Council jointly issued in 1981 the "Decisions on Strengthening Education of the Staff and Workers." As a result of these policy decisions, the literacy, post-literacy and continuing education have now returned to normal and have gained headway along with the cause of socialist reconstruction.

The Strategy Adapted by the Chinese Government to Overcome the Problem of Illiteracy

In educating the staff, workers and the peasants, the Government of China's main approach is to develop Secondary and Higher professional education and conduct continuing education in junior middle schools for some of the younger staff and workers. As for educating the peasants, the Government has adapted a two pronged strategy: one is to eradicate the illiteracy among the peasants totally and the other is to impart them primary and secondary education in culture and technology and initiating them into higher professional education.

Accordingly the Government laid down a well-defined plan for the staff and workers and peasants separately.

Goals for the Education of Staff and Workers

1. To complete the first phase of training for the staff and workers in a planned and systematic way.
2. Elimination of the remainder of illiteracy.
3. 60-80 per cent of workers, whose education level is lower than that of the junior middle school graduates, shall reach the level of the junior middle school graduates. One-third of the staff and workers who are at the level of the junior middle school graduates shall reach the level of the senior middle school graduates or the professional secondary school graduates. Likewise it is planned to elevate a considerable number of staff and workers who are at the level of the senior middle school or the professional secondary school graduates shall reach the level of college students.

Goals for the Education of Peasants

1. To completely eliminate illiteracy among peasants both young and the middle aged in keeping with the variations in topographical and socio-economic conditions of the region where the level of primary education also correspondingly varied among them.
2. To promote by education 80 per cent of young people among farmers whose education level is less than that of the primary school graduates to higher than that of middle school graduates except where the socio, economic and cultural conditions bar such quick transformation.
3. To organize the low ranking cadres, the peasant technicians and the young peasants with education equivalent to junior and middle level to go up the ladder of education by

combining various forms of education in culture, science and technology so that they all attained the level of secondary vocational or technical school graduates.

The Criteria to Declare one as "Illiterate" or "Literate"—The Chinese Definition

The Chinese could since eradicate the illiteracy among the staff and workers by vigorously pursuing the policies enunciated above. However, the efforts to eradicate the illiteracy among the peasants has become a Herculean task for the government. The Government has taken the target group in the age of 15-40 as illiterates. Those who do not possess minimum skills of written vocabulary or vocabulary level less than 500 Chinese characters are called as "illiterates". Similarly semi-literates, with a written vocabulary larger than 500 Chinese characters but below the standard of literacy, children below between 12-15 years of the who do not go to a full time school or who dropped out before completing five years of school or without completing grade 3 are also considered as "illiterates".

A person is considered 'literate' in Chinese if he or she is able to read and write 1,500 characters, understand popular newspapers, keep simple accounts and write informal notes. The literacy criteria for the minority national language are laid down by the relevant province or autonomous region. For such literacy education the teaching materials include simple Reading Primer produced by the concerned province or autonomous region by its own authors and such reader relates the contents mostly to the local work and life. Similarly the local teaching staff of the schools and colleges are drafted for the purpose of these anti-illiteracy programmes on some payment basis. On successful completion of the Primer, an examination will be held in the skills of—reading, writing and reading of Chinese characters. Those who succeed in the examination by securing 60 per cent and above would be given a certificate by the local province or autonomous government.

Units

The population comprising illiterates in the age group of 12-40 years is considered as a Unit. If 85 per cent of the literacy learners of the unit have completed the above-mentioned examination, then it is said to be a unit, which reached the standard of evaluation and a certificate, would be awarded. There is a production brigade, which examines the individuals first. Then the local people authorized by a commune would examine people cleared by the production brigade. In order for the commune to conduct examine for these the minimum population must be 50 per cent of the unit. Further, the department comprising a higher authority would examine these people.

But the department would consider examining these only if they are one-third of the unit. After all this process is accomplished, a unit having 85 per cent of the literacy learners would be declared as literate unit.

In order to achieve high literacy growth China has a well-defined educational hierarchy and administration. Educational commissions for staff and workers and workers and peasants have been established both at national and regional level extending down to rural areas. At the central level there is a department of adult education and at provincial level there is a Bureau of Education. A certain number of full time staff members are present in all these administrative departments. The Chinese Government has a "walking on two legs policy" which means an all out effort both from the Government sector as well as sectors comprising people, factories, companies, trade unions and many other voluntary organizations. All these run schools under them. There is a lot of flexibility in the structure and the content. The students who are learning through the adult learning centers are given special leverage to leave the work spot earlier than the others. For those who are pursuing the primary and secondary education, spare time study is another concept followed.

Radio, TV and Correspondence Courses

In developing secondary and higher education, radio and television played a very important role in China. Correspondence courses are widely used in addition to direct instruction. In the countryside, short-term training courses and lectures on special subjects are adapted for spreading the knowledge of science and technology. Teachers are hired on contract basis to take full time responsibility of adult education programmes to see to the elimination of illiteracy. This apart there are several motivation strategies such as treating acquisition of next higher qualification as a criterion to get an increment in pay or as a criterion for promotion to the next position in the hierarchy.

The Chinese Government broadly considers the movement to eradicate illiteracy as the movement of the people and calls for the active involvement and participation of the masses.

Major Techniques for Post Literacy and Continuing Education

In order to conserve and consolidate the literacy levels achieved, the Government of China has adapted a number of techniques, which are mentioned here briefly. Firstly, they have inculcated the idea in the minds of literates and neo-literates that they need to expand their knowledge and that their education did not and should not stop at the level of mere literacy. Secondly, the Government organized diverse study groups according to individual and local conditions. They are:

1. To form study groups with production team as a unit while organizing centralized study once a week under the aegis of the production brigade.
2. To organize a spare time study groups for the production team.
3. To guide self-study.
4. To fix one-day once a week for the neo-literates who are working in a specialized team to study while reading books or newspapers in their leisure time.
5. To hold broadcasting classes every two days in the commune. The league group leader of the production team is responsible for the organization of the neo-literate listeners.
6. To organize family study groups.
7. Unfolding the teaching activities of the "four enhancements" and "four improvements" by compiling new teaching materials with new contents that is *(i)* to practise copying and dictation and improve learners' knowledge of 1,500-2000 basic Chinese characters through exercises, *(ii)* to enhance guidance in reading by organizing the pupils to read extensively newspapers and popular books so as to develop vocabulary, broaden the scope of their knowledge and improve reading and comprehension skills, *(iii)* to enhance writing practice so as to improve writing ability and *(iv)* to enhance arithmetic.

In line with these techniques, books like Peasants' Reader, Textbooks of Individuals Characters and Characters Commonly Used in the Countryside have been compiled.

8. Launching a movement of 'hundred, thousand and ten thousand' reading and writing activities on a grand scale. It means to read a hundred articles, to write a thousand sentences and to copy ten thousand characters.
9. Enhancing the understanding and memory further by applying what they have learned to actual practice in production and in daily life. Integration of learning with the practice and learning while practising are encouraged.

Main Players in the Field of Adult Education

The Government as already mentioned has formed a number of schools with well-defined objectives to achieve the target of eradicating the illiteracy. The schools set up by it are the major players. Different schools are designated to promote the literacy in various spheres of knowledge. They are:

1. Spare time Literacy and Technical Schools for Primary and Secondary Levels.
2. Spare time Universities and Colleges.
3. Correspondence Courses and Night Universities.
4. Broadcast and Television Schools and Universities: Central Broadcasting Television University and Central Agricultural Schools (CABS).

In spite of all out efforts, China admits that the level of Adult Education it had launched for the workers and peasants was not sufficient and did not eradicate the illiteracy from its soil. Still a sizeable portion and percentage of the total population is languishing in illiteracy in the remote and thinly populated areas of the country which are economically and culturally backward. The inability to achieve 100 per cent universalization of Primary education still continues to breed new generation of illiterates, which is what the crux of the problem that China faces as a major challenge in the 21st century.

India: Tryst with Destiny – Nehruvian Era

India is the second largest and highly populated country in Asia next to China. It too had undergone the trauma and the bitter experiences the Mughal invaders and the British colonialists unleashed on it for over centuries. At the time of Independence India was left with 32 million population reeling under abject poverty with only 17 per cent of them being literates. The foreign marauders and the colonialists virtually stripped the country of its every valuable available natural resource and left the county in a state of misery and grief. The economic repression that the world had seen immediately after the Second World War had its devastating effects on the country's economy. Further, the drought and floods that nature had brought in its fold had crippled the nation that had been the victim of many scourges already. Soon after Independence India had to struggle one side with rebuilding the nation, rehabilitating the huge influx of refugees surging their way into India from all the three sides, north, east and west and revitalizing the economy and combating the other side with Pakistan, which, out of vested interests fuelled with religious fanatism, attacked Kashmir and India on its Northern and Western frontiers.

The incessant wars with Pakistan and China, coupled with border disputes and unrest, had left their own deep scars on the nation's economy and virtually diverted the Government's all efforts to rebuild the nation. Yet the Government of India never missed its targets. On one hand, the government constructed heavy dams for water conservation and irrigation, besides hydroelectric projects and on the other it established heavy engineering units in the area of steel, iron, coal, medicines, fertilizers and oil with the collaboration of the US and the USSR. By 1990, India had about 243 heavy engineering industries in various sectors under the operational control of Government of India. These are in addition to the postal, railways and the defense, the largest Central Government sectors.

In fact, during the formative years, the country's economy was modeled on the lines of the Soviet Plans and the aim of the Constitution of India primarily is to usher in a Secular and Socialist Republic of India. Apart from pursuing the Five Year Plans, of which first Three Five Year Plans did go futile without realizing the intended targets due to wars, drought and floods, the government of India adapted a mixed economy in which the Government and the Private Sector both had equal say in the nation building.

Capacity Building and Capital Investment in Education Sector

Amidst all these the Government of India kept on concentrating fighting against the illiteracy. It had multipronged approach towards eradicating the illiteracy in the country.

In the first-two decades of post-independent era it had concentrated on the capacity building and the capital investment in the education sector. Thousands of schools, primary, secondary and the Government Junior and Degree colleges, besides a number of Universities have been established and constructed in the phased manner. By 1990 there have been nearly 200 Universities in India, which are working under the watchdog body called the University Grants Commission. More than 12 Universities are established by the enactment of a special Act by the Parliament. These are called the prestigious *central universities* to which admissions are done on a nationwide basis with special provision of reservation and economic support for the students hailing from the remote backward areas and backward economic groups. The other Universities are enacted by the law of State Legislatures and yet they are funded by the Central Government. All Universities are autonomous in nature of administration, though political interference rose to high levels of late.

Education has been the subject of concurrent list and both the State and the Center had equal role and share in promoting the education and eradicating the illiteracy. Yet, the major part of the role, such as planning and funding, has always been that of the Central Government and the States complimented the Center's efforts by launching and implementing these programmes in their utmost backward areas. The greatest achievement of India in the Education sector is its pronouncement of a national educational policy followed by the enactment of a comprehensive educational law. The States under the Federal Administration have their own independent Educational acts and laws governing the both private and state sector. The Central Government had established a number of educational bodies to cover the education administered in the Central Schools and the Schools, which follow the pattern of the Central schools.

There is a Central Advisory Board of Education (CABE) which worked directly under the Ministry of Human Resource Development and advises the government on all its policy matters of Education.

The government also established a Central Board of Secondary Education (CBSE) and Indian Council of Secondary Examination (ICSE). These are regulatory bodies established by the Statute of Parliament to regulate the administration and governance of schools following the pattern of 10+2 education on the lines of Central schools. The Government allowed the Private Sector also to run the schools under the aegis of these regulatory bodies. Today the standards of these schools are so established in the world, that many countries in the Middle East, Arab world and in the Asian islands follow either CBSE or ICSE pattern of education.

The States have the pattern called Secondary School Certificate (SSC) or Matriculation or equivalent to 10th class. In so far regulating and formulating the country's educational curriculum in the formal education sector, the Central Government established an apex body called the National Council of Educational Research and Training (NCERT) which offered a corporal guidance to the State Units—State Council of Educational Research and Training with regard to establishing the curriculum at the State level.

Both the NCERT and the SCERT together formulate and update periodically the curriculum and see to the dimensions of enriching them from time to time keeping in view the contemporary global developments in all subjects, especially in the field of Social Sciences and Sciences and Technology. The country's educational policy in the early days of independence was very incoherent and each state followed its own pattern of education. This has led to a confused pattern of education looked from the national perspective. As a result the Central Government quickly came to rescue the situation by appointing a Commission of Education which recommended a rapid restructuring of the education system stressing the need to bring in a uniform policy throughout the country. The commission, which worked with the concurrence and involvement of the Federal States, adapted 10+2+3 pattern and three-language policy at all levels of education in all states. This is the foremost development in so far the reforms in the education sector is concerned.

In 1986, the youngest ever Prime Minister of India, Mr. Rajiv Gandhi, pronounced the revised National Educational Policy in which the emphasis is on achieving the Universalization of Primary Education and the vocationalization of education. Also to reach the underprivileged sections of the society and the rural areas of the country, the Government of India announced the plans to start Jawahar Vidyalayas also called Navodaya Vidyalayas where education is fully residential and at the expenses of the Government. Admissions are made on the basis of entrance and reservations are provided for the backward and under privileged sections of the society.

Another notable reform in the sector of education, brought about by the Central Government in the Central Pattern of Education is to elimination of marks system. In the place of marks grades are indicated. This has eliminated unhealthy commercialization and competition in the private and the public sector education. Nevertheless this unhealthy practice is still continuing in many Federal States unfortunately making the primary and secondary education very burdensome to the parents especially middle class and lower class people. This apart another revolutionary step taken by the Rajiv Government was to equip the rural schools with teachers, Black Boards and books for the school libraries. The whole programme was called the operation black board.

Under the scheme every state has been entitled to recruit in all single teacher run schools one more teacher and furnish all schools with the Black Boards, chalks and books. Where there were no schools earlier and the classes were taken under trees, the scheme enabled the state to open new schools and provide right from the inception a minimum of two teachers. It was Rajiv who first realized the importance of computer in education and advocated a curriculum based computer education in all the central schools. The steps taken by Rajiv Government during his short tenure indeed help consolidate the progress achieved in the primary and secondary education but remained far behind achieving the intended goals such as achieving Universalization of Primary education by 2000 AD.

From Directive Principles of State Policy to Amending the Constitution: The Right to Primary Education—A Fundamental Right Now

Though the country's Constitution, in its **Directive Principles of State Policy**, included under **Article 45**, expressly states that, *The State shall endeavor to provide, within a period of ten years from the commencement of this Constitution, for free and compulsory education for all children until they complete age of 14 years* this could not be translated into the reality due to the reasons stated above, coupled to lack of political will too. In the last 50 years of post independent era, only 70 per cent illiteracy could be wiped out. The reason obviously attributed to the staggering 30 per cent of illiteracy is the ever-increasing population. Another thing which is very important to note here that the country's average expenditure on education sector did never exceed two per cent of its whole GDP since independence despite strong criticism from all the political and apolitical organizations. The funds crunch was one of the worst causes always cited by the officials for the failure of the many schemes and programmes launched by the Central or State Government.

Whereas the Government's unrelenting efforts indeed brought down the percentage of illiteracy in a linear proportion the geometric growth of population had outwit the efforts. The Government's argument has been always that there are other priority areas such as rural roads, health and sanitation programmes, family welfare schemes etc., where the government has the annual recurrent budget expenditure purely as a welfare measure of the State. To meet the educational needs of the growing population, which by the turn of 2000 AD touched one billion, the Government had to double or treble its average expenditure of 2 per cent GDP every year. Even then it would be difficult to meet the intended goals and objectives. This has necessitated the Governments both at the Center and the States to think in terms of relinquishing part of their control over higher education in favour of Private sector. Beginning with the Primary Education upto the level of post graduation, including such important areas like Engineering, Medicine, Law and Business have been passed on to the private sector and slowly government started wriggle out of this expenditure. However, the Government could not escape from its objective and commitment to achieve the Universalization of Primary Education, in keeping with the objectives of Education For All (EFA).

As a result the present BJP led coalition Government in 2001 introduced a bill into the Parliament making the right to Primary Education a fundamental right, making primary education compulsory besides banning the child labor, which means employing children below the age of 18 years a punishable offence. All the Federal states have been requested in line with this to initiate action against the parents who do not send the children in the age group of 3 to 18 years to schools and the employers who employ such children in their establishments. Though this is purely a social movement, the teething of the movement by law is a welcome sign for the officials of the Education department who have had to struggle a lot to convince the parents to send their children to school.

Not to be outwit by the Center, even the States like Tamil Nadu and Andhra Pradesh have launched several attractive schemes like – *Mid-day meal, let us go back to school, let us light the lamp of literacy, Education for All*. Most of these are meant to encourage the children for education and to attract the dropouts back into the fold of education. Despite all these efforts, what one basically notices is that the Center and the State have failed in convincing a rural child about the need and importance of education in so far his or her life is concerned. If a rural child asks a question as to why should he study when he is able to work and earn his livelihood by working along with his parents in the fields or farms or factories, there is no apparent answer from the Government. It only makes the government to look at the education programmes which when linked with economic prospects sounded different to the rural people.

For quite a long time this resulted in a situation of static equilibrium and of late the programmes of eradication of illiteracy picked up the momentum again when government revised its strategies of adult education and non-formal education based on their previous experience of economy linked literacy movements. In order to achieve best results in the eradication of illiteracy, the Government of India had devised and implemented various strategies of unique nature, some of which remained a model for the rest of the developing countries later.

Economy Linked Literacy Movements: India's Unique Strategy

For instance the Government of India's SITE project of 1975, dedicated to promote the rural educational programmes for farmers and the youth, combined with the programmes meant to enriching the skills of the rural natural science teachers and the professional skills of the rural youth, had been a unique success story by any standards of judgement both from the West and the East (enough of this has already been described in the earlier chapters). This apart there are a number of unique schemes and projects which the Government of India has come up from time to time based on the contextual needs and contemporary demands. The Radio Schools and the Radio Forums started by the All India Radio way back in 1950s in Gujarat, were meant to educate the illiterate peasants, small farmers and agriculturists as to better farming practices, had revolutionized the entire agriculture sector in India.

The media role, especially through Radio and the Newspapers, wall posters, pamphlets, booklets and other support materials, in agriculture is immense that it complemented the efforts of the scientists led by M.S. Swaminathan *et al.*, and the farmers in bringing about **the Green Revolution.** Similarly **the White Revolution** brought about by the cooperative sector in the Anand area of Gujarat by Professor Kurien and others owes its success partly to the supplementary efforts of the State Government and the Central Government.

Thus, there is an apparent uniqueness in India's educational strategy which is always combined with a movement linked to revolutionize the individual as well as national economy.

Thus the success stories of the Green Revolution in Punjab and Chandigarh, and the White Revolution in Gujarat clearly sent a clear message to everyone involved in the exercise of literacy programmes that any effort of the Government, be it State or Central, to eradicate illiteracy must be in a position to convince the rural masses that such education would bring economic prospects not only to them but to their village too. Unfortunately the Government of India could not read into this message and gain out of the spirit of these success stories. As a result, though the Government of India launched incessantly a number of programmes and schemes to educate the rural masses, there is always slackness and an indifference towards many of these. From the above, it is clear that if any third world country plans to implement adult education programmes or comes up with plans to promote educational programmes for the elimination of illiteracy, it should weigh the social relevance of such programmes by implementing which would there be rapid economic boom to the individuals and to the State. Otherwise these educational programmes are more likely to end up as mere dress rehearsals.

Post Globalization Strategies: DWAKRA a Self-Help Women Movement in the State of Andhra Pradesh

In the context of post globalization, there is a need to revise the strategies and the educational programmes to convince the rural people the importance of the education. Particularly in India, the education is passing through the toughest times of privatization. At this time, for a government to achieve eradication of illiteracy is not very simple and easy task. Firstly, the post globalization has demanded a market-oriented growth and this has caused ever-increasing expansion of the towns and cities. Secondly, India achieved the unique distinction of transferring the urbanization from the Metro cities to towns and district headquarters which at one time was thought to be impossible for Asian giants like India. Even then the mobility of the rural youth from villages to towns for employment purposes is very hard to restrict. The demographic composition of the country is thus fast changing. At the time of independence, India was having 80 per cent population in the rural areas and 20 per cent in the Urban areas. If the effects of Globalization could not be restrained in terms of the flow of rural youth to towns and urban centers, the complex and intricate composition of the demography of the countryside will undergo drastic and irreversible change. This may lead to much more complex problems in future.

Therefore, in keeping with this philosophy in mind, the Federal Governments like Rajasthan and Andhra Pradesh have come up with the schemes like DWAKRA a self-help women group, which emerged as the largest cooperative movement with the aid of the State Government initially. Today this women movement not only successfully operates the entire state but also offers educational programmes for their members in computer literacy and programmes of literacy which go far beyond the minimal literacy programmes offered earlier by the Central and State Government. The principle of White Revolution and Green Revolution reappeared in this cooperative movement. The Amul cooperative movement of Gujarat and the Single Window Movement for the Farmers in the State of Andhra Pradesh are such notable movements, which provided education beyond the definition of literacy programmes.

The Traditional and Modern Educational Strategies of India: Formal and Non-Formal Education

Since independence India has pursued the traditional and conventional education system. Like any other country India too had a strong kindergarten education followed by Primary, Secondary and Higher education. Though Kindergarten was a new entry into traditional education (by 1970s in Metro cities) in the early 1980s (in the towns) in India, the original traditional education in the rural areas continued to begin only at class 1 at the age of 5 years. Though there were 11th class and 12th class at School level in many states in the country upto 1960-70s, gradually the entire country came into one pattern of 10+2+3 system of education. Along the sidelines of the traditional education, the Governments in the State are encouraged to start Industrial Training Institutes for those, who either discontinued their traditional education or dropped out due to personal problems, in several trades such as fitter, mechanic, welder, cutter etc. Several institutes of similar stature have been established in the fields of sculpture, theatre arts, drawing, painting, music, tailoring, embroidery, gardening and interior decoration. These institutes are established to meet the various aptitudes of the dropouts who did not find any taste in sailing with thousands in the traditional education. These institutes issue certificates which are recognized for the employment in the State and the Central or Private Establishments.

For the benefit of dropouts, after completing the 10th class, the Polytechnic Institutes have been established. This would serve the cause of middle class families in two ways. Firstly, it offered education in Engineering courses which could be continued to University level depending on one's own economic and academic interests and created opportunities of employment in the government and private establishments. The post 10th class education included two years junior college education called intermediate education, which acted of late as a "bridge education" connecting the successful candidates with any professional course of their choice such as Engineering in IITs, Universities, Medicine in Medical colleges or Agriculture in the Agriculture Universities or Bachelor's Degree in the University affiliated Colleges. Students who complete the courses in these institutions are offered a Bachelor's degree in the chosen field and are permitted to pursue their next higher education for a Master's Degree either in the Universities or in the University affiliated Post Graduate Colleges. Besides, there are a number of established and internationally reputed Institutes of Professional Studies like Indian Institute of Management (IIMs), Advanced Research Centers like Bhabha Atomic Research Center, Tata Institute of Fundamental Research, Tata Institute of Social Sciences Research.

Almost all the Universities in India have world ranking Scientists and Philosophers and all of them offer programmes in research leading to the award of Ph.D. This apart there are State and Central bodies also which offer a number of courses at the Post Graduate level or Professional level and even offer programmes in different fields leading to the award of Doctoral degree.

To sum up the whole scenario of the traditional education, the following would suffice:

1. Kindergarten Schools.
2. Primary Schools.
3. Middle Schools.
4. Secondary Schools or Matriculation Schools.
5. Junior Colleges or Senior Secondary Schools.
6. Degree Colleges affiliated to Universities.
7. Universities.
8. Specialized Institutes like Regional Engineering Colleges, Indian Institute of Technology, Indian Institute of Science, Indian Institute of Management etc.
9. Universities of Agriculture.
10. Universities of Medicine—All India Institute of Medical Sciences, JIPMER—Pondicherry, PGMER—Chandigarh, NTR Health University, Andhra Pradesh.
11. Specialized Institutes offering Ph.D. and Postgraduate Programmes—ICAR., IARI, ICMR, BARC, ICSSR etc., NBRI, CSIR, CCMB etc.

    This apart there are many specialized institutes, which function under various corporate bodies that offer postgraduate programmes and Ph.D. programmes too.

The Schools offering Vocational Education are as follows:

1. *Industrial Training Institutes:* ITIs offering certificates in various trades mentioned above—admit students with 0 qualification to 7th class pass or fail. Some courses or trades are offered to those with 10th class simple pass also.
2. *Polytechnic Institutes*: Offering Diploma in Engineering courses—admit students with 10th class pass and Intermediate pass or fail qualifications.

    All those who succeed in the above courses have to apply for apprentice job training for 18 months in the Public or

Private Sector and after completion of the apprentice service, they must appear for National Apprenticeship examination. Qualifying at this examination finally entails them to a full time permanent job on a regular time-scale.

Formal and Non-Formal Education through Distance Education Programmes

School Education

There is an ample scope for every child, who discontinued or failed or dropped out for various personal or socio-economic reasons, to appear for 7th class common examination conducted by the District Common Examination Board or 10th class examination (SSC) conducted by the Board of Secondary Education as a private candidate after obtaining exemption from regular attendance and qualify in it. The student can study at home or take the help of Private tutorials. Once he/she qualifies in this examination he can join the regular stream. There is no restriction on him as to his/her further studies. The Federal Government keeping in mind the economic and social problems of several sections of the society provided ample opportunity for a child to study his entire school education at home itself and appear for annual examination along with the regular students by paying some nominal amount as exemption fees from regular attendance. Likewise a child can pursue any class right from classes I to X and still get the same value and recognition to his childhood and school education.

National Open School Education

This apart, as part of National Policy of Education of 1986, a number of open schools are established in entire country which worked directly under the operational control of the Ministry of Human Resource Development. These schools offer one-year correspondence cum contact education through their resource personnel in the Federal States (through SCERT) to the students who could not pursue their regular education in the schools. At the end of one year they conduct examination and those who qualify in the examination are awarded a certificate equivalent to SSC (Secondary School Leaving Certificate issued by the States) examination of the States. From their on they can pursue their Jr. college or Technical Education such as Polytechnic.

University Education

1. All the Universities in India including specialized Universities like Indira Gandhi National Open University (IGNOU), New Delhi, modelled on the lines of the British Open University, Dr. B.R. Ambedkar Open University, Hyderabad, AP offer distance education programmes in a variety of both conventional and non-conventional courses leading to the award of Bachelor's Degree, Master's Degree and Postgraduate Diploma, besides Diploma and Certificate courses. Some of these Universities offer M.Phil and Ph.D. programmes also through Distance Education.
2. Most of these universities offer educational programmes through Open University system also. It means the programmes offered by the Universities are of two kinds: *(i)* Those who had some level of previous education which would qualify as a minimum level of qualification for the university to consider admission into a specific programme of study. These are qualification-based programmes and would have the same weight and value as those offered on the regular stream. *(ii)* The other is to allow an entry into any level of the course or programme without any previous background of education. There is an age limitation for such an admission into Open University system and the University conducts an entrance examination to those who wish to gain entry into the Open University system. Based on attaining the qualifying mark prescribed the University, the admission is granted. However, those who qualify through Open University system are not eligible for any employment on the basis of it. Almost all employers, private or government in India insist on the regular educational records commencing from the School level. Hence such an Open University education is seen as a measure of satisfying the unfulfilled educational ambitions. Particularly the housewives, who could not pursue their higher education during their youth days, prefer such system of qualifications to fulfil their academic and spiritual ambitions.

Adult Education Programmes and Schemes

With nearly 30 million population (as per national census data of 2001) still groping under illiteracy, the Government of India is desperate to launch various programmes for the eradication of illiteracy. The aim to wipe out illiteracy from the soil of India is a long cherished dream. The Government of India initiated steps to implement the adult education right from the first five-year plan under various names e.g. Social Education, Farmer's functional literacy programme and non-formal adult education. In 1978, it was launched on a massive scale and it was included in the 20-point economic programme as well as the Minimum Needs Programme. The Sixth Five-Year Plan Document envisaged coverage of the entire 110 million adult illiterate population by 1990. Accordingly all the Federal states have prepared operational plans to achieve this target and also have made special plans to cover women and weaker social groups.

Strategies

- Correlation and integration of formal and non-formal education with each other as in countries like in India formal education through schooling alone cannot by itself be sufficient for achieving major educational objectives.
- Development of non-formal educational programmes at all levels for all categories of learners—children, youth and adults—each separately.
- Every child in the age group 6-14 shall continue to learn—provision must be made to allow the child to change from full time to part time study at school also.
- The twin programme of adult education (15-35) and non-formal education (6-14) would be organized simultaneously to strengthen and supplement each other.
- Designing of the programmes must concentrate on enhancing the capacities and abilities of the individuals to contribute to greater productivity and earning capacity in their fields of work.

In line with the above strategies, 4 important programmes have been conceived for rapid implementation and transformations.

Programmes

(a) *Programmes for Children and Youth With Some or no Formal Schooling: (i)* part-time education for non-school going children in the age groups of 6-11 and 11-14, *(ii)* offer education to make-up deficiencies in learning, to integrate literacy skills with the needs of learners and development activities such as functional literacy for women in the age group of 15-40, functional literacy to farmers and farm women, and adult education for persons in the age group of 15-35.

(b) *Programmes for Improving Work Performance: (i)* Short-term courses for illiterate and semi-literate workers, peasants, farm labour, craftsmen, artisans, tradesmen and women to help upgrade their skills and the management abilities, besides get financial incentives.

(c) *Continuing Education Programmes: (i)* offering courses, which are related to vocational education such as home sciences, drawing, painting, gardening, embroidery, painting, toys making, basic computer skills, interactive English and Communicational skills to help individuals to develop confidence in the profession e.g. Receptionists, Caterers, Security personnel, customer care personnel, liasioning personnel, kindergarten teachers etc., *(ii)* offering correspondence courses, *(iii)* conducting evening schools, and *(iv)* providing libraries and reading rooms.

(d) *Programmes with Emphasis on Health and Promoting Community Leadership: (i)* offering instruction in health, sanitation, child-care and nutrition education; *(ii)* Forming local groups which promote community efforts such as farmers', workers' or cooperative associations; *(iii)* short training courses for local leaders and members of organizations.

(e) *Programmes of Post-Literacy and Lifelong Continuing Education: (i)* to involve all sorts of folk forms—dances, songs, ballads, dramas to keep the messages of the need to continue the education lifelong alive among neo-literates, *(ii)* organize these activities through Nehru Yuvak Kendras, Chetan Sanghs and other rural literary youth associations and *(iii)* to involve the media, print and electronic as far as possible and this should include the local small scale newspapers and FM Radio and TV stations run on Battery or Solar Cells.

In keeping with the above strategies and programmes the Government of India has been making relentless efforts to curb the illiteracy and even wipe it out from the soil of India. But as mentioned earlier, all the programmes and strategies have failed in short to convince a rural parent or child as to what wonder would happen if he/she learns something to write or read. Basically the Government failed to see that unless the rural parent and child is convinced of the need to study, the success keeps eluding ever. It must look back at the success stories of the economy-linked literacy movements, which could successfully integrate the rural life with the need of education. Until unless such movements occur on a large scale area wise, the rural population hardly get convinced of any need of education.

Indonesia

Indonesia, an archipelago, presents a classic example of how the unsustaining political will of a Government can put its own national educational programmes to jeopardy. The country is essentially a large cluster of islands with a vast variation in the population density per square kilometre. The average population density is 77 per square kilometre. It has about 13,667 islands of which only 992 are only populated reasonably. About 60 per cent of the total population of the country would live in Java itself with the population density of 690 people per square kilometre. The highest density is found in Jakarta with 11,023 people per square kilometre. The lowest was found in Irian Java with 3 people per square kilometre. The country's economy is more farm based or agriculture based though the country has been marching towards manufacturing and modern industry. At the time of independence in 1945 the country was having about 50 per cent illiterate population.

The country's Constitution clearly states that, "every individual was entitled to education." This has been further reiterated in the General Policy Directions (GBHN) that, "education should be a life long process and should be implemented within as well as outside the school system." Thus, education became the responsibility of the families, the communities and the government.

The educational objectives and goals are so delineated that they extend beyond the ordinary instruction of literacy and numeracy skills and encompass the development of positive attitudes towards learning the skills, identify and solve problems, create new employment opportunities for themselves and others so that they can lead a prosperous and happy life.

In accordance with this the Government developed a national system of education consisting of complementary programmes for formal and non-formal education. Formal education is implemented through a standardized structure at the Primary, Secondary and Tertiary levels. However, the formal education failed to reach the entire school population. The 1971 census revealed that more than 21 million illiterates over the age of 9 did never attend their school during 1960s. Some of them who went indeed to school also ended up as dropouts and lost their skills altogether, whatever little they learned.

All this clearly held a mirror to reflect what one could call as the failure of the political will due to its own unsustainable programme of action. The plan of action to eradicate the illiteracy from the country began indeed on a true nationalistic spirit but ended up in a political fiasco. It happened unfortunately twice in the history of Indonesia once in 1949 and another in 1960-64. Were it not to be so probably Indonesia would have been the first Third World country in South Asia that successfully eliminated the illiteracy way back in 1950s or 1960s. The reasons for this are obvious; firstly, steps to initiate follow up literacy or post literacy programmes have been ignored and secondly, the political propaganda to gain the public will took precedence over the educational achievement.

In view of this the Government came-up with a firm planning and programme of action that remedied the above stated two drawbacks. But the literacy movement never picked up the momentum of 1949 or 1960s afterwards, the progress achieved at slow pace however, notwithstanding. Nevertheless there is something unique of the structure, planning and organization of the non-formal education programmes. First and foremost that one could recognize, among other things, is related to its comprehensive and well-defined establishment. The establishment not only includes the printing and production of materials of non-formal education but also oversees its distribution throughout the country. A brief outline for the general appreciation of its meticulous and well-defined is given here.

The Ministry of Education and Culture contains four general directorates: *(i)* Elementary and Secondary Education, *(ii)* Higher Education, *(iii)* Non-formal Education, Youth and Sports (PLSPO) and *(iv)* Culture.

The Directorates concerning the Elementary and Secondary Education as also Higher Education oversee the planning, development and administration of the conventional education or traditional or formal education.

Conventional Education

Like any other Third World country, the Government of Indonesia has also opted for conventional or traditional education system with 4 tiers:

1. Kindergarten.
2. Primary and Middle School Education.
3. Secondary Education.
4. Tertiary Education.

Non-Formal Education

The non-formal education is administered by the Directorate of Non-formal education, Youth and Sports (PLSPO). It is again divided into 4 Directorates:

1. Community Education (PENMAS).
2. Youth Guidance.
3. Sports.
4. Technical Support and Development.

The Employment-Oriented Learning Programmes (EOLP) is an integral part of the total PENMAS (Directorate of Community Education) programme. PENMAS has two different structures. One is regular and oversees the whole programmes. The other deals with the various wings of the programme planning organizations.

PENMAS–I

It takes care of the administration, planning and development of the following:

1. Basic Education, Literacy programmes etc.
2. Women's Education, Family Life Education Programmes.
3. Vocational Education, Sewing, Automobile Mechanics, Typing etc.
4. Mobilization of Community Resources; Skilled persons in the community are recruited for PENMAS learning groups and courses.

5. Educational Technology; Development of learning materials and aids.

A Financial Division of PENMAS through Funds and Grants supports all these.

PENMAS–II

It is as mentioned earlier a structure, which encompasses various wings, and bodies that offer support to PENMAS–I. It is a very carefully planned group of bodies that perform well-defined functions without a clash or overlapping.

1. *Programmes:* Research and Development and implementation of EOLP, literacy and other programmes primarily through local learning groups established by the PENMAS field worker.
2. *Learning Materials:* Research, Planning and Production of Printed and non-Printed learning materials for use in training PENMAS staff and in NFE learning groups.
3. *Secretariat:* Procurement of hardware and software for various training centres and financial administration.
4. *Evaluation:* Evaluation, Supervision and monitoring of learning group activities as well as those of the PENMAS staff of training programmes and procurement within the project.
5. *Training:* Training of PENMAS staff from national to sub-district levels to plan, implement and supervise PENMAS programmes; training of non-PENMAS and PDK personnel (Ministry of Education and Culture) on their rôle in the implementation of PENMAS programmes. The training of tutors and facilitators of learning group.

Target Population

The programmes of PENMAS are directed to the following target groups:

- Those who do not attend the schools due to poverty or other reasons.
- Those who are illiterates.
- Those who dropout from various levels of schooling.
- Those who have completed the basic level education.

Programme Objectives

To eradicate simultaneously three kinds of ignorance – ignorance of literacy, numeracy and national language and ignorance of Basic Education.

- To prevent new literates from relapsing into illiteracy.
- To foster positive attitudes towards development and changes.
- To help learners acquire relevant skills needed to improve their standard of living.

Delivery System

In order for achieving the above objectives, the PENMAS has developed a unique delivery system, which runs on the following lines: *(a)* Courses, *(b)* Apprenticeship, *(c)* Self-learning and *(d)* Learning Group (Kejar).

(a) *Courses:* A course is designed to teach a group of 10 to 20 people a variety of skills. The curriculum is set-up PENMAS at the national, provincial and district levels. The government provides finance to design courses and implement the PENMAS curriculum, while private individuals or non-government institutions may organize similar skill-learning courses funded by the learner's tuition charges.

(b) *Apprenticeship:* This learning process emphasizes acquisition of certain skills through working with and under the guidance of someone (e.g. tutor) who has specific knowledge and skills needed by the learner. By giving his/her labour, the learner does not burden the resource person or tutor nor does she/he suffer a loss of earning because of acquisition of skills in return.

(c) *Self-learning:* This method of learning applies to those who completed basic literacy. It does not mean the isolation of individual. Self-learning is thus planned through a group in the presence of a resource person. This is done through a learning group called, *Kejar*. At the end of all, the whole learning process occurs through the participation of community based groups.

(d) Learning groups form and develop activities on the basis of

work-related needs and interests. It is aimed in such a way that it would promote the positive attitudes and motivates them towards their development and life improvement.

The Lessons from the Experience of Indonesia

There are a number of lessons that one can learn from the experience of Indonesia.The most important one, among others, is that it is not sufficient enough to simply launch and implement the literacy or non-formal education programmes. What is most important is to follow it up with simultaneous post-literacy and lifelong education programmes. It is here the Government of Indonesia has put all its efforts on the mat twice. Secondly, the impetus or momentum given to any educational programme to pull out the illiteracy from its grass roots from a country should not take the political overtones. If politics get mixed up with the campaign for eradication of illiteracy, the consequences of such political precedence would be devastating and sometimes undoing the little good done too. Thirdly, the entire efforts of the State of Indonesia in the implementation of the non-formal education programmes are community based which is what the need of the hour in the newly liberated countries like Eritrea. Further the involvement of community as a learning group of 20 would present an ideal size for any course or for organizing a self-learning group. Fourthly, the organizational planning for the implementation of the non-formal educational programmes is very ideal to emulate. Fifthly, the literacy programmes are mostly work linked or economy linked and keeping the Indian experience in mind, definitely these strategies are going to cut ice with the rural people and motivate them to take up the non-formal education in a national spirit and broader perspective.

A Review of the Strategies of Countries of Latin America and Africa

A broad review of learning strategies of other Asian countries such as Nepal, Thailand in Asia, Brazil and Mexico in Latin America and Algeria and Egypt in Africa—suggest that almost all the countries have faced enormous problems concerning the growing illiteracy, dropouts and post-literacy and have broadly followed similar format of Educational Strategies to overcome them. Irrespective of degrees of differences in the magnitude of these problems, it sounded as though illiteracy, dropout and relapse into illiteracy due to lack of post-literacy follow up are universal.

All the countries, among these continents, have also primarily recognized that there are certain common constituents or instruments that would go to help counter these effectively the economy or global differences notwithstanding. They are:

(i) Community Centres or Village Centres or Village Reading Rooms are best suited for complementing the formal and non-formal education in any country, as all the countries faced the problem of illiteracy more localized among the rural side of their countries rather than the Metro or Urban side.

(ii) All the countries, confronted with illiteracy problem, could not make rapid progress in their efforts unless they combined these programmes with economic prospects of the individuals involved. Otherwise these programmes showed a very little impact on the rural people. The progress thus achieved was very minimal and not commensurate with the funds spent on it.

(iii) All the countries used a well-defined Organizational and Administrative apparatus to eradicate the illiteracy of all forms. The establishment of this apparatus – top to down – from the Central level to the grassroots level plays a vital role in the success of these programmes. All realized the importance of involving the voluntary bodies and non-governmental organizations mostly comprising women groups or women cooperatives.

(iv) All the countries used Radio as the best means of mobilizing the masses into literacy programmes and the Radio offered a range of programmes including correspondence courses. Very few countries of late began to use TV educational Channel also to supplement the school and college level education. Even the UNESCO recommended the involvement of Radio and TV, mostly the latter, for the direct teaching, where there is dearth of qualified teachers or instructors. The fact the Media can play enormous role in changing the literacy patterns of the country gets additional force if it is supplemented by the Print Materials and allowed to be studied through group study, group supervision under the spirited leadership of the village heads or instructors or monitors.

(v) All the countries have taken note of the fact that non-formal educational programmes and adult educational programmes

yield best results if they are carried through self-learning groups of 10-20 or through community oriented groups, than individual-centered.

(vi) All the countries have realized the importance of simultaneous implementation of post-literacy programmes.

In relation to Eritrea, the above scrutiny of the Educational Strategies offers a number of insights. Firstly, there are many similarities between Eritrea and India, if a true comparison is made to the times of India, when the latter became independent. Especially both are agriculture based countries. But the differences arise in identifying the right agricultural practices. Especially in Eritrea the rearing of cattle and their extensive grazing of available grass lands and the fields in Eritrea have over a long period resulted in the soil erosion leading to the bareness of the lands. Further killing of cattle for beef and mutton etc., had adversely effected the milk production and the production of milk related products. Cattle are particularly grown for the production of meat. As such soil conservation as also production milk or milk related products both have taken a back seat or step motherly treatment.

If this problem is taken advantage of to convert it into a *green and white revolution*, as a cooperative movement on the lines of Indian experience, it would certainly serve the cause of education and economic prosperity of the poor peasants including poor woman of Eritrea. It may temporarily affect the beef or meat market, but it would begin to produce lots of milk and milk related products, both of which are presently scarce. But it is certain that soon it will grow into a nation wide cooperative movement bringing unpredictable profits to the poor farmers and their families.

When their economic interests are combined to their need to get educated, the plans of Government of Eritrea would succeed in eliminating the illiteracy among the women and poor peasants. Otherwise, it is very difficult to keep the poor peasants confined to formal or non-formal educational programmes and still to forge ahead an initiative or drive among them.

Further, the experiences of China, though it has a proletariat administrative set-up, could be of immense help in relation to its rigid plan of implementation and evaluation. For instance its definition of literacy is one which ensures no scope for relapsing into illiteracy once a level of functional literacy is achieved. The normal level of education that forbids one to relapse into illiteracy is 4th class level. It is generally considered in Asia as an ideal level of literacy acquisition. This definition ideally suits Eritrea where the scope for pursuing further education is enormous in view of the limited population and expanding educational horizons. Further, the Chinese way of dividing illiterates into units and evaluating them through a systematic scheme of examinations is a pointer to the efficient system of implementation.

In this regard many developing countries including India has to draw the lessons from the Chinese evaluation of neo-literates. At the same time, it needs to be mentioned that the curriculum and content that China adopted in its primers and the methodology of instruction it pursued is worth following in any developing country. The contents and the materials are easy to learn, at the same time, reflect a high quality and standard. Compared to China's Adult education materials, the Primers followed in many other African countries such as Kenya or Tanzania fall much below the desired level. (UNESCO, Paris: 1990—Reports of IIEP Workshop on Tanzania and Kenya, 1989-90). It is advisable if Eritrea takes note of this for its programmes are in the stage of commencement.

It has become of late a tendency to call one literate, if one acquires the knowledge of writing his own name and affix his signature. But, such kind of literacy is a false literacy and based on that, a country cannot or should not reel out the figures of literates in one's country. The definition of 'literate' is fast changing today. It is advisable if UNESCO standards of definition are taken into consideration and extend the adult education programmes beyond the functional literacy and even acquaint the definition with the computer literacy and visual literacy.

6

Correspondence-cum-Contact Programmes for Rapid Educational Transformation

The Challenge of Meeting the Nation's Teaching Needs and Keeping Pace

The main problem of newly liberated countries or developing countries is that they have to keep pace with the fast changing scenario of the world and bridge the gap between the developing and the developed. Particularly the changes that occurred all over the world in the last one decade have brought the newly liberated States under tremendous pressure. The struggle to reform a nation's economy by bringing in structural reforms through the nation's educational planning has thus become an urgent priority for all the newly formed countries. But "how" is the big question. To get the highly skilled or educated manpower, in addition to infrastructure and funds, at a time and in a short time is an uphill task for any developing nation or a nation in the making. Especially the compulsory achievement of Universalization of Primary Education and attainment of the Millenium Development Goals imposed by the developing world on the newly formed countries built up a tremendous pressure on the meagre resources these countries had at their disposal. In a short span of 10 or 15 years of post independence, these countries had to not only combat with the serial drought, wars, famines but also with the large educational structural reforms to achieve these targets by 2010.

It means they must have to turn out large numbers of teachers in a shortest time to meet the challenge of transforming the nation's education sector into a production-oriented economy. How to do such wonders is the moot question. It is here the past experiences of many Third World countries act as torchbearers to other newly liberated countries. To be more precise most of the Asian, Latin American and African countries, in order for achieving this goal, have fallen back on the Media—either Radio or Television. They have no option but to use the radio and television to educate and train the teachers as also turn out millions of students, who in turn strive hard to bring generation after generation into the nation's main stream. By launching distance education programmes, in addition to several other educational programmes, Third World countries across the world are grappling hard.

The scope of this chapter thus centers round the experiences of some of the countries, Asian, Latin American and African, in relation to their planning and organizing media education for the manpower training and to quickly catch up with the pace with which the reforms in education have to be carried further. If the media were to do the manpower training, then it would be certainly the shortest one and cost effective one than any other programme. But there are different ways and means that media could help execute this. It had already been discussed in the chapter two along with some examples of how

Table–18

Some Out of School Enrollment Data in Some Third World Countries

Institution	*Year of most recent data*	*Enrollment (000s)*	*National secondary enrollment 1995 (000s)*
Mexico: Telesecundaria	1998	575	7589
Malawi: Study centres	1994	57	142
Zambia: Study centres	1990	11	290[a]
Zimbabwe: Study centres	1992	23	661
India: National Open School	1998	130	66634
Indonesia: National Open School	1996	172	12224[a]

Source: For Mexico: International Bureau of Education, *World Data on Education,* Geneva, 1998: Malawi: Basic Education Statistics 1995; Zambia: Siaciwena 1994; Zimbabwe: *Secretary for Education and Culture Annual Report 1992; India: National Open School Profile 1999; Indonesia: Sadiman and Rahardjo 1997.* [a]1994.

Courtesy: World Education Forum: Thematic Studies.

certain nations implemented them effectively. Thus, in the present chapter, it would be the main aim to focus on the planning and organizing of various courses through the Media rather than dealing with the different ways and means.

Planning and Organizing Through Media: Distance Education Mode

In the context of Planning and Organizing the Media Education, the target groups would be either the teachers or the students and the mode is primarily distance education, though it too involves contact programmes between those who offer the course and the learners. As any State has to gear-up its teaching community first to see the results of their enrichment would pass on to its student community, there are various ways the teaching community could be equipped with necessary educational credentials. For instance, there could be Certificate Programmes, Diploma Programmes, Degree Programmes and Postgraduate Diploma Programmes. Further, they could be for Formal and Non-formal sectors. They could be extended to Vocational sector to strengthen the efforts of the much burdened Technical Schools. A certificate, diploma or Degree or a PG Diploma in Computer skills and applications—Software and hardware, bioinformatics etc., would go a long way in raising the self-employment potential of a nation's youth.

Therefore, for a country in the making, the requirement of teaching community from the grassroots level to the highest level becomes an indispensable urgency. Particularly the teachers who are supposed to sow the seeds of qualitative education at the lower rung of education such as Kindergarten need to be well-informed of the fundamentals of Child Psychology, Educational Psychology, Basics of Pedagogy (Teaching Methodology) and Philosophical Foundations of Education.

Formal Education Sector: Distance Education

Kindergarten Education

As for the training of the Kindergarten teachers, there are two established models of education. One is Froebel's method established by Froebel Friedrich Wilhelm August (1782-1852) and another is Montessori's method founded by Maria Montessori (1870-1952). Many schools across the world follow more Montessori method than Froebel's method. But of late many International schools, modelling themselves on the lines of Froebel's method, are preferring to offer education to tiny tots by Play-way method. Many a time, a mixture of both the schools is followed in many countries without being aware of the ill effects and pains such an exercise would cause to the children.

In fact, the Montessori's method would look more like a conventional education though it deals with all physical and mental developments of the child without inflicting tiresomeness or annoyance on the child. It depends on a set of didactic materials that arouse interests in the child spontaneously. But, for many thinkers and supporters of progressive education, this is burdening the child with a number of curricular subjects of topics which in fact in the age of commercialization turned out carrying a heavy load of books on the back at such a small age.

As a reaction to this, many schools all over the world began implementing the Froebel's method, which is more child-centered and progressive than the Montessori's method. It is modelled on the lines of a Play-way education, with the basic premise, learning while playing.

As for Eritrea, it is not clear which model does the Ministry of Education prefer with reference to the above two, in its National Policy of Education or in Rapid Transformation of Eritrean Education System. Hence it is a matter which would be decided in the due course. However, the Ministry is keen to train a thousands of teachers, as did Tanzania, Niger, Nigeria, Kenya, Uganda, Zambia (African), Nepal, India, China, Papua New Guinea (Asian), Brazil, Gautemala and Mexico (in Latin American) in the next couple of years to meet the teaching requirements at this level in view of the expansion plan it is pursuing.

The various courses that the Radio or Television could offer the Teachers are mentioned below:

1. *Certificate Courses for Pre-primary Teachers or Kindergarten Teachers in Either Montessori Method or in Froebel Method:* They can be one-year courses as they are offered on the Media either by Radio or by Television. If the need to recruit more teachers in a short time is felt, then the length of the course

could be reduced to a minimum of 6 months. In any case there should be provision for practical or apprentice training on stipend if the candidates admitted are fresh and without any previous background of experience. If the course is offered to the existing teachers to enrich their skills, then the practical training and observation could be relegated to their school Director and on the successful completion of both the course and practical training, the candidates, both the in-service as also freshers could be awarded the certificates.

As for the course curriculum, depending on the choice—the State makes between the above mentioned two methods, curriculum could be designed. But the importance of subjects like Child Psychology, Educational Psychology, Foundations of Educational Philosophy and the salient aspects of Child Pedagogy etc., should be kept in mind while preparing the curriculum, be it any method.

Salient Features of the Certificate Programme—Through Media Radio or Television

Objectives of the Programme

To train Kindergarten Teachers to meet the tiny-tots educational and psychological needs.

Description of the Teacher Educators' Target Group

Children of 3-5 years age group. Very tender age with or without Nursery School Background.

Intended Behavioural Goals or Learning Outcomes (For Teacher Educators)

(i) The teachers must tend to give the motherly care and as such they must develop the desired aptitudes and attitudes by the conclusion of the programmes. *(ii)* They must be in a position to identify the students with physical or mental deficiencies not noticed by the parents or friends. *(iii)* They must have the knowledge to distinguish the case studies who require special attention due to the problems at home such as lack of parental or elderly care, wrecked home or fighting parents etc. *(iv)* They should have the knowledge to identify the brilliant child from the Gifted Child and slow learner. *(v)* Develop friendly disposition with the children, must be playful, paying adequate attention to their psychological and physical needs in the school.

Specific Objectives to be Achieved (for Teacher Educators)

Behavioural

Ability to impart basic skills of conversation and living, to inculcate friendly attitudes and aptitude for mutual adjustment and compromise, tolerance and empathy among/with other children.

Academic

To offer the children knowledge of written and spoken skills along with songs and dance, besides games.

Cultural

To seek the all round development of the child by offering expertise in mechanical and psychomotor domains through toy making by papers, clay toys making, drawing, painting and by word games etc.

Sports and Games

Helping children play various games and watch animation or cartoon films to increase the width and depth of their imagination besides cognition.

Curriculum of Instruction

The teachers of Kindergarten must have the basics of the following in order for achieving the above General and Specific Objectives:

1. Basics of Child Psychology.
2. Basics of Educational Psychology.
3. Basics of Philosophical Foundations.
4. Basics of Pedagogy or Methodology of Instruction in subjects: *(i)* English, *(ii)* Local Mother Tongue, *(iii)* Mathematics, *(iv)* Sciences–General, and *(v)* Social studies.

Duration of the Course

Six months for in-service teachers or nine months for freshers.

Mode of Education

Distance Mode through Radio or Television. Correspondence and contact method.

Table-19
Some Distance-Education and Technology Projects in African and Latin American Nations

Country and institution	*Date established*	*Basic education functions*
AFRICA		
Botswana: Department of Non-formal Education	1973	Adult basic and non-formal education
Core d'ivoire (and 9 other countries): INADES-formal	1962	Basic education in farming and rural development
Kenya: University of Nairobi Department of Education and Extension Studies		
– Ministry of Education/Voice Kenya	1980	Interactive radio project for English teaching
– Ministry of Community Development	1978	Distance-teaching training of literacy workers
– Aga Khan Foundation	1983	Experimental computer education project
Lesotho Distance Teaching Centre	1974	Basic education for herdboys
		Support for national programmes of teacher education
– Ministry of Education/School radio		Interactive radio project for English teaching
Malawi: College of Distance Education	1965	Primary and junior secondary programmes Teacher training
Mali: Institute Pedagogique National	1962	In-service education of teachers
Nigeria: National Teachers' Institute	1976	Large-scale in-service education of teachers to upgrade whole-national teaching force
SOMALIA	1993	Teacher training for teachers in nomadic communities
Sudan: Open Learning Unit	1984	Basic education principally for refugees
United Republic of Tanzania: Co-operative Education Centre	1964	Basic education for co-operative movement
– Teacher education project	1978	Training of primary school teachers

(Contd.)

Country and institution	*Date established*	*Basic education functions*
Zambia: Co-operative College	1980	Basic education for co-operative movement through radio campaigns
– National Correspondence Institute	1964	Out-of-school junior secondary education
Zimbabwe: ZINTEC	1981	Distance-education programme for primary school teachers
LATIN AMERICA		
Bolivia	1986	Interactive Radio Instruction project in maths, health, child development
Brazil: Minerva Project	1973	Radio-based secondary equivalence courses for adults
Colombia: Accion Cultural Popular	1947	Basic education for rural adults and children
Costa Rica, Dominican Republic, Ecuador, El Salvador, Guatemala	1988	Interactive Radio instruction in Maths and Spanish
Dominican Republic Santa Maria	1972	Out-of-school basic education for young people
– RADECO	1981	Non-formal programme using Interactive Radio methods
Honduras: Accion Cultural	1974	Radio school programmes for rural families
– Popular Hondurena – Radio Learning Project	1987	Interactive Radio Instruction in Maths, Spanish, English
Mexico: Radioprimaria	1970	Rural basic education by radio
– Telesecundaria	1965	Television-based rural education at junior secondary level
Venezuela: Instituto Radiofonico Fey Alegria	1976	Primary and secondary equivalence courses for adults, using radio and print

Courtesy: World Education Forum: Thematic Studies.

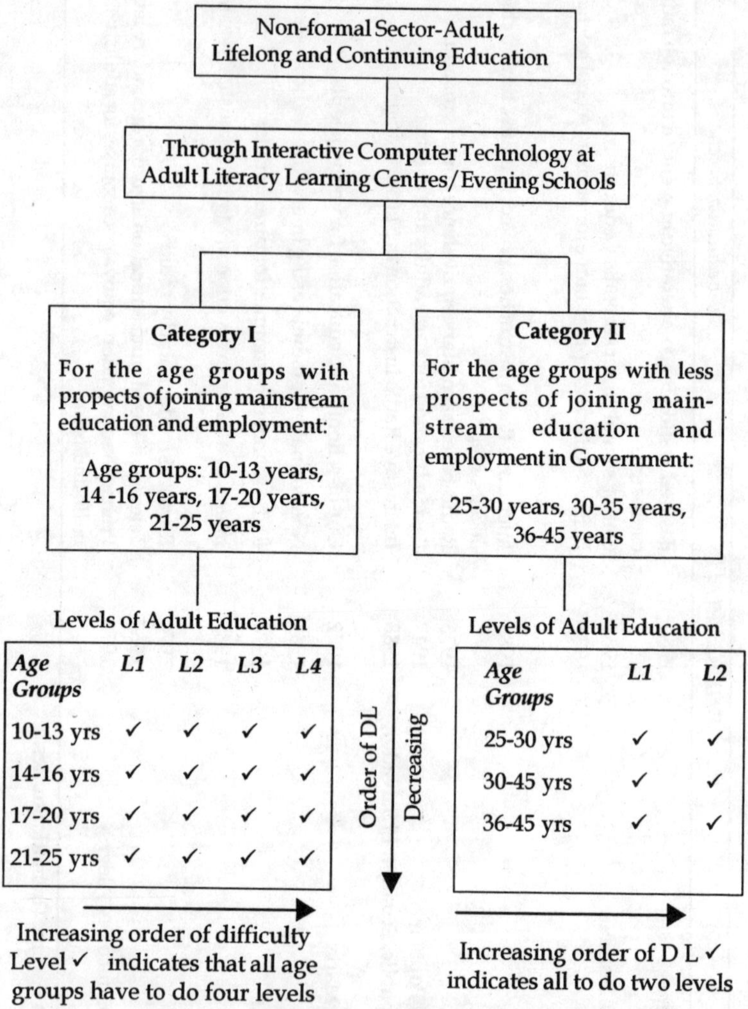

Figure 3: Flow Chart of Implementation of Non-Formal Education (Proposed by C.S.H.N. Murthy, 2004)

Practical Evaluation and Supervision

The Director of the School and the local parents committee.

Theoretical Evaluation

By evaluation of self-study materials and by holding Annual Written Examinations.

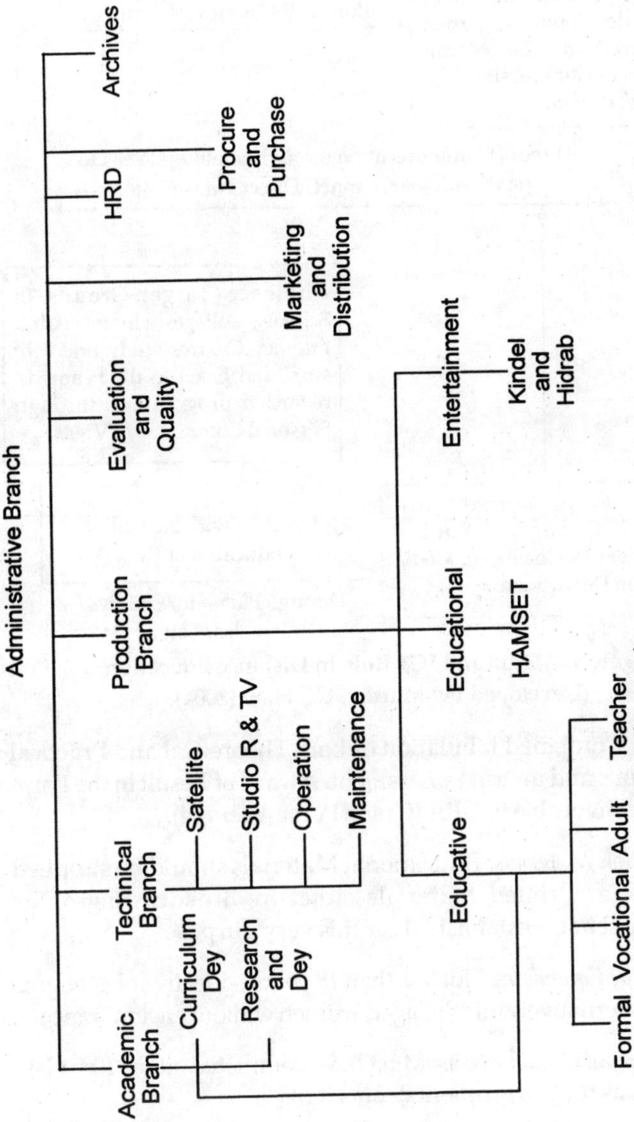

Figure 4: Media Organisation—Structure and Tasks
(as proposed by C.S.H.N. Murthy)

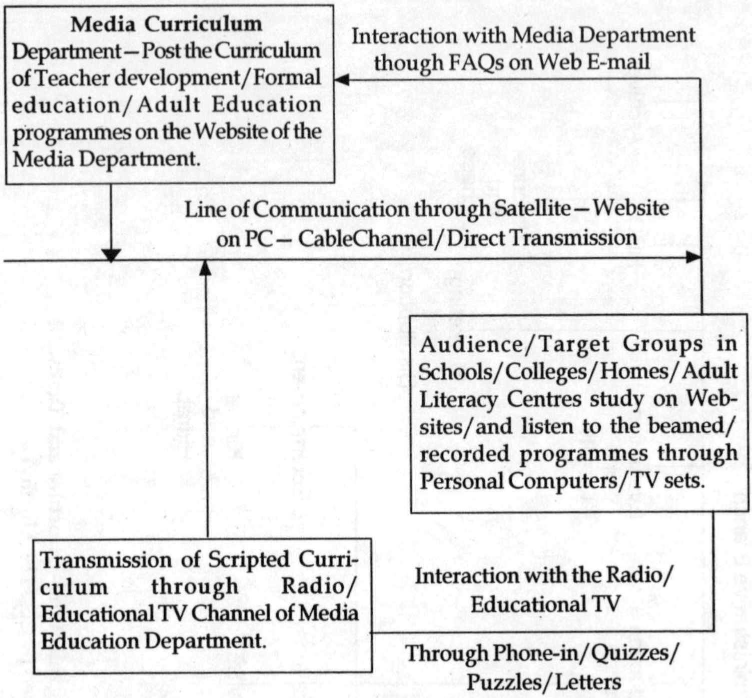

Figure 5: Media and ICT Role in Distance Education
(Developed by: Murthy, C.S.H.N. (2004).

Result: Combined tabulation of both Theoretical and Practical Examinations and internal assessment. Award of Result in the Form of Grades convertible to GPA (Grade Point Average).

Education Materials: Educational Materials should be supplied in advance as Printed Materials either by Broadcasting or by Telecasting schools established for this very purpose.

Age of the Candidates: Not less than 18 years—ideally spinster girls or boys or alternatively middle-aged women without encumbrances.

Educational Qualifications: Must have completed either 10th class or 7th class as the government deems it fit.

Diploma Courses in Teacher Training Education—D.Ed.

The need to train the Primary Teachers or Middle School teachers in large numbers to meet the increasing Gross Enrollment Rate cannot be overemphasized. There are important reasons for this. One is to help curtail the number of illiterates who are otherwise to be admitted to Adult Education or Non-formal education. Secondly to bring down the rate of dropouts. If teachers in the local area are trained, they would help motivate the children around and would be in a position to maintain individual attention which dropouts need more. Further, they would be able to offer home tuitions, remedial classes for the dullards or slow learners and participate as Adult Educators in the schemes being implemented by the Government. As such the presence of a trained teacher makes a lot of difference to a rural setting. The Diploma in Education is thus quite handy and has thus many advantages.

The Salient Features of the Diploma in Education

Objectives of the Programme

The programme is meant to train the Teachers for the Primary and Middle Schools (Junior Schools) or for Basic Schools.

Description of the Teacher Educators' Target Group

Children in the age group of 5+ to 12+ years. Not having crossed the age of adolescence. Prone to heavy ego disturbances between the age group of 10 to 12 especially due to development of secondary sexual characters.

Intended Behavioural Goals or Learning Outcomes (For Teacher Educators)

(i) The teachers must tend to give the motherly care and as such they must develop the desired aptitudes and attitudes by the conclusion of the programmes. *(ii)* They must be in a position to identify the students with physical or mental deficiencies not noticed by the parents or friends. *(iii)* They must have the knowledge to distinguish the case studies who require special attention due to the problems at home such as lack of parental or elderly care, wrecked home or fighting parents etc. *(iv)* They should have the knowledge to identify the brilliant child from the Gifted Child and a slow learner. *(v)* Develop friendly disposition with the children, must be playful, paying adequate attention to their psychological and physical needs in the school. *(vi)* Develop interactive communication skills and be able to offer a variety of cultural and social themes for active communication process between and among them. *(vii)* Must be

possessing expertise to conduct quiz, puzzles, experiments and making models etc for offering different learning experiences to the children. *(viii)* Must develop an elderly and dignified personality to inculcate values of life and education without which the learning experience would prove a meaningless burden of mind.

Specific Objectives to be Achieved (for Teacher Educators)

Behavioural

The teachers must achieve the level of competency, desired traits as professionals and develop appropriate attitudes and aptitude for the profession as a matter of commitment and policy. They should develop the skills to inculcate among children a sense of brotherhood and sisterhood, social adjustability, mutual tolerance and appreciation and allegiance to the country's integrity and constitution. They must be in a position to teach children the ways and means of developing self-confidence and self-actualization, besides self-respect not by percept but by practice. They must have a rational approach to life and by demonstrating the logical reasoning in every act of their day-to-day behaviour, they not only act as role models for the students to emulate but also give a scientific orientation to the wouldbe citizens of future. They must be in a position to exploit the imitation skills of the students for the wider academic and intellectual experience and growth. The target groups of children, whom these teachers handle are of impressionable age, and as such every care must be taken by the teacher on his or her part of behaviour as to the habits, language in conversations and attitude towards his or her colleagues including the elders and head of the institution.

Academic

The teachers must be in a position to perform a reasonable level of communication with the students both in the mother tongue and English and inculcate in them the desire to learn a reasonable level of standard of language, both written and spoken form, with special reference to accent, pronunciation spelling and syntax. This is very important objective that every teacher must achieve in view of the greater role he or she plays in shaping the future careers of their students, who more or less are going to end up in professional line in view of the fast changing global scenario. The teachers must develop special taste for histrionics and theatre arts as these forms are still having their lasting impact on the impressionable minds of these age group children. Skills necessary to enact a play of the lesson, a poem of an author, a ballad of a writer—must be on the fingertips of the teacher. Similarly the skills and abilities to relate the social and science subjects with a practical and scientific bent of mind are to be achieved or developed at the end of the course. Skills to integrate the media and contemporary developments with the classroom curriculum are to be acquired by the end of the conclusion of the programme.

Cultural

The teachers must have expertise in offering the all round development to their children in various aspects of the State or Regional Culture. The abilities of the teachers in co-curricular activities such as essay writing, debates, discussion, elocution, story writing, poetry writing, dance, drama and skits would go a long way in preparing the children for the annual and occasional cultural programmes. This apart the teachers must be in a position to take the students on cultural tours to various places within the province and outside the province for real life experiences, which are called extracurricular activities. Organizing science exhibitions with social relevance would give an added advantage to enhance the cultural values of life.

Games

Teachers must be in a position to participate in the sports and game, in door and outdoors and must encourage all, including the handicapped and crippled, physically weak. They must possess the knowledge of the science of sports, as today sports are no more mere games of some entertainment. Today sports are viewed as body and memory building scientific exercises, with specific objectives and outcomes. Hence, all teachers must possess some knowledge and skill related to indoor or outdoor sports. There are many indoor sports, which enhance the memory power of the children without being aware of it. This is especially very much important in view of the fact that there are many schools, which are run without physical education teachers.

Curriculum of Instruction

The Primary Teachers or Middle School Teachers must have the basics of the following in order for achieving the above General and Specific Objectives:

1. Basics of Child Psychology.
2. Basics of Educational Psychology.
3. Basics of Philosophical Foundations.
4. Basics of Pedagogy or Methodology of instruction in optional Subjects: *(i)* English, *(ii)* Local Language, *(iii)* Mathematics, *(iv)* Sciences–General, *(v)* Social Studies.
5. Curriculum Development and Planning for Elementary Level—including Blooms Taxonomy of objectives with special reference to appreciation of values of the content.
6. Basics of Educational Administration and Planning (Maintenance of Attendance Registers, evaluation of examination sheets and principles of valuation, preparation of scholastic data, lesson plan and annual plan writing, time table planning—individual and for entire faculty—organizing the academic calendar—integrating media schedules etc).

Duration of the Course

Six months for in-service teachers and nine months for the freshers.

Mode of Education

Distance Mode through Radio or Television. Correspondence and contact method.

Practical Evaluation and Supervision

The Director of the School and the local parents committee.

Theoretical Evaluation

By evaluation of self-study materials and by holding Annual Written Examinations.

Result: Combined tabulation of both Theoretical and Practical Examinations and internal assessment. Award of Result in the Form of Grades convertible to GPA (Grade Point Average).

Educational Materials: Educational Materials should be supplied in advance as Printed Materials either by Broadcasting or by Telecasting schools established for this very purpose.

Age of the Candidates : Not less than 18 years – ideally spinster girls or boys or alternatively middle-aged women without encumbrances.

Educational Qualifications: Must have completed 12th class or those who completed the Graduation or discontinued the Graduation due to different reasons or as the Government deems fit.

The Degree in Education – B.Ed. (with Specialization in various optionals – Languages, General Sciences – Natural Sciences or Physical Sciences as Specialization or Social Sciences or Mathematics).

The teachers of the High School dealing with classes higher than 7th are expected generally to be very proficient and authoritative in view of the increasing standards curricular subjects. Firstly, there is an upward revision of the curriculum in all subjects including Languages world over – both in terms of the content and teaching methods. For instance the Physics of 1970s and 1980s vary with the Physics of 2000s both in the concepts as well as in the presentation and interpretation. So is the case with the Biochemistry and Natural Sciences. Many new concepts like Biotechnology, and Bioengineering have been added to the textbooks of biology. Even the approach of subjects has undergone a thorough change. For instance at one time subjects like Botany and Zoology are studied systematically in the order of their classifications. But the present approach or trend is to study the same in an interdisciplinary manner. It means under the heading of nutrition, today the students would learn the different nutritional systems of both the plants and animals at a time. Similarly under the heading or respiration or reproduction, all the different systems among plants and animals would be learnt together. Thus a biology teacher today needs a very comprehensive and latest knowledge of the plant and animals sciences to meet the challenges posed by the textbooks. Most of the latest researches in Physics, Chemistry and Mathematics have become soon textbook facts. The explosion of knowledge in almost all branches including Economics and the changing geographical boundaries of many countries have quickly been added to the curriculum.

For instance prior to 1991, the USSR was a geographical reality. But, after 1991, the USSR began disintegrating. Today some of the former States of the former USSR became new members of European

Table–20

Costs and Effects of Some Teacher Education Projects (Currency: Constant 1998 US$)

Country project date[a]	*GNP per capita at time of study*		*Student numbers*	*Average cost*	*Educational and cost impact*
	Date current US$	1998 US$			
United Republic of Tanzania, TTD, 1979-84	1982 310	524	15,000 p.a. 45,000 total	1,863 per student p.a. 7,316 per graduate	Effects comparable to conventional education; cost about half conventional education
Brazil, Logos ll, 1976-81	1978 1,650	4,125	24,400	211 per student p.a. 741 per graduate	80% pass rate; costs lower than alternative
Sri Lanka, 1984-88	1986 410	610	c5,000	116 per student p.a.	Cost 1/6-1/3 of alternative; more effective than alternative for some subjects but less effective for others
Indonesia, 1985-88	1986 530	788	c5,000	805 per student p.a.	Cost about 60% of equivalent; more effective than alternative in languages but less so in mathematics
Nepal, RETT Basic teacher training course, 1978-80	1979 130	292	3,000	196 per student p.a.	Cost slightly lower than alternative; completion rate 83%, pass rate 57%; no evidence than less effective than alternative
Nigeria, National Teachers	1984		20,327	79 per student p.a.	Cost probably lower than regular colleges;

(Contd.)

Country project date[a]	*GNP per capita at time of study*		*Student numbers*	*Average cost*	*Educational and cost impact*
	Date current US$	1998 US$			
Institute, 1978-89	730	1,145			completion rate estimated 42% pass rate estimated 27%, both rates higher than those of regular colleges
Pakistan, Primary Teacher Orientation Course, 1976-86	1981 330	592	83,658 total enrolment 31,674 completed	107-149 per successful completer	Cost per AIOU graduate 45-70% of conventional university
Kenya, in-service teacher training, 1968-77	1972 180	661	790	806 per subject equivalent p.a.	Cost relatively high, favourable effect on access
Kenya, University of Nairobi B.Ed., 1986-90	1988 370	510	515	1,096 per student p.a.	Cost thought to be lower than cost of residential equivalent
Nigeria, COSIT University of Lagos 1980-88	1984 730	1,145	2,000	345 per full-time student equivalent 1304 per graduate	If opportunity costs are omitted then cost per graduate slightly lower than residential campus cost
Uganda, NITEP project, 1993-97[b]	1995 240	257	2,750	2,000 per successful student	Lower cost than equivalent

Source: Perraton, 1993, pp. 386-87 except where shown, with costs converted to 1998 US$.
[a] The end date in column one refers to the period reported, not necessarily the end date of the project or programme.
[b] Wrighrson, 1997, p. 5.

Courtesy: *World Education Forum:* Thematic Studies.

Union. Similarly former Czech Republic and Yugoslavia in the Europe got disintegrated into smaller nations like Bosnia, Serbia, Croatia, Slovakia etc. Similarly prior to 1991 Eritrea was the State Federated with Ethiopia. But due to prolonged independent struggle, Eritrea was liberated in 1993 and became a Sovereign nation. These changes would also result in the concomitant changes in the Economy and Geography, which deal with the availability of natural resources. For instance Ethiopia has no more access to Mossawa or Asab seaports now. As such the entire income accruing out of the Fishing and Shipping industry now goes to Eritrea. All these changes call for greater capabilities of interpretation on the part of the Social Sciences teachers. Particularly the changed role of UN in the unipolar world would need to be highlighted for the better understanding of the global equations by the students.

The above background only gives how important the role of a Secondary School Teacher, in the context of fast changing order of events on every front. Thus the importance of equipping these teachers with all the modern content and techniques of each subject cannot be easily ignored. Further, the importance of curricular reforms along the sidelines of upgrading the qualifications of the teachers is always to be underscored. At the same time for a developing country to achieve this in a short time, it is possible only through Media education.

The Salient Features of the Bachelor Degree in Education

Objectives of the Programme

The programme is intended to train the teachers with desired skills to handle the students of higher classes from above 8th class to 12th class. It is also meant to upgrade the teachers with Certificate or Diploma in Education. It is further intended to train the teachers who are working without suitable qualifications.

Description of the Teacher Educators' Target Group

The students are of the age group of 12-15 years passing through the phase of puberty or adolescence and are prone to have ego and hormonal instability. This is the phase of confusion due to the conflict between several ideas and ideologies. The effect of the peer group would be more than the elderly guidance and learning by experience is more accepted than by the doctrine.

Intended Behavioural Goals or Learning Outcomes (For Teacher Educators)

The teachers are expected to develop a genial disposition towards the students as the target group is in the age of making quick judgements, moral as well as academic, about their teachers. They must be developing the competency to offer different learning strategies to the students of different IQ levels. They must be able to discern the physical and mental shortcomings of their target group and selectively offer them the suitable alternatives to overcome their setbacks some of which are permanent and some of which are developed due to wrong pursuit of thought and direction of the mind. They must have a clear depth of the student psychology, personality problems and disorders and help them cure on time before they become fixtures in their life through appropriate counselling (for instance addiction to smoking and drinking, narcotics, lose moral values, succumbing to the biological temptations and indulging in lewd and immoral talk and acts etc.).

Develop interactive communication skills both in the Mother Tongue and English especially as the latter begins from the middle school and children need a lot of support in promoting their knowledge in a foreign language. Develop an elderly attitude and act as philosopher and guide to the students. Urge to combine latest developments of the world, with the curricular topics and to focus rational outlook in the analysis of day-to-day teaching and learning activities. Especially the teachers must develop a scientific approach to distinguish between the faith, superstition, sentiment and scientific reality as the survival of civilized society mainly depends on this discriminatory power.

Specific Objectives to be Achieved (for Teacher Educators)

Behavioural

Commitment and love for profession is the most important attitude that is expected to develop in the conscience of the teacher. Especially for a developing nation, it is impossible to achieve the intended targets without having this spirit at the substratum of the mind. Teachers themselves must act as role models to students in achieving the social adjustments that ease any possible tensions in the society. In a secular State education must go with the imparting of training to the children how to adjust, compromise and make a peaceful living. Without this kind of constructive principle, the whole education turns out to be a destructive force when social disturbances erupt and tensions mount as a result. They must be able to give guidance to the students to develop self-confidence and self-actualization, both of which are the permanent assets that go a long way with the students. They must develop the skills to exploit the imitation habits in the children to inspire them in the academic direction such as expression, body language, poise and persuasiveness.

Academic

Teachers must possess an all-roundness in their profession to the extent it is required. They must have the potential to conduct quiz competitions, debates, discussions and elocutions to keep the spark of academic interests live always. They must be good at conducting practicals, organizing science, social and mathematics clubs and exhibitions. They should be in a position to prepare models working and non-working, besides being sagacious enough to use audio-visuals for the enhancement and betterment of understanding among children. The use of Over Head Project is of extreme importance for the quick explanation and quick revision of the entire subject. They must have the knowledge to integrate the media education with the formal and conventional education. They must develop the taste for histrionics and relate it to the classroom teaching to enhance the level of teaching in subjects like languages and history or science.

Cultural

The teachers must possess the cultural base of the country and the region, which they should utilize for the promotion of fine arts among the children. Folk songs, folk dances, ballads, songs – classical and modern from the film world, are to be known to the teachers at least in their elementary form, if not deeply as to encourage students in these forms of tradition. They must be in a position to conduct cultural competitions in these forms of arts among the students and judge them for the best first and best second awards. They must also lead their students teams for botanical and science tours to give the students of a first hand account of experience – what they mean to the nation.

Games

Teachers must be themselves good in various sports – indoor and outdoor. They must help students understand the importance of sports and physical education. They must help the physically disabled and crippled also to participate in the games depending on their aptitude and attitude.

Curriculum of Instruction

The Secondary School Teachers must have the basics of the following in order for achieving the above General and Specific Objectives:

1. Educational Psychology.
2. Curriculum Development including Blooms Taxonomy of objectives.
3. Philosophical foundations.
4. Educational Administration.
5. Pedagogy: *(i)* English, *(ii)* Local Language, *(iii)* Mathematics, *(iv)* General Sciences – Natural Sciences or Physical Sciences, *(v)* Social Studies.
6. Practicals. *(i)* Preparation of Models – Art on cardboards, charts, sheets, clay or paraffin, working models – with paper or alternative materials, thermocoal, pith etc., *(ii)* Preparation of lesson plans and annual plans, *(iii)* Preparation of Time Tables etc., *(iv)* Case Study and *(v)* Action Research.
7. Research, Innovations, Statistics and Interpretation. (Research includes Action Research and Case Studies etc.)

Duration of the Course

10 months for the in-service teachers and 16 months for the freshers.

Mode of Education

Distance Mode through Radio or Television. Correspondence and Contact Method.

Practical Evaluation and Supervision

The Director of the School and the local parents committee.

Theoretical Evaluation

By evaluation of self-study materials and by holding Annual Written Examinations.

Result: Combined Tabulation of both Theoretical and Practical examinations and internal assessment. Award of Result in the form of Grades convertible to GPA (Grade Point Average).

Educational Materials: Educational Materials should be supplied in advance as Printed Materials either by Broadcasting or by Telecasting schools established for this very purpose.

Age of the Candidates: Not less than 22 years.

Educational Qualifications: Must have completed a Bachelor's Degree within any of the optional subjects—English, Mother Tongue, Sciences—Natural or Physical—Social Studies or Mathematics. Must have secured not less than 45 per cent in the case of English or Mother Tongue Subjects and 50 per cent in the case of optionals or as the Government deems fit.

So far the courses described in the foregoing are meant to train the teachers through Media, through Distance education mode (C.S.H.N. Murthy, 2006). These are conceived as part of overall efforts to rapidly change the man power situation on the teaching front. By following the above courses, the Ministry of Education can turn over thousands of teachers without compromising the quality of Education. If need be there can be refresher programmes and faculty improvement programmes as a follow-up to these to make the teachers' education viable and sustainable for longer terms. Usha and Sanjaya Mishra developed a handbook for Teacher Developers as to how to teach the students Multi-media. This is an important step towards enabling the student teachers to perform creatively at the classroom level. Som Naidu (2006) also produced a learning module on E-learning programmes as to make the teacher learners more effective while handling course modules of interactive learning of various subjects using computers in the classroom. (Usha Vyasulu, R. and Sanjaya Mishra 2003. Usha Vyasulu, R., pp. 1-25, *CEMCA*, 2003).

Correspondence-cum-Contact Programmes for Vocational Education (For Students Only)

Now the courses, which are going to be dealt with, here are meant for the students only and not for the teachers. It does not mean that is no way of improving the teachers' competencies and skills through the Media Education. Once the Government of Eritrea arrives at a definite idea as to what qualifications are required for the teachers working in vocational schools and how many they need in terms of man power and the time span within which they are required, accordingly the Correspondence and Contact programme for the TVETs could also be launched with General and Specific objectives, besides course curriculum, duration of the course and evaluation system.

The importance of this programme stems from the fact that there is a high percentage of dropouts, at various levels of the educational ladder in Eritrea, who need to be brought back to the productive line of national economy. There is also reason to believe that the compelling conditions, which led them astray, have not vanished even now. There may be many problems, like poor family income, need to go for menial jobs to meet two square meals of the day or to go for pastoral work and agricultural field work, which would not allow them to a regular formal education even in the TVETs (Technical and Vocational Educational Training Centres, working under Ministry of Education) established by the Government.

The TVETs are presently offering a variety of courses at various levels. Apart from TVETs there are SDCs (skill development centres) also. But all of them together could not meet even one hundredth of the requirement to achieve the targets of Rapid Transformation of Eritrean Education. To offset this widening gap, it is proposed to offer Vocational Education through Correspondence Courses, which would enable these poor youth of the country to look after their family economic needs and attend these programmes during their spare time at home itself as these are offered through Radio or Television and no regular attendance is required.

Though there is no mention of the Government's intention to use Media Education for the promotion of Vocational Education for Rapid Transformation of Eritrean Education in any of policy documents including the World Bank Report, many Third World countries, where the native skills are felt extremely important for the revival of nation's economy, have used Media Education as a means of quickly putting back the rural youth on the task of national reconstruction through the promotion of the rural native skills. The programmes thus offered often combined the economic interests that accrue out of pursuing such native skills in the context of global economy. Enough of this has been discussed earlier itself to show how education linked to one's economic growth curries favour than the education which remains much as a mere tinsel or ornament of decoration. Examples of Russia and China point to this kind of education. Even the Indian experience has been successful against this backdrop.

However, there is a lot of concern, expressed by the Ministry of Education in all its reports, with regard to achieving equitable access to TVETs at all levels above the gender stereotyping and gender disparity. Similarly one can discern a great concern clearly in all its reports as to the certification measures and standards of the Technical Education offered and making it more market oriented. Establishment of more TVET schools at all levels, primary, middle and secondary, may also prove very costly for the Government as the maximum percentage of the aid received towards TVET sector would go for the investment (capital and capacity building) itself. Further, there a number of native skills, which are very exclusive and unique of the superb workmanship of the Eritrean rural men and women. Any neglect of these would equally prove hazardous to the nation's economy and would help only these great handicrafts soon vanish from its soil. So, the exclusive concentration of the nation's youth in certain select areas may not prove to be a fertile programme viewed from this angle.

A glance at the courses presently offered through TVETs and SDCs would suggest that a number of native skills found across Eritrean countryside have not yet got the due attention they deserve. The courses, which are being offered at best, may absorb only a section of the youth who would like to go for a cosmopolitan or industrialized life. But what about the youth who would for various reasons could not move out of their native places and yet would very much like to pursue their traditional forms of profession not only as a means of living but also as a measure of producing them in bulk for sale outside their region or zoba. They may need to employ so many youngsters under them in large-scale handcrafts industry and need to give them the training. Hence it is very important to have a holistic and multi-pronged approach to this very crucial branch of education sector. One formal educational approach may not meet the length and breadth of the whole sector.

At present the Government is offering a few technical courses through its TVETs to those who have completed the 9th grade. Most important among them are: 1. Metal Works. 2. Machine Shop. 3. Wood Works. 4. Automechanic. 5. Electricity. 6. Electronics. 7. Survey. 8. Draughtsman. 9. Construction. 10. Agromechanics. 11. General Mechanics. 12. Horticulture. All these courses are offered on a well–planned pedagogy and most of them have a component of practical experience included in them. They have to work in the industry for a stipulated period before they earned their certificate.

There are also courses offered through SDCs under Adult Education programme. These courses are offered to those without any educational background also and they are not with any defined curriculum and pedagogical instruction. These courses are: 1. Wood Works. 2. Metal Works. 3. Construction. 4. Plumbing. 5. Electricity.

From the above it is very clear that the Government of Eritrea has not yet formulated its comprehensive educational policy to encompass the entire gamut of vocational education. Admittedly it has to look into many gray areas which are yet to be explored to usher in a sweeping coverage of all the facets of it.

Two Categories of Programmes through Media

(i) Single Episode Programs (Based on undefined curriculum) for various skills and handicrafts, and
(ii) Series of Programmes (based on defined curriculum) for the courses offered through TVETs.

Against this backdrop, it is proposed to involve Media Education for the promotion and integration of vocational skills and educational training with the nation's economy. There are for the time being two ways that Media could achieve this:

Single Episode Programmes (Based on Undefined Curriculum) for Various Skills and Handicrafts

These are the programmes, which are complete by themselves in a single episode, either by Radio or by TV, and would cover all those skills and handicrafts that need not have a curriculum and pedagogical instruction. During the contact programmes, the practicals for this category could be done by the target groups there itself. E.g. pottery, carpentry, wooden toys with miniature art, sculpture, drawing and paintings general and Eritrean styles, basket making, pottery making with design and art, embroidery, tailoring etc. At the end of this programme, evaluation would be held for various skills to find out whether any deficiencies still exist after all.

Series of Programmes (Based on Defined Curriculum) for the Courses Offered Through TVETs

These programmes are to be produced for those skills and courses for which a defined curriculum and pedagogical instruction are required. These programmes may have to be produced as a series to cover the entire curriculum and pedagogical instruction. At the end of the programmes, the contact programmes are offered to check any deficiencies that may have crept into the learning of the target groups. This category target group must do the practicals along with the mainstream or formal stream in an industry for the stipulated period before they appear for the examinations to acquire the qualifying certificate. This would automatically ensure the quality of education being offered by the Correspondence and Contact programmes through the Media.

For instance Distance Education programmes through Media in information technology would be of immense help at this stage now. The Government has a long cherished dream to start an ICT training Institute of Eritrea in conjunction with Telecommunications. The plan as such required a lot of funding to the tune of $142 million dollars and a five-phase programme of action is being contemplated. The Government wants to implement this simultaneously. However indications are that it may take some more time to actual take off. But the Media can immediately begin it if the Government finds favour with the proposal. Firstly, certificate courses in Computer Applications could be launched, both in the software and the hardware. Then it could be followed by Diploma in computer applications and postgraduate diploma in computer applications. The students in the remote rural areas also could instantaneously avail the benefits of these programmes offered on Media, either Radio or TV. Similarly Certificate and Diploma Courses in subjects like Horticulture, Metal works, Electronics, Electricity and Survey etc., could also be planned in a short time.

If this approach is in principle accepted by the Ministry of Education and the Government of Eritrea, then the programmes could be developed for each course offered under second category with clearly defined objectives, curriculum, duration of the course and mode of evaluation etc., as was done for the courses with defined pedagogical instruction in the foregoing. For the first category, the programmes could be developed as single episode programmes, though their production could still be based on defined objectives, systematic planning and development, and with defined learning outcomes. The only difference is that they do not have a long strategic curricular planning such as units, sub-units and concomitant development of programmes on the basis of them.

National Open School Education for National Grade Examination and Eritrean Secondary School Certificate Examination

This is one of the greatest alternatives that the modern Third World countries have chosen to use to advance the rapid educational transformation to bring those who have fallen behind in the stream of formal education. It is a boon for the dropouts – boys and girls, who could not prosecute their studies for various reasons. It does not call for any basic fulfillment of education. There are two stages in the National Open School (NOS) which would directly work under an autonomous institution for all administrative and executive functions and is funded by the Ministry of Education: One is to appear for the National Grade Examination equivalent to 8th class. The other is to appear for Eritrean School Secondary Certificate Examination equivalent to 12th class. In Asian countries like India, the National Open School does not impose any restrictions of eligibility criteria on the perspective applicants. In India, there is even 12th grade examination, equivalent to Intermediate offered by the Regional or Provincial Governments. Even age limitation is not prescribed. In the context of Eritrea, it is for the Ministry to take a policy decision in this regard. The Media like Radio and TV in India offered the course programmes based on the prescribed curriculum. They are beamed in the early morning hours both on Radio and Television.

The course outline is very simple and comprises 4 or 5 curricular papers with difficulty level less than 50 per cent. After the successful completion of these courses, they can join the mainstream of education from any level, either National Grade Examination to Formal education or from Secondary School Certificate Examination to University level. Earlier it has been

Table–21
Costs of Some Adult and Basic Education Projects, Currency: Constant 1998 US$

Project	*Scale and duration*	*Cost per learner*	*Cost comparison*
Radio schools in Latin America (e.g. Accion Cultural Popular, Colombia, Radio Santa Maria, Dominican Republic)	ACPO: 190,000 students RSM 20,000 students One-year course offering equivalency to primary education	In range 50-$88 per student per annum	Cost at ACPO less than for primary schools. At RSM comparable with primary, lower evening than classes
Zambia radio education campaign on co-operative movement	4,730 participants Ten weeks of meetings, once weekly	$22 student	Cost per learner lower than cost of training at farmer's centre, higher than primary school costs
Functional Education Project for Rural Areas, Pakistan	1,500 students Eight meetings at weekly intervals	About $46 per student	Cost probably low in comparison with alternatives, high as compared with primary schools
Telesecundaria Mexico	Running for 30 years in 1997-98,817,200 students in 12,054 schools and with 38,698 teachers (16.6% of national secondary enrollment)	In range $441-589 per student[a]	Cost per learner has been relatively stable over a long period. Costs understood to be of similar order of magnitude to costs in conventional schools.
National Open School, India	Year enrolment 130,000 (1998-99) 400,000 in full roll Weekly tutorials, one hour per subject	Cost per learner $10 (1997-98) Cost per graduate $92 (97-98) (graduation rate 43%)	Comparative cost per learner in formal schools is $27

Source: Perraton 2000; Castro *et al*, 1999; Bradley and Yates forthcoming.
[a] Figures from three studies in 1975, 1988, 1997. One further study in 1981 had figured of $927.

Courtesy: *World Education Forum*: Thematic Studies.

discussed how in Indian context the private study or private appearance for any level of examination from classes I to XII has been allowed and how the students are allowed to join the mainstream from any level onwards after qualifying in any of these exams even at the provincial levels or the state levels.

It is therefore pertinent here to know briefly the outline of courses of these programmes in the context of Eritrean Education and certainly these would be immense help to quickly bring back those who got alienated from the mainstream of education. As the courses are offered on Media, they are economic and do not call for any additional infrastructure. With less than 20 per cent of the cost inputs of the conventional or formal educational system, any government can achieve wonderful results. The main cost input would be the print materials cost. It is a quicker and short way to implement the Rapid Educational Transformation.

The National Grade Examination or 8th Class Examination

It is meant to offer shortest means to join the national mainstream of education by directly and privately appearing for the 8th class Examination offered by the National Open School. It does not call for any prior fulfilling qualification. Simple knowledge of literacy, numeracy and awareness of contemporary developments are enough to enable a student or an adult or a drop out to build up confidence to appear for the examination. The syllabus is very general in nature and difficulty level is less than 50 per cent. The treatment of curriculum is on the conventional lines but dealt with in popular terms and popular language minus the difficult side of it.

Salient Features of the National Grade Examination or 8th Class Examination

General Objectives of the Programme

The programme is meant to encourage or bring back the dropout boys and girls into the mainstream from any level of their past education. Dropouts of Primary or Jr. Middle School or the students with simple literacy, numeracy and logical reasoning with social awareness from the Adult Education Centres (AECs) are also allowed to appear for the examination straight.

Specific Objectives of the Programme

1. The target group would acquire the knowledge, understanding and appreciation of subjects like English, Mathematics, General Sciences and Social Sciences. 2. They also develop logical and analytical reasoning skills from the subjects studied in relation to life situations. 3. They also acquire some written and spoken skills 50 per cent above their earlier level. 4. They would be informed the minimum measures of health, hygiene, environment, history, and civics. 5. They would be able to do the self-study and build up desired skills further. 6. They would be in a position to understand the global developments in relation to their life and society. 7. They would be able to rely on themselves in dealing with the governmental and non-governmental agencies.

Description of the Target Group

The target group comprises both the children and adults, as it is not a formal educational programme for a homogenous age group. Secondly, it is highly individualized as the programme is offered as correspondence programme over Radio or TV.

Intended Behavioural Goals or Learning Outcomes

1. At the end of the programme, the students develop a mental poise, body language, communicative and reasoning skills on the basis of what they studied or learnt. 2. Their confidence levels would go up and they become better self-reliant than ever. 3. They would be able to show better appreciation of subjects like health, hygiene, environment, economy, history etc. 4. They would have better spoken and written skills than earlier. 5.They would have broadening of mind and adjustability compared to earlier. 6. They develop a democratic spirit and sense of secular tolerance towards the others and dissent.

Curriculum of Instruction

The following would be the part of the course curriculum:

1. English
2. Mother Tongue
3. General Mathematics
4. General Sciences
5. Social Studies.

Medium of Instruction

English or Mother Tongue as the Government of Eritrea deems it fit.

Mode of Instruction

Distance Mode either by Radio or by TV or by both supported by the Print Materials. Self-study at home by listening to these programmes and recorded cassettes and by taking some home tuitions under the elderly care of some educated persons such as Teachers or Adult Education Supervisors or Organizers.

Duration of the Course

One year.

Method of Evaluation

The evaluation is done on the basis of the performance of the students both in the Self-Testing Material assignments sent home nd on the basis of the performance in the written examination. Generally the pass mark is kept low to encourage more and more to join the course and discourage the dropping out. The pass marks for all subjects on an aggregate should be not less than 30 per cent but if any one gets less than 25 per cent in any one paper also, he is promoted or passed.

Result: 30 per cent aggregate pass. Usual A, B and C grades would be awarded for successful candidates on the basis of their combined performance. D Grade for failure to pass in the examination.

Eritrean Secondary School Certificate Examination

It is an excellent opportunity for all the dropouts and the fresh learners from the Adult Education to join the mainstream of education by appearing through the National Open School Examination. There is no stipulation of any qualification as a minimum eligibility for appearing for this examination. The course materials are offered in the form of printed materials. Both the Radio and the TV would broadcast the curricular programmes. The course materials are of very general nature, simple in language and offer logical insights into the subjects being offered. They are not hard or tough in terms of the content and analysis. However, the treatment of curriculum is on the general lines of the conventional education as to enable them fall in the groove of formal education subsequent to their successful completion of this examination.

Salient Features of the Eritrean Secondary School Certificate Examination

General Objectives of the Programme.

The programme is meant to encourage or bring back the dropouts—boys and girls, into the mainstream of education from any level of their past academic background including educational background from the Adult Education Centers. Simple knowledge of literacy and numeracy, basic analytical and reasoning skills and the ability to interact and communicate are considered basic requirements for a comfortable study throughout the course.

Specific Objectives

1. To ensure the minimum learning levels in all the school subjects. 2. To impart the minimum knowledge, understanding and skills in all the subjects as to enable the learner to specialize later on in further education. 3. To impart minimum vocabulary, terminology and analytical skills to cope with the increasing complexity of day-to-day life. 4. To develop coping skills with the changing trends of the world and tune the individual to adapt to the changing global perceptions. 5. To provide the basic requirements of social life such as to live a life free of social tensions with tolerance and democratic spirit of appreciation of the views of others 6. To develop a scientific spirit as to allow himself and his family and friends—a civilized life with enough caution for health, hygiene and environment. 7. To develop self-confidence and self-actualization 8. To enable one to development mental faculties required for the self-study and lifelong education. 9. To acquire written and spoken skills 50 per cent above their earlier level.

Description of the Target Group

The target group is not a homogenous mixture of the same age group. They are people from various walks of life, engaged in various professions during the daytime including pastoral and agricultural life. Some of them may have a hardened mind and some may still be sensitive to the niceties of education. It is their spare time that is targeted for this education programme offered over Media. It is therefore individualized rather than group study.

Intended Behavioural Goals

1. At the end of the programme, the increase in the general awareness will be manifest in the self-confidence. 2. The coping skills of the individual increase in day-to-day life situations. 3. The ability to interact and communicate would develop better than earlier. 4. The degree of self-reliance increases. 5. The analytical and reasoning skills improve. 6. There would be an orientation to scientific spirit of inquiry. 7. There would be better adjustability and degree of tolerance than earlier.

Curriculum of Instruction

The following would be the part of the course curriculum:

1. General English
2. Mother Tongue
3. General Mathematics
4. General Science
5. Social Studies

Medium of Instruction

English or Mother Tongue as the Government of Eritrea deems fit.

Mode of Instruction

Distance Mode either by Radio or TV or by both supported by the Printed Materials. Self-study at home by listening to these programmes and recorded cassettes, and by taking home tuitions under the elderly care of some educated persons such as Teachers or Adult Education Supervisors or Organizers.

Duration of the Course

One year.

Method of Evaluation

The evaluation is done on the basis of the performance of the students both in the self-testing material assignments sent home and also on the basis of the performance in the written examination. Generally the pass mark is kept low to encourage more and more to join the course.

Result: It is generally in the form of grades: A, B and C for the successful candidates on the basis of their combined performance.

Non-Formal Education—Distance Mode Adult Education Programmes

In a country like Eritrea where the per cent of illiteracy is as high as 70-80 per cent, the need to press into service the Media Education for the promotion of Adult Education programmes can never be over emphasized. It has been a policy of the Government to give thrust to the Adult Education programmes by resorting to various strategies, which included Media education too and underscore its role as one of the efficient means of eradicating illiteracy. The Department of Adult and Media Education has already launched several programmes, the details of which have already been dealt with in the earlier chapter, through its 10kW MW transmitter to enhance the awareness and educational levels of the illiterate masses across the country.

The Government therefore targeted the Adult Education Programmes towards the people, under the age group of 15-45, without or with some education background. As of now, since a decade of independence, there is no specific course work prescribed for this group of learners. There are many problems confronted by the government in targeting this large group, which is a heterogeneous one. The problems become worse confounded when the learners of different age groups come to the same place for their learning. The Primer being followed one is a much old one and it helps to attain only a minimum literacy and numeracy level. As there are learners of many backgrounds, the government has to develop the curriculum for meeting their needs. As such lack of a variety of combinations in the curriculum in a way alienates the learners from the very adult education programme itself and constitutes a major setback. This apart, there is another gray area in the whole of this programme, which centers round the age group of 10-14 years, who do not fall under the definition of either the Adult Education programmes or have scope of admission in formal education according to the latest educational policy.

Table–22

Adult Education Programme—Institutional and Technical Support: Indian Model

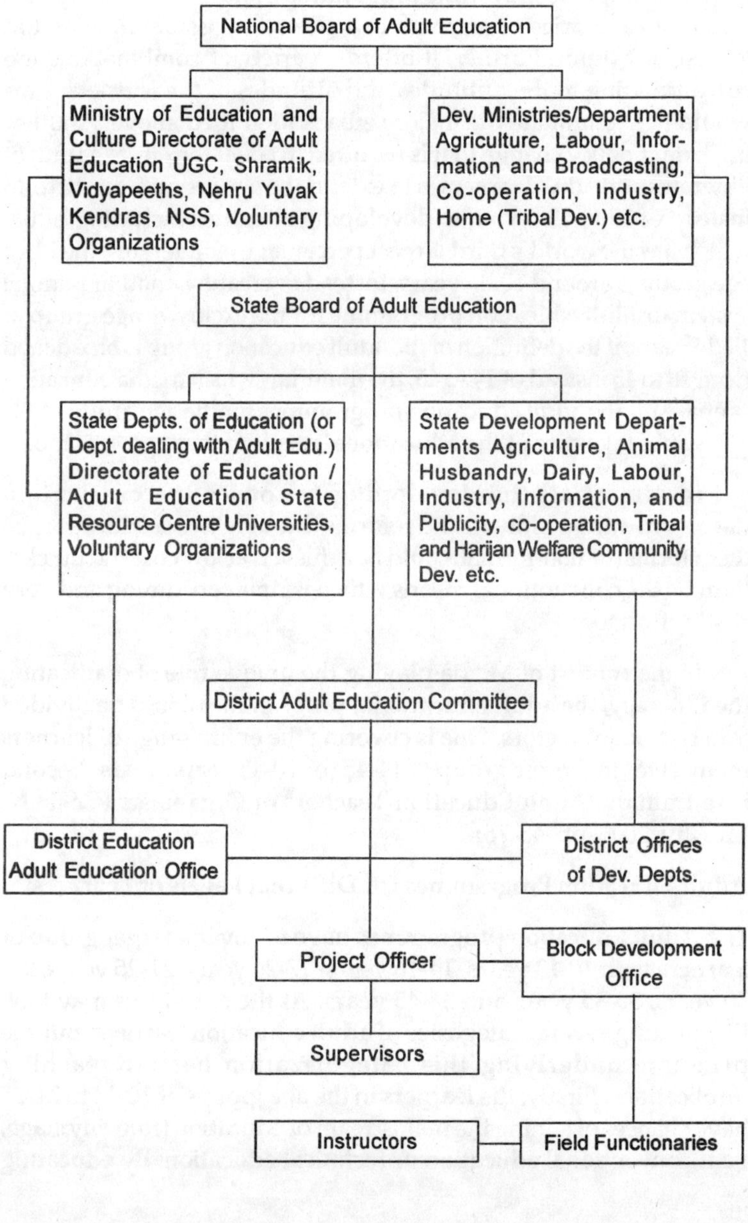

Against the backdrop the Government of Eritrea wanted to utilize the media education in a manner that covers the whole gamut of Adult Education with low cost infrastructure. The Media education provides ample scope for the preparation of the curriculum for the different categories of learners in a shortest possible time and at lowest cost input. Further, it offers a variety of combinations too corresponding to the aptitudes and attitudes of the learners. This would help eliminate the major setback identified above. Another important policy change that is required to cover the entire gamut of illiterates and adult learners is to extend the age group from 10 to 45 instead of 15 to 45. In many developing countries including India, which has the world's third largest percentage of illiterates, the ideal age group is around 10-45 years. Instead of creating another parallel system to adult education programme for the exclusive age group of 10-14 years, if the definition of the adult education group is broadened from 10 to 45 instead of 14 to 45, the materials which media education prepare for the adult education programmes for the age group of 14-45, would take care of the educational needs of these groups too.

In almost all the developing countries the curriculum development, enrichment and reforms through Media education, be them formal or non-formal, could be achieved at low cost and quicker than by the conventional means which is time consuming and very costly effort too.

In the context of Media playing the unique role of eradicating the illiteracy, the adult educational programmes could be divided into two major sectors. One is covering the entire range of learners themselves in the age group of 14-45 (or 10-45 years) years. Second is to train the Adult Education Teachers or Organizers (C.S.H.N. Murthy, 2006, pp. 45-76).

Adult Education Programmes for Different Levels of Learners

The Adult Education programmes have to cover a target group of learners with 10-13 years, 14-16 years, 17-20 years, 21-25 years, 25-30 years, 30-35 years and 36-45 years. At the outset this may look like making several categories of adult education learners. But the principle underlying this categorization has far reaching implications. Firstly, the learners in the age groups of 10-13 to 21-25 have chances of joining the mainstream of education from any stage, be it conventional education or technical education. By educating these groups of learners there is an immediate benefit both for themselves and in turn to the nation through increasing productivity. Further, they would be the future citizens of the country and help bring their next generation with educational values and contribute to the national growth vertically. Secondly, those who are above the age groups of 25 to 45 can sustain very well with functional literacy levels and can help bring their children in an environment of education. There chances of getting into mainstream of education at that age is indeed low. However, if anyone is desirous of carrying forward his education, the correspondence courses offered through the national open school and the Media are always available. As such for a miniscule population of the age group of 25-45, the functional literacy level is reasonable both in terms of need as also the spending of the Government. In addition to the programmes offered by the Media Education in the form of lifelong Education and Continuing Education would always act as back up programmes and refreshing programmes without giving scope for relapsing into illiteracy and stagnation of intellectual growth (the *categorization done here is based on the concepts of Anthony Bates on Non-formal and Social Education in "Broadcasting in Education,* p. 99 *and "Onion Phenomenon").*

If the above logic is to be formulated then the whole scheme of Adult Education programmes could be divided broadly into two categories.

Category I: Adult Education Programmes for the Age groups: *(i)* 10-13 years, *(ii)* 14-16 years, *(iii)* 17-20 years and *(iv)* 21-25 years with prospects of joining the mainstream of education and employment in the Government Sector.

Category II: Adult Education Programmes for the age groups: *(i)* 25-30 years, *(ii)* 30-35 years and *(iii)* 36-45 years with less prospects of joining the mainstream of education and employment in the Government Sector and can benefit from the Media programmes of Lifelong Education and Continuing Education for sustainability of literacy levels.

Salient Features of Category I

Homogeneity and Different Levels of Adult Educational Programmes

For the purpose of achieving homogeneity, the Category I is divided into several subgroups across a range of age limits. As such they can be assigned to different levels of Adult Education Programmes. For all these age groups to go through an ideal environment of education, it is possible to design the educational programmes as L1, L2, L3 and L4. All the age groups mentioned above have to proceed through these levels essentially to arrive at a reasonable level of proficiency that stands as a qualifying mark for them to join the mainstream of education at any stage. All of them have to undergo an examination in the written and oral skills at the end of the completion of each level and obtain a certificate of satisfactorily completing it. This is very essential to ensure the quality the programme being imparted. Each level will have defined General Objectives and Specific Objectives with intended behavioural goals and outcomes. There will be well-planned and realistic course content in each part of the curriculum. Designing of course content should be made in such a way to offer reasonable opportunities for the overall development of the individual personality. There should be a gradual increase in the level of the course content and curriculum from L1 to L4.

The curriculum must include such topics, which offer practical experience in their day-to-day situations and involve their day-to-day work skills. It needs a clear survey of the local activities of the people and the professional skills. From these the sciences and social studies involving the general principles of science and social studies must emerge. Against this backdrop must emerge the principles of health and hygiene. Examples involving mathematics in day-to-day life situations should form the basis for formulating the course content of Mathematics. This should be carefully adhered to in formulating the course content for all levels—L1 to L4. Many a time, there is a tendency to give academic touch to the course content and curriculum of the Adult Education Programme by the planners who tend to justify it on various grounds. At the end of all this programmes come up as croppers or non-starters.

Evaluation and Quality Assurance

More often than not, the Government and the machinery that implement the Adult Education Programmes gloss over the evaluation part of the programmes offered by them for various reasons. This in fact resulted sometimes in the total failure of the programme itself and over years the illiteracy situation remains unchanged in spite of heavy spending of a lot of donor money.

Table–23
New Adult Education Nationally Networked Television Programmes Produced in UK, 1981

	BBC CE (Jan-Dec., 1981)			*ITV (Apr. '80-March '81)*			*OUCE (Jan.-Dec., 1981)*		
	Series	*Programmes*	*%*	*Series*	*Programmes*	*%*	*Series*	*Programmes*	*%*
Disadvantaged									
Basic and coping skills	1	10	4	0	0	0	0	0	0
Physically and mentally handicapped	4	37	15	1	7	3	0	0	0
Women's studies/ young adults elderly ethnic minorities	3	25	10	6	45	22	0	0	0
Sub-total	**8**	**72**	**29**	**7**	**52**	**24**	**0**	**0**	**0**
General interest									
Family, community & health education	3	33	13	7	50	24	1	4	36
Crafts, leisure and household skills	3	20	8	7	54	26	0	0	0
Environment/nature	3	19	8	0	0	0	0	0	0
Sub-total	**9**	**72**	**29**	**14**	**104**	**50**	**1**	**4**	**36**
'Up-market' work training industry, management	4	25	10	0	0	0	0	0	0
Literature, arts, history	2	16	7	1	13	6	0	0	0
Public affairs, political education, media studies	4	18	7	4	25	12	0	0	0
Education	3	23	9	2	7	3	1	7	64
Modern languages	2	20	8	1	6	3	0	0	0
Sub-total	**15**	**102**	**41**	**8**	**51**	**25**	**1**	**7**	**64**
Grand Total	**32**	**246**	**100**	**29**	**207**	**100**	**2**	**11**	**100**

Courtesy: Anthony, W. Bates: *Broadcasting in Education.*

Somehow a feeling of implementing the Adult Education Programmes without appropriate checks has crept into the machinery which oversees the execution of these programmes in many developing nations. There is no scientific study of the reasons, which led to the formation of this feeling among the personnel of the machinery, done anywhere in the world. However, many tall claims and rosy talks about the success of the implementation of the programmes ended up at the end of the day with ever increasing and perhaps even threatening figures of illiterates in most of the Third World nations. Hence a word of caution with regard to the quality of evaluation at the end of each level of the programme is to be borne in mind more importantly.

Quantum of Learning Corresponding to Each Level

Curriculum Planning

This is very important of all. It calls for a careful planning of curriculum at each level. The experiences of many Third World and developing nations would help guide in the proper formulation of the objectives of curriculum for each level. For the sake of ready reference and convenience of the reader, good deal of details regarding these are mentioned in the foregoing chapters. There are many aspects that should be looked into such as local relevance and relevance to their day-to-day life situations. Above all the content should be inspiring rather being academic and boring. This difference in the treatment of curriculum should be perceptible and must be exploited to the hilt for the sake of holding the attention of the target group.

Attractive

Formulating the curriculum in an attractive and acceptable measure corresponding to the age group is an utmost important factor in whose of the scheme itself. There should be different introductory readers at each level keeping in view the age group of the target groups. Keeping one introductory reader at level one for all the age groups indeed makes the whole exercise futile, as what is attractive for one age group is not the same for another age group. The inability to recognize the psychology of the each age group with respect to its educational needs is one of the major factors of the failure of the Adult Education programmes at the inception level itself. Many a studies conducted by the UNESCO, Paris in various developing Asian and African nations have proved that the Educational Psychology plays a very important role even in respect of the Adult Education programmes and it is this which is grossly overlooked by many developing nations on one ground or the other, most importantly the lack of resources and the political will.

Illustrative

The readers designed with regard to each level and subject must be mostly illustrative and mostly compatible with the running text. The text should be brief, pointed and must be relying mostly on the illustrations. Therefore, there should be a match between the text and the illustration. If the illustrations are coloured and properly labelled there can be no major attraction than this. In the case of languages, the illustrations and the course content must be related to local folk stories or war heroes who sacrificed their lives for the cause of nation's freedom or related to stories from Bible or Koran which offer a sense of moral value to life too.

Language

The language of the texts or readers must be very simple and carefully written. Avoiding long and complex sentences should be one of the characteristic features of the text. The letters must be in the same font and size and the same script (e.g. no cursive script of English) should be followed at all levels.

Scope for Exercises

There should be sufficient scope for the in-built exercises with all the hints necessary. The exercises should be of different kinds enhancing the cognition and memory levels of the learners. They should help reinforcement and recapitulation. They must lead to the right and the intended learning outcomes or behavioural goals.

Multi -reader or Multi-optional Approach

To ensure success the Multi-reader approach or Multi-optional approach offers a lot of flexibility to the learners of different age groups. For each age group, there should be different introductory language readers and course readers at same level. It is not proper to offer the same set of language readers and course readers in view of

Table-24
BBC Adult Literacy Broadcasts

Target group	*Title*	*Medium*	*Length (min)*	*No. of programmes in senies*	*Channel*	*Transmission times*	*Years transmitted*	*Average audience size*	*All*	*National Figure Seeing/hearing at least one programme socio-economic Group D/E*
General audience + adult illiterates	'On the Move'	TV	10	50	BBC1	18.05 Sundays 12.15 Thursdays 10.25 Saturdays	1975-78	1,500,000 0 70,000 525,000	67%	63%
Adult illiterates	'Your Move'	TV	25	20	BBC1 BBC2	12.05 Sundays 19.05 Thursdays	1976-78	500,000 250,000	12%	11%
Adult	'Next Move'	Radio	5	20	Radio2	17.50 Sundays 18.45 Thursdays	1977	500,000 500,000	3%	3%
Adult illiterates	'Move On'	Radio	5	20	Radio 2	17.50 Sundays	1978	500,000	No information	No information
Tutors	'Teaching Adults to Read'	Radio	30	8	Radio 3	19.00 Tuesdays 19.00 Tuesdays 19.99 Tuesdays	1975 1976 1977	No information	8%	5%
Tutors	'Helping with Spelling'	Radio	30	4	Radio 3	19.00 Tuesdays 19.00 Mondays	1977 1978	No information	No information	No information

Source: Hargreaves, 1980, Jones and Charnley, 1978.

the wide range of differences in the Educational Psychology. This will not cause any difficulty in the Evaluation and Examination system as the latter two are conducted based on the skills not on the content. Alternatively the multiple option approach will also boost the morale of the learners. There would be a wide range of introductory language readers and course readers available at each level. The learner is open to choose the language reader and the course reader from among compatible with his learning attitudes and aptitude. At the end, he would sit for evaluation and examination in the optionals he has chosen. In fact, the Multi-reader or Multi-optional approach would help curtail the dropouts better than the single reader and single optional system.

Curriculum Development

The curriculum planning, designing, development could be done directly by the Media Department unless the State desires it to be otherwise. But Curriculum development and enrichment could be cheaper if done by Media.

Mode of Instruction

Distance Mode-Media based along with the Print Materials.

Language of Instruction

Local Languages or English Medium as the Government deems it fit.

Scheme of Evaluation and Examination

The scheme of Evaluation and Examination can be conducted by the authorized independent board or independent body by oral and written methods. There should be sufficient marks allotted to practical or internal assignments. The result should be combined assessment of both the examinations—internal assignments and annual written examinations.

Alternative Channels

Those who qualify in these examinations can choose to continue to the next level or can join the mainstream of education either by regular schooling or by national open school or by privately appearing directly for the National Grade Examination or Eritrean Secondary School Certificate Examination. Alternatively, they can opt to join the technical schools below 9th Grade or above 9th Grade and become professionals in their chosen field of profession.

Salient Features of Category II

This category consists of 3 age groups, all of which fall outside the sphere of any hope of joining the mainstream of education or government employment. However, they must receive the training at L1 and L2, both of which should make them self-reliant with regard to functional literacy. They can be given option to break from the Adult Education programmes after successful completion of the L1 and L2 levels. They may also have a choice to join the mainstream of education or technical education by appearing for an entrance examination. Both L1 and L2 levels would suffice their day to day life needs and ensure reasonable level of literacy, numeracy including computer skills. They can further update themselves by following the programmes of Lifelong Education or Continuing Education that Media would keep transmitting from time to time. If need be to prevent their returning to illiteracy, it is possible to offer the refresher programmes instead of L3 and L4 levels.

The designing of L1 and L2 levels could be different than those for the Category I for these age groups keeping in view the principles of educational psychology. Though the course content could be broadly same, the treatment and approach could still be different in view of the age constraint of these age groups. Each increasing level of age will acquire additional complexities and difficulties in its wake and in keeping with this advanced age the designing should be done. The tastes, attitudes and aptitudes would vary considerably from age to age, as individuals keep acquiring higher age. So, these factors cannot be over looked and a blanket approach is not advisable.

As such one major task remains as to the whole scheme of Adult Education Programmes. It is formulating, planning and designing the Curriculum and the Course Contents of the Curriculum. A Plan of Action with or without funding could also be hammered out to meet the challenges in a short time. This would be done at the appropriate time by the concerned authorities after obtaining the necessary mandate from the Ministry of Education. The scheme outlined above thus is in the form of a concept in the offing and is subject to further consideration by the Ministry of Education and the Government of Eritrea.

Policy Laying for the Implementation of the Scheme of Media Education for Adult Education Programmes

From the foregoing, a number of questions arise as to how to organize the Media Education, which is otherwise thought to be quite informal and uncontrolled, for the Adult Education programmes. Firstly, there is an existing administrative structure which has employed Adult Education Facilitators, whose level of education too is very low. Further, the existing infrastructure has acquired an almost a decade's experience as to the factors which are dragging down the process of implementation of adult education programmes. An effort is underway to consolidate this experience and a plan of action is being hammered out to offset these identified gaping holes. At the given moment the Department has only conceived a supportive role for the Media Education rather allow it a full-fledged independent role. But the above scheme of Media Education, though not exhaustive, is a comprehensive as to the scientific formulation of the implementation of Adult Education programmes.

Yet, it needs two things: one is a plan of action about the development and implementation of the programme as outlined above and the second is the policy framing by the government to give full effect to the Media Education as an independent agency, rather than a supportive agency, to quickly implement the scheme to achieve a rapid transformation of educational scenario of the State to achieve the Millenium development Goals and Education for All. In view of the above the following important major decisions are to be taken by the Ministry of Education as to translate the above scheme into reality. Firstly, the Government of Eritrea is conceiving the present report as a basis and a right step towards according a major role to the Media Education as an independent agency rather than a supportive agency. Its independent and autonomous standing is pivotal to the whole concept of Media Education in view of the magnitude of targets the State is contemplating to achieve. Against this backdrop the following policy decisions required to be laid down:

1. The Media Education should be conceived as a major mode of education to achieve the rapid transformation of education rather than supportive one to the existing structure of education, which has already completed a decade's existence and making a slow pace of progress. The result

intended to achieve here is a quicker and rapid one and not time-taking one.

2. The scheme is intended to include both Adult Education facilitators and the learners at a time to avoid loss of time to train the facilitators once and then on their target group.
3. The Media assumes almost a formal role like what is conceived in respect of other correspondence-cum-contact programmes for teachers, Technical and Vocational Education for Students, National Open School for Dropouts etc.
4. This automatically calls upon a systematic enrollment of illiterates and dropouts at all grossroots levels in a prescribed application form along with their national identity cards and a complete data is developed as to the requirements, options and the levels at which Media Education should be offered to them. The feedback would be sent to the Media Education department by electronic mode through computers from the local Adult Education Centres or by post if the dearth of funds is felt.
5. The beaming of the programmes by Radio and TV would be done as per the levels identified based on the feedback zoba-wise and are strictly in accordance with the curriculum developed for each level subject and each level primers or readers.
6. The transmission of the programmes are supported by the Audio-Video Cassettes which would be distributed down to all the grassroots levels to cater to the listening needs of the students of the Adult Education.
7. There should be regular evaluation and conducting of examination for each level at the end of the stipulated period.

The above matters need to be viewed by the Ministry, in addition to development of an action plan for the rapid curriculum designing, for laying policies in regard to the governance of the scheme by the Media Education independently.

Preparatory Steps or Foreground for the Launch of Media Education

So far an exhaustive and comprehensive discussion is being done on the multi-faceted approach of the Media education in the context of the world scenario in general and in the context of many developing or Third World countries including Eritrea in particular. Dealing with the Media education as such on a holistic basis is one thing and to prepare a launch pad for its take off is another one. The installation of technical infrastructure involves wherewithal besides the recruitment of technical personnel for launching the Media channel. At the same time, there is a need to prepare the manpower to meet the software demands of the Media Channel. In other words, a lot of groundwork has to be done to ensure that there are suitably trained manpower to perform various tasks without much loss of valuable investment or time. Since the educational channel could be launched both on the Radio and the Television, both of which have certain advantages and deficiencies in their own perspective it is felt better to discuss the preparations for the both separately.

A. Preparatory Steps for Radio

Any educational channel becomes operational if the manpower required for the various levels of operations are suitably trained. As Radio is a blind medium, the preparation for the Radio Educational programmes is different from that of Television. The following steps are very crucial for the launch of the Radio Educational Channel.

I. Awareness Programmes

1. Awareness Programme of the Unique Characteristics of Radio in General and their exploitation for the educational programmes.
2. Awareness Programme of the Formats of Radio—Conversation, interviews, phone-in, dramas, songs, single presentation (called as a radio talk), group programmes such as children programmes and especially creating classroom environment.
3. Awareness of Various Roles—As a Presenter, Producer, Writer, Character and as Director. Awareness of maintenance of voice levels compatible to mike reading and modulation etc.

II. Workshops for Training

1. Conducting workshops for the interested participants (teachers, writers, journalists, editors and intellectuals) in writing for the Radio in general and for various formats in particular e.g. Writing as Talking and Conveying the Messages within the time limit effectively.

Table–25
Instructional Television System

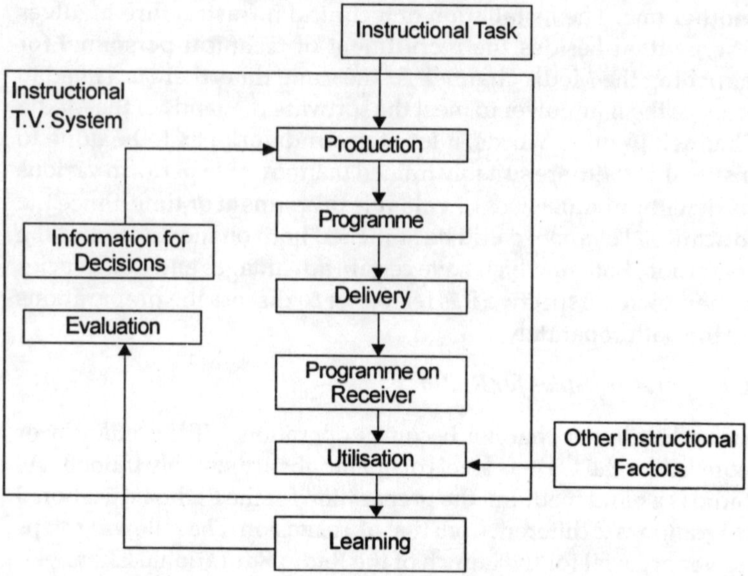

Courtesy: Peter Combes and John Tiffin: *TV Production for Education:* A Systems Approach.

2. Writing for literary and non-literary styles: e.g. Poetry and story writing (literary) and non-fiction such as essays, Thematic programmes such as environment creation by background voice and music etc. (especially in the case of history of Literature, Science and Social Studies).
3. Popular Writing (health, agriculture, environment and hygiene) and writing for general educational programmes (women's welfare, children welfare etc.) for Lifelong and Continuing Education.
4. Writing for Popular Sciences (latest discoveries, old discoveries of immense value, Nobel prize winning personalities and their works etc.) and Social Sciences (contemporary developments including Economics, World Stage of Politics).
5. Writing for the Curricular Topics – Various ways of developing curricular themes and contents into different formats – how many formats one can develop for a given curricular theme or content – how to determine which is the

correct, low cost and effective one that can be prepared in a shortest possible time – All subjects including Mathematics.

III. Training Programmes for Special Planning for Radio

Writing for Print Medium and writing for Radio are not one and the same. The latter becomes all the more significant in respect of educational programmes for one needs to plan all special effects associated with the theme and the content. Keeping in mind the special effects that go with the content, the script and the vocabulary should be planned. Therefore, it is a very specialized planning. The script preparation and presentation both should go together with careful and special planning, if any educational programme were to be successful. For instance, the Radio Mathematics Project of Nicaragua would speak immense the Special Planning they had done in developing the project as a role model for all the Third World countries.

IV. Training for Radio Planning of Curriculum (Compatible to its characteristics)

The curriculum prescribed by the State would undergo modifications in view of the limitations the Medium like Radio imposes. Therefore,

Table–26
Television Planning System

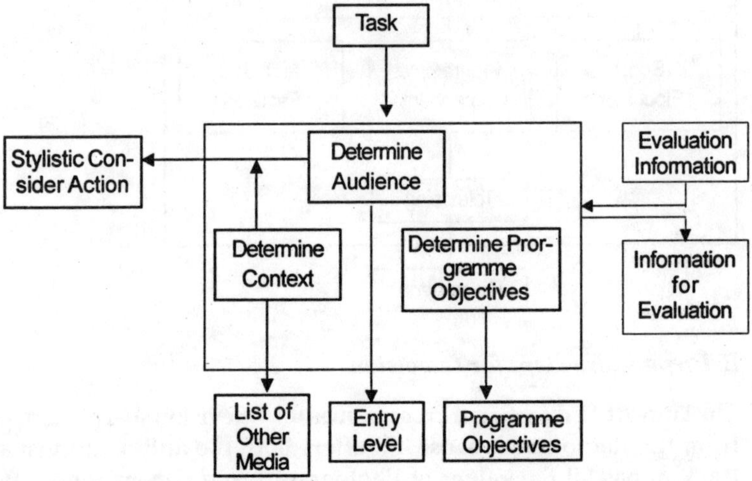

Courtesy: Peter Combes and John Tiffin: *TV Production for Education:* A Systems Approach.

how to plan the curriculum compatible to Radio, how to enrich it and how to use it both for direct teaching and non-direct teaching including as a learning resource – the criteria for sub-dividing the curriculum into different sub-units etc., associated with special planning for Radio as outlined above would be dealt within the programme.

These are the broad action programmes, which should be taken up before the launch of the Educational Channel in Radio.

Table–27
The Television Production System

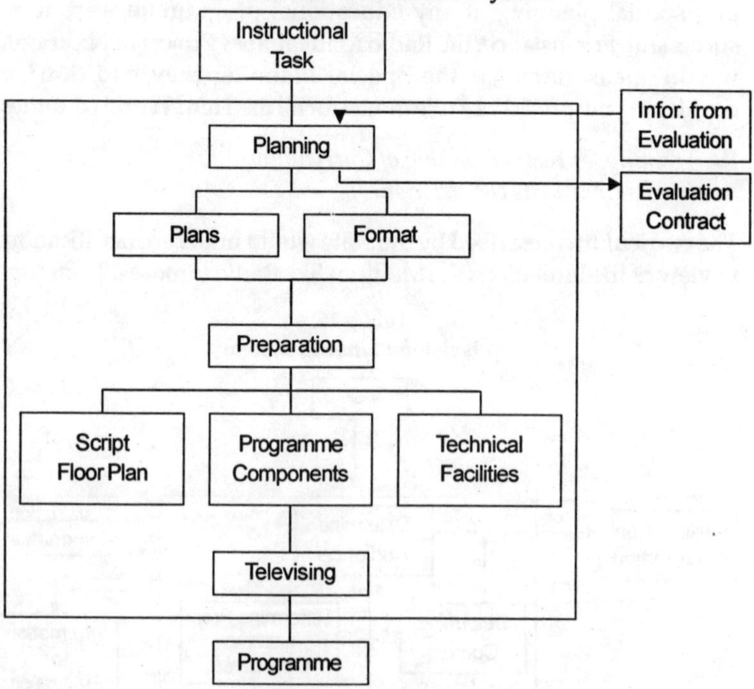

B. Preparatory Steps for Television

The launch of Educational Programmes for Television sharply differs from the Radio in the sense TV offers both the audio and visual track. It has all the values of Photography and Cinematography. The viewers have world over established certain norms of relishing or enjoying an educational programme. Unless a whole lot of exercise comparable to Cinematic values goes into play, the effort to produce an educational programme may end up with no viewers or audience at the end. Writing for the Radio is not the same for the TV. Similarly planning for the TV educational programme is not the same for planning for the Radio. Precisely put, one who has the background of Cinematography can quickly do the educational programme but one who does educational programme cannot shoot a film. It means familiarity with the entire range of cinema production is essential for producing the Educational Programmes. Script writing for a TV educational programme is possible if one has familiarity with the advantages and the limitations of the lens of the Video camera, digital or non-digital. One must know precisely what could be translated to a film or could be composed into a frame. It calls for a special eye and orientation. The following steps could help train the manpower in the launching an educational channel.

I. Awareness Programmes

1. Awareness of the Advantages of Television both as an Audio and Visual Medium.
2. Awareness of the Cinematographic Techniques – Planning film production (cost value in relation to time) and Shooting Schedules and Direction values.

II. Workshops for Training

1. Conducting workshops for Television Script writing including language skills for brevity and presentation.
2. Conducting workshops for Selection of Materials and Locales (including selection of background scenery, images and photographic pictures or paintings etc.).
3. Conducting workshops for various Theme development – compatible to formats like Drama, Abstract Anchoring (anchor not seen on the screen) or Concrete Anchoring, documentary etc.

III. Training Programmes for Special Planning for TV

1. Training for Planning the Special Effects or the Special Materials – settings, photographs, painting, pictures including graphics and sound and light effects.
2. Training for script preparation for the above special effects.

IV. Curricular Planning for Television

1. The Curriculum Planning Techniques Compatible to the Special features of TV.
2. Criteria to divide and sub-divide or combine the Units of the Curriculum to develop it into a single theme.
3. Ways and means to enrich the Curriculum—Curriculum Reforms—Develop learning resources for the Teachers.
4. To Formulate Curriculum compatible to TV for Various Correspondence Courses of Teacher Education, and National Open School/TVET/Adult Education Programmes. *(The Curriculum for the Correspondence Courses for all programmes including Adult Education Programmes could be developed Straight without prior formulation by the State as did by American Samoa, Brazil etc.).*

Establishment of Educational Technology

At the time of writing this report giving emphasis on Media oriented Correspondence Courses both for the teachers and the students, and Media administered educational programmes for the formal and non-formal courses, with the independent curriculum or with the curriculum prescribed by the National Curriculum Development Board, the popular criticism on the limitations of the Distance Education as documented by Ljosa (1988) is well-known. At the same time the profound history and evolution of the Distance Education as characterized by its Correspondence Courses and by the features of "industrialization" and privatization of "institutional learning" over the "conventional learning" have offered it a great resilience and strength to withstand all such criticism. In the process, arguments emerged both in favour and against combining the Distance Education with educational technology as to give the Distance Education a conventional touch to permit a two-way flow of communication between the teacher and the student similar to classroom experience which permits a dialogue between the teacher and the students (Keegan, D., 1986 and Holmberg, B., 1986).

However, eminent scholars like Garrison and Shale (1987) argued against laying over emphasis on the mere technical term "distance" and trying to explore the demerits of it on basis of the physical separation of the two important partners—the teacher and the student. On the other hand, they favoured to place emphasis on "education" – though it is non-contiguous. However, they too argued in involving two-way communication between the teacher and the students and to achieve this they advocated the use of technology to mediate the necessary two-way communication.

Citing the Wedemeyer (1981) model (which is the first to identify the crucial role of the communication mode in distance education) which states that, "Teaching and learning can safely and effectively be carried on with no loss of interaction, through various communication means, even though the teacher and learner are separated in space and time", Doug Shale and D. Randy Garrison sought to make the model more participatory and distinctive. This model is based on the premise that there is no two-way communication process in the existing correspondence course education offered through the Distance Education. As a remedy to it, the model assumes that "the teacher generates information which is captured by some enduring medium (such as Print, Audio-tape, laser disc. etc.). The medium carries the content forward to the student who may then be regarded as having received information. The "negotiation of meaning" required to close the communication loop is an activity separate from the transmission of information and frequently is supported by a medium different from that used to distribute the content. The negotiation clearly will be mediated by a technological medium, and depending on the technology, exchanges may either be delayed or direct. It is however the communication loop that unifies the concepts of distance (with its focus on technological structures) and education (with its focus on instructional activities).

Garrison has described and discussed the various distance education technologies from the perspective of their communication characteristics. Communication technology is classified into two categories: 1. Two-way communications technology consists of three generations or distinct types – Print (correspondence), Telecommunications (teleconferencing), and Computer based. Though Media Education through Radio and Television, as pioneered by the British Open University and Japanese Educational Radio and Television, is considered an advancement, it still left the meaning of "education" far behind the conventional experience of the word "education". The apparent print mode complementing the Distance Education programmes characterized by its correspondence courses did not give it the complete meaning acceptable to the educational methodology and teaching techniques. It needed therefore, something else to add to make the communication loop complete. The use of telecommunications in distance education marked a new generation in fulfilling the definition of educational methodology of the correspondence courses offered through Distance Education even by the Media—Radio and Television. The second-generation technology of telecommunications such as Teleconferencing has come to play a lead role in complementing the efforts of Media Education. Its ability lies in its two-way communication among several individuals at a time. Teleconferencing conjoins two or more groups through telecommunications technology. Telecommunication channels may be simply telephone and cable transmission or advanced innovations such as satellite and fiber optics.

Teleconferencing

There are two primary kinds of teleconferencing: one audio and another video. From an instructional standpoint of view both of them are capable of providing group interaction. The dynamics of the group are often essential to explore and convey aspects of certain curricula. It also provides opportunities for social support and informal evaluative comparisons among the students. It has also advantage of being close to the conventional system of education where the teacher deals with a group more than an individual student. Hence, it gains acceptability easily among teachers who usually offer resistance to any modernization or innovation which would threaten their role as a dominant character in the teaching profession.

Audio-teleconferencing is currently the most prevalent form of teleconferencing in distance education. Its cost effectiveness is another added advantage. Hardware costs are relatively less and could be obtained on lease for pilot trials. The hiring of the services of the instructors is not going to be very costly than the hiring in conventional teaching. The time and money spent on the instructors almost parallels the conventional teaching system. The curriculum and delivery of the instruction are almost identical. Long distance charges are likely to affect the cost inputs but if the counselling centres are located close to the target groups, this could be minimized. It is a matter of logistic plan independent of the potential of Audio-teleconferencing. If number of students involved in the exercise is less, audio-teleconferencing would be much cheaper.

Video-conferencing is a complicated and costly exercise than the audio teleconferencing or enhanced audio-teleconferencing. Two-way exchange of video images between two or more sites and three or more individuals would be complicating the technological process though such a system allows a direct eye to eye contact between the student and the teacher just as it happens in the educational setting. Therefore, to reduce the costs most of the Video-conferencing techniques apply one way video-conferencing where the students only can see the teacher keeping the audio both ways interactive.

Computer Based Educational Technology (CAL, CML, ICAL and Cyclops)

Computer Association with regular classroom learning has become an added responsibility to both the students and the teachers. However, this has been of less help to the present conventional education, as it did not bring in as many innovations in the teaching and learning experiences of the students, as does the Distance Education. All the technological innovations and advancements found their place only through correspondence course studies and distance education.

Communication through Computer based technology, a third generation support to educational technology, is of two types with regard to distance education applications. The first type is the transmitted or online method in which the computer is integrated with telecommunications technology. The second type is the local or off line mode. Together they offer the distance educator an enviable range of teaching opportunities – methods and techniques. Out of the two, it is the transmitted mode, which is having most immediate application in distance education. This allows computer conferencing, electronic mail, accessing electronic data bases, and administrative contacts such as online applying for admissions and examinations etc. They would constitute the expanding services, which conventional mode would not offer, available to the distance educators and learners. This would further reduce enormous manpower employment.

Using the computer in local mode offers a great promise in the future for distance education. It offers packages of materials or learning kits and tools to the individual learner, which he could directly, control himself. This is now being evolved as Computer Managed Learning (CML). CAL, CML and intelligent computer assisted learning—ICAL are all going to be the important tools in the distance education for correspondence studies.

Cyclops

It is a microcomputer processor based simple technology, which can be operated easily by the people even not familiar with the computer operations. It will allow teachers to create their own sophisticated audio-visual materials very simply without needing the computer programmeming skills. It converts digitally simple color videographics—handwriting, text, diagrams and very simple animation—into sound codes. These graphics can be very easily generated using a combination of a standard computer keyboard and an electronic light pen which writes on a standard television screen or an electronic writing pad which also displays graphics on the TV screen. Still images from a video-camera can be similarly coded. As the video signals are converted into a sound-code, they can be stored on audio-cassette or transmitted down standard telephone lines, they decoded back into a video-signal. Using either standard stereo audio-cassettes or two telephone lines, full sound can be synchronized with the visuals.

This system has been successfully utilized by the British Open University and its associated schools for 3 years for running the distance education programmes' tutorials. Cyclops is basically a "peripheral" system for a standard micro-computer since its core can be made available as a cartridge or a ROM to be added to a standard micro-computer. The probable configuration for a Cyclops is to consist of a Standard Television receiver, a stereo-cassette player, a microphone, a light pen, or an electronic writing pad and a standard micro-computer. This will allow incorporate a Cyclops-type facility.

Sustainability of Media Education

All said and done Media Education is an excellent alternative both in terms of cost effectiveness and rapid transformation of the State Education and Economy. But coming as it does the question of funding the whole range of programmes that Media Education can offer is sometimes very disillusioning. However, if the Media

Education has be to sustainable, the Ministry of Education must look at the alternative ways of raising the funds for the programmes to continue uninterruptedly. With the GDP touching as high as 90 per cent it is not possible for the Government to spend heavily on this core sector for a long time. At the same time it is not possible for the Government to do away with the idea for want of funds. Nor can the government implement the programmes of Media Education in a limited way as they do not lead anywhere and objectives of EFA can hardly be realized.

One of the finest alternatives to make the Media education financially viable and long lasting is to open the doors of privatization, which offer a wide market of advertising. It is through the revenues of this advertising that Media Education can become self-sufficient. But being a small State, the possibility of garnering high revenue through advertising appears to be bleak for the business development in Eritrea is passing through the infancy stage at this time. Most of the businessmen are small traders and have to go a long way to build themselves into big business houses. As such many multi-national firms may not immediately find Eritrea an ideal place for any business investment. But some big business houses organizations in Europe and the UK or the US could sponsor some advertising programmes on philanthropic considerations as the State of Eritrea is a newly formed country and requires a lot of international support. Whatsoever may be the way of raising the funds, the State of Eritrea can ill afford to lose an opportunity at the present time.

However, the Government has expressed its intention to open the doors for privatization in the sector of general education and technical and vocational education. If this becomes a reality the advertisements from the private educational institutions themselves become a major source of revenue. As such some international schools in Asmara are offering advertisements in Eritrean Profile. This only points to a ray of hope on the horizon. Further, the baby and children products—eatables to the skin care products, the products of health and hygiene, beverages—such as Tea and Coffee, Cool drinks, Cakes etc., can offer a wide range of market for advertising for the Media Educational Channel of Radio and Television. Even Cell phones, flat screen TVs and some electronic items could be promising sources of income. What all is required to employ the marketing agents on commission basis to garner the advertisements.

This should open the doors of self-sustainability of a most vital instrument of reforms—namely Media Education. The earlier it happens, the greater it saves the State exchequer, which can divert most of its funds for other developmental activities.

7

Establishment of Corollary Institutions

Nodal Institution or Body to Coordinate and Monitor—Educational Programme of Radio and Television

A Look at Similar Institutions

Once the role of Media Education against the background presented here is accepted, then the question of the need to establish a number of support institutions to meet its all requirements arises. Media Education does not become effective without taking the support services of these institutions. For instance, as we know, the Media Education involves Print and Electronic Media, both of which require certain criteria as also a set of operations being accomplished, either simultaneously or before, based on the development of curriculum design and enrichment both for Radio and TV. The other operations necessary to be completed prior to the launch of the Media Education have already been discussed in the preceding chapter. In this chapter, the need and the importance of these nodal institutions would be discussed in their in-depth detail.

Most importantly questions concerning.......*what educative programme should be broadcast, what should be the criteria underlying for classifying the educative programme against the backdrop of the country's needs, what should be the curriculum for formal and non-formal sectors, the criteria for formulating the curriculum for various correspondence courses and for vocational and national open school, the curriculum planning and development for the non-formal distance mode of education, how are they being prepared and broadcast, who are the personnel to be involved and how to evaluate and assess the quality of these programme*—are to be met with objectively with the help of these nodal institutions.

The nodal institutions would have the primary and secondary objectives related to the above questions. Almost all the developed and developing countries, which are dependent on Media Education, have formed these nodal institutions which would effectively coordinate the activities of the Media Education. Each country has established its own network of Media Education. In some developing countries, the Ministry of Education directly involves itself in discharging all these large-scale operations without going for independent or autonomous bodies for various political reasons. On the other hand, some countries prefer to establish nodal institutions to aid and support these independent or autonomous bodies so that the Government interference is minimum. For instance BBC has an independent nodal institution which would oversee the administrative as also academic, including the research and development on the quality of the content of the educational and educative programme broadcast by it.

The Structure of BBC

The BBC is an autonomous body with the Government partnership less than 50 per cent and is dependent mainly on the license fees collected from all its Radio and Television networks. It competes with the Private Sector Television Channels operating under the Independent Television Agency (ITA). There can be more structural details, which are not necessary in the context of the scope of this chapter and hence it is felt worth to focus on the educational broadcasting service itself.

The BBC has four educational broadcasting departments fully funded from its license revenue: Schools Television, Schools Radio, Continuing Educational Television and Continuing Education Radio. The Independent Television Companies (ITC) are required to Provide schools programme, continuing education programme and a specified amount of social purpose programme from their own revenues under the framework of Independent Broadcasting Agency (IBA).

Both BBC and the ITV companies and some of the local radio stations employ full-time education officers responsible for liaison with local educational establishments and for providing feedback on educational programming. *Both the BBC and IBA have appointed their own advisory bodies for educational programming. The BBC has appointed an Educational Broadcasting Council (EBC) which is serviced and financed by the BBC and which has a small research department attached to it. This research department provides both the BBC and ITV companies with annual equipment and utilization figures for education based on annual surveys of schools and further education institutions. The EBC also carries out special research for the BBC.*

In addition to the above a new system of TV and Radio audience research has recently been established in Britain. In accordance with the recommendations of Annan Committee on the Future of Broadcasting, *audience measurement* is introduced. Immediately after this the Broadcasters' Audience Research Board (BARB) was established in 1980. It is a limited company jointly owned by the BBC and the Independent Television Companies' Association (ITCA). There is a board of three directors, of whom, one is an independent chairman, with one member each from both the BBC and ITCA. There are two services provided by BARB. The first is *audience measurement* and the second is *audience reaction.*

The British Open University

Established in 1969, with its own royal charter, it is another important institution, which caters to the educational broadcasting. It is fully autonomous and degree awarding institution and provides education upto degree level and offers continuing education courses for adults on a part-time basis. The British Open University and BBC educational have sowed seeds of similar experiments in many other developing Asian and Latin American nations. The undergraduate programme are financed by the Department of Education and Sciences—which is a wing of the Ministry of Education in Great Britain, although students pay the fees which amounts to 15 per cent of its budget. The continuing education programme are self-financing.

Students study through a mixture of specially designed correspondence texts (which provide the core teaching material), television broadcasts, audio cassettes, correspondence and face to face tutoring, and on some courses summer schools, home kits, radio or computer-aided learning are also available. Courses are designed by teams made up of academics employed full-time by the open University (sometimes assisted by external subject consultants), educational technologists, editors, course managers, staff tutors responsible for regional tutorial arrangements, and broadcast producers. The broadcast producers are employed by the BBC, which has a unique partnership arrangement with the Open University. The BBC established a separate department, BBC/OUP, devoted entirely to the production of television, radio and audio programme for the Open University. Each year this department produces upto 250 television programme and over 300 radio programme or audio programme. For the services the BBC does for the Open University, the Department of Education and Sciences of the Ministry of Education would defray the costs.

The above information only confirms the fact the Media Education could be launched as a collaborative effort and requires support services from different nodal institutions. Countries like Japan and India too have launched Educational Television Channels exclusively to meet the educational requirements of the country.

Japan's Educational Channel (NHK and NET—Private Channel)

In case of Japan, there are two channels owned by NHK of which one is educational. Among the four private networks, there is a Nippon Educational Television (NET), which is the only educational network as a private broadcaster. The Tokyo Broadcasting System is the strongest of the four private networks with 20 affiliated companies, followed by Nippon Television Network Co., Fuji Television and Nippon Educational Television (NET). NET is composed of some 21 affiliates and the contract to its affiliates is made on a per-programme basis, which means that all the stations need not broadcast the same educational programme. Most of the Japanese educational channels' revenue system is modelled on the American Educational Television system. However NET (1959) being a private channel operates on profit basis though it offers only educational programme. The Government run autonomous and independent NHK educational channel however is a non-profit one. The universities assist all these channels and the Educational Agencies help in preparing the curriculum based instructive programme both for educational programme and social education programme.

The textbooks for the broadcasts are prepared with the cooperation of an advisory body in which the senior high schools having correspondence courses are represented. The broadcast texts thus prepared are used together with the usual correspondence textbooks. NHK appoints lecturers from among the authors of the textbooks. A second committee composed of lecturers and representatives of correspondence schools as well as NHK makes the final decision. Other committees made up of representatives of the above two committees decide on the detailed content of programme for broadcasting. Each subject is assigned to one committee that meets twice a year.

The NHK Correspondence School

It is organized for and covers the whole of the country. Located in Tokyo, it consists of about 70 teachers and 50 clerical staff. It also houses a two-story dormitory to accommodate nearly 100 students for the contact programme. In the rest of the country about 75 high schools are commissioned as learning centres for the distance education students where the Correspondence School appointed resource personnel offer guidance to the local students with regard to their educational needs. Though NHK Correspondence School is administratively considered as part of the NHK, there is no scope at any point of time for the NHK to interfere with the functioning of the Correspondence School. It is an independent juridical person responsible for educational programme and activities. The NHK's role is confined to accessing these programme prepared by the Correspondence School to the TV screen. The Educational programme prepared by the NET often overlap the programme of NHK as both NET and NHK prepare the programme based on the same school and college curriculum prescribed by the Ministry of Education. The broadcasting law of Japan forbids any deviation from conforming to its educational law.

The NET School Broadcasting Division

The procedure in producing the School Broadcasting programme is as follows. The NET School Broadcasting Division always proposes the original programme of action. It then goes to a School Broadcasting Committee. After that, the advisory organ of each local station examines the plan, which goes back to the NET School Broadcasting Division for re-examination. The Broadcasting

Division and the local committee make a final decision about the plan. The Planning Committee of School Broadcasting then takesover and prepares the production of each course.

Poland – National Radio and Television University for Teachers

Poland is another European nation, which utilized the Radio and Television exclusively for the upgradation of teachers without having to give up their teaching profession. In order for achieving this Poland has established a National Radio and Television University for Teachers in 1974 as part of its reforming of the education system. It is meant to expand rapidly the secondary education and modernize the teaching methods and techniques. At this time out of a total teaching force of 3,60,000, about 1,60,000 (i.e. 44% approximately) were not even graduates. Therefore, the immediate task of the NURT is to provide a Graduate Course equivalent to 4 years to these teachers. Another important aspect of this is not to impose any entry-level qualification restrictions. As a result by 1977 about 75,000 had enrolled themselves. Teachers receive three television and two radio programme a week, and broadcast would be at the end of the school day. The programme are made and broadcast by the Polish National Broadcasting System in consultation with NURT. The curriculum for students following NURT courses is so fully integrated with the curriculum for full-time student-teachers at universities and teacher colleges that the NURT programme are also a compulsory part of the full time student-teacher curriculum. In a way NURT offers more Radio and Television programme than the British Open University, which also offers non-graduate, working teachers with the opportunity to achieve graduate status through part-time study.

India – IGNOU-NCERT-SCERT-SITE

India is one of the leading nations next to Japan in Asia in offering the Educational Broadcasting since the inception of Radio and the Television. It has established a well-defined administrative and operational infrastructure to fulfill the obligation of transforming a predominantly illiterate country at the time of independence to present 70 per cent highly literate country. Its educational broadcasting network is fully integrated with the educational agençies of the Federal States and the Centre. The central organizations like NCERT (the National Council for Education and

Research and Training) and the SCERT (State Council for Education and Research and Training) have perfectly coordinated the curriculum development for these Media institutions. Further Satellite Instructional Television Experiment (SITE) is one of the pilot institutions in helping these programme reach the rural areas. The course for the SITE projects was designed by the National Centre for Educational Technology.

A number of Radio Stations of Tamil Nadu and Kerala offered even correspondence courses for the rapid teacher training and teacher upgradation in the early 1970-80s to remove the dearth of teachers in all regions of the State. Indira Gandhi National Open University (IGNOU) established in 1985, considered an apex body for all the open universities and distance education institutions had taken further leads in accessing hundreds of thousands of underprivileged and deprived to the higher and modern education. It is modelled on the lines of British Open University. Even professional and vocational courses are being offered by it to the women, girls who hitherto remained mere household entities. Indira Gandhi National Open University along with the Council of Scientific and Industrial Research (CSIR) has been regularly broadcasting the educational programme for the benefit of all the students including its own clientele during the early hours of the day everyday. Most of its programme are styled on the lines of the British Open University and the BBC. The quality of the programme is also very high and rich in content and presentation. The video- cassettes produced are available from its own marketing agencies and from private agencies. Copy right problem is one that is acutely felt in this sector. But, unfortunately, even developed countries are no exception to it.

The AVRC and EMRC

The Audio-Visual Research Centre (AVRC) and the Educational Materials Research Centre (EMRC) are two bodies, which are established in a number universities like Osmania (AVRC), Pune (EMRC), Delhi (EMRC) and deemed universities like CIEFL (EMRC) etc., not only involved in training the personnel in the production of educational programme but also in producing the educative programme of high standards for the benefit of the students of IGNOU and CSIR institutions.

Kenya – University of Nairobi – Correspondence Course

The Government of Kenya in order to meet its requirement of the teaching staff set-up a Correspondence Course Unit in the University of Nairobi to provide courses through a combination of correspondence teaching, and radio broadcasting with occasional residential seminars. This has helped turn out one-third of its unqualified teacher force to qualified ones in a short time.

Algeria

It is another African nation, besides Tanzania, Zimbabwe and Zambia, which utilized the Media Education as distance education for offering the Correspondence Courses to teachers to turn out the qualified teaching force in the country without depending on the expatriate teachers. Algeria not only used Radio but also pressed into service the Television quite effectively. Over six years, more than 20,000 teachers at the primary level have been trained. Apart from Radio and Television, printed materials are supplied and group meetings are often held to clear their doubts.

Institutional Objectives

The nodal institution established to control, regulate and monitor the Educative and Educational Programme is expected to function against the objectives outlined here:

1. To decide the nature and the scope of each educative and educational programme required against the backdrop the country's educational needs.
2. To lay down the criteria for each programme and work out the number, nature and scope of programme for each curricular subject of formal and non-formal education.
3. To plan for the programme based on the curriculum of distance education programmes – for teachers at various levels from Kindergarten to Graduation level.
4. To develop the programme for Vocational and Technical education by distance education.
5. To organize the programme for different levels – L1, L2, L3 and L4 of Category I and Category II of Adult Education programme.
6. To work out the number, nature and scope of the programme of National Open School.

7. To plan the overall scheme of production of the programme for various courses without giving scope for any over-lapping.
8. To plan for the script writing for all these programme based on the curriculum (The curriculum for the Media Education be assigned by the designated National Curriculum Development Department or the Media could be allowed to develop curriculum straight as many developing nations did as part of reduction of the costs).
9. To organize and plan for the shooting (TV) or recording (Radio) of the programme.
10. To form a panel of teachers and media experts, both within and outside for regular consultancy and interaction for the effective production of the Radio and Television.
11. To check, assure and certify the quality of both the inputs and outputs at the beginning and end of the programme.

Administrative Functions

1. To recruit and organize the manpower required for various levels of work.
2. To regulate the process of preparation and production of the scripts by streamlining the operational procedures by assigning specific tasks at each level.
3. To conduct audience research and elicit information on the quality of the products.
4. To ensure timely planning and production without giving scope for the administrative or technical delays.
5. To ensure the installation and commission of proper infrastructure.
6. To regulate the services of the manpower engaged in the performance of specific tasks.
7. To ensure the maintenance of the technical infrastructure from time-to-time, and replace the wear and tear.
8. To ensure the proper flow of finances toward the budget meant to perform the specific tasks.

The above nodal body is central to the entire concept of Media Education. Presently the Government of Eritrea is planning to establish a full-fledged TV Educational channel. Most of the above functions could be assigned to the channel to be established shortly. Further, the Ministry of Education has approached the UNESCO for funding to establish a full-fledged AVRC for the Production of Educative and educational programme. If the launching of TV channel and the AVRC would synchronize, it would give a major impetus and boost to the educational strategies of the Ministry of Education. At the same time, the Ministry approached the World Bank to finance the erection of a 10kW Short Wave transmitter with Multi-directional Antenna. This would give a major thrust to the Radio Educational programme presently being done by the Department of Adult and Media Education. It would further help launch a number of Educational programme on full time basis round the clock in various languages, besides launching of the ELT programme and Teacher Development Programme.

Nodal Institution to Administer Examination to All the Trainees/ Learners/Target Groups of Various Courses Offered by Electronic Media—Radio and TV

It is a very important institution as far as Correspondence Courses and courses through Distance Mode are concerned. In many countries, to avoid duplication of curriculum, one for the conventional and the other for the Distance Mode, the Governments have tried to synchronize both the conventional and distance mode. As such the examination could be conducted simultaneously for both streams. In certain countries, though the Media offered Correspondence Courses for various target groups, formal and non-formal, the examination responsibility is entrusted to either an Open University or to a Department in the National or a State University. In respect of some countries, specific designated bodies or departments of the Ministry of Education carried out this responsibility. Whatsoever may be the institution, the mandate of the institution is to be clear. It should conduct regular and supplementary, either semester or annual, examinations for the target groups of all the courses and declare results on time.

Institutional Objectives

1. To plan and organize the examination schedules in accordance with the academic calendar for various courses both in the formal sector and non-formal sector.
2. To recruit such staff as may be necessary and train them for the organization of examinations on a larger scale, say, entire country.

3. To develop systems for coding and decoding of answer scripts, tabulation of marks and tabulation of results – either manual or electronic such as Computer systems.
4. To budget the requirements of the Institution for the conducting the examinations – stationery and other support materials like threads, or tags, punch machines, staplers etc.
5. To get the appropriate stationery printed in the name of the institution for the conduct of examinations such as envelopes in which answer scripts, question papers, confidential materials should be preserved or dispatched or received.
6. To empanel the experienced and senior teachers or professors for the preparation of different sets of question papers as per the syllabus for the range of courses offered through distance education.
7. To lay down the criteria of different grades or divisions for declaring results such as failed, passed, promoted, 1st Division, 2nd Division etc.

Administrative Functions

1. To lay down the criteria for planning the appropriate examination network for the entire country.
2. To interact with the concerned authorities and appoint or designate the local heads for the liaison work further.
3. To work out the logistics for the conduct of the examinations entire country at a time smoothly.
4. To prepare the Administrative Machinery such as Controller of Examinations or the Branch of examinations to do coding of the examination centres identified and allot the applicants of various courses to the nearest places or centres of examinations.
5. To set the assignments to the individual staff for conducting the Examinations and to plan for the invigilation duty of the available local staff for the smooth conduct of the examinations.
6. To lay down the criteria of administering the examinations by appointing local custodians, transit officers and Chief Superintendent of Examination Centres.
7. To appoint people fully accountable to the smooth and accurate conduct of the examinations.

Nodal Institutions to Provide the Raw Materials—Print Materials, Tapes, CDs, Transistors, Radios and TV Sets—Low Cost Education and Adult Education

It is very important institution as its sole goal is to procure and provide the Raw Materials for all the efforts done by the Media Education. Without these Raw Materials the messages produced by the Media Education could not be carried forward to the intended target groups. Especially a nodal institution like this is very important for it affords a reasonable time to plan not only effectively but also cost effectively. There are many ways of following the low cost techniques. One is to seek the help of Donor Agencies such as Donor nations and NGOs to liberally donate the Stationery for the Printing of Broadcast materials, Blank Tapes, CDs, Transistors, Radios and TV sets in bulk. The equipment and materials thus obtained through donations could be sent to the educational institutions and the community learning centres. Many European nations would certainly be able to give in kind than in cash. It all needed diplomatic and bilateral efforts in addition to the existing efforts through various UN agencies like USAID, UNESCO or World Bank etc.

Table-28
Schools Television and Radio in UK: Equipment and Programme Use

School Year 1981-82 *Radio*	*Primary and Middle*	*% of UK Schools Secondary*	*All Schools*
VHF receivers (total)	99%	97%	99%
Average number per school	3	4	
Audio recorders (total)	98%	99%	98%
Average number per school	4	10	
Schools using school radio	95%	66%	90%
Average number of series/school	6.4	5.1	
Television	97%	99%	97%
Television receivers (total)			
Average number per school	1	3	
Colour television receivers	82%	94%	84%
Average number per school	1	2	

(Contd.)

School Year 1981-82 *Radio*	*Primary and* *Middle*	*% of UK Schools* *Secondary*	*All Schools*
Video recorders	24%	96%	36%
Average number per school	1	2	
Schools using BBC television	95%	90%	94%
Average number of series/school	5.2	9.4	
School using ITV television	85%	80%	84%
Average number of series/school	3.4	3.7	
Total number of schools	27,993	5,743	33,736

Source: Educational Broadcasting Council, 1982.
Courtesy: Anthony, W. Bates: *Broadcasting in Education.*

Most of the developing nations both in Asia and in Africa are the recipients of such benefits. Countries like—Australia, Japan, Germany, Netherlands, Norway, Britain and the US in the past gave several such donations for the development of education and Communications network to developing Third World countries. Alternatively, a number of countries including India, Japan, Britain, the USA, produced a wide range of audio-video cassettes on the curricular subjects. Though Eritrean national curriculum may vary in respect of the main units and sub-units, and in emphasis and explanation, the facts of English, Science and Mathematics do not change in respect of major heads, explanations and content. Further, they offer insights into the artistic presentation of the curricular topics which may serve as models for furthering the value of indigenous production. Even these cassettes could be obtained through diplomatic channels from these countries gratis under bilateral agreements and cooperation.

Further right to copyright free could be obtained from these countries to produce them in the bulk at low cost. In India for instance each audio-video cassette produced by IGNOU or UGC-CSIR, or by any other Audio-Visual Centre would cost around 300 rupees which is equivalent to 125 nakfa in Eritrean currency. If the copyright permission is procured for all the range of educative cassettes produced by the Educational Agencies on curricular topics, locally they could be produced at a very low cost either in CDs or on Tapes. Then what remains is the procurement of raw materials like CDs, Tapes, Radios and Transistors.

In many developing countries today, Radio has almost become silent on the advent of Television. As such the bulk producers of such nations today could find Eritrea a good market and could produce them at the costs accessible to them. If the donor countries could afford to offer them gratis, these instruments and raw materials could be obtained in a short time. As this is all linked to bilateral tie-ups and diplomatic channels, the need to keep this nodal institution with separate agenda and mandate is very essential. The mandate of this institution could not therefore be assigned to any ministerial department which gets bogged down with so many administrative protocols and procedural wrangles. If the institution is autonomous and serves as a nodal agency, then it is easy to convince the donor nations of the social cause and purpose behind.

Institutional Objectives

1. To plan and liaise with donor agencies or donor nations for the free procurement of the raw materials required for the supply to all the educational institutions in a short time.
2. To plan for the low cost procurement or production of the printed tapes either by obtaining copyright permission free or obtaining the printed tapes on curricular topics free from the donor agencies or nations.
3. To plan for the procurement of multiple decks and CD writers for the bulk production though donor agencies and donor nations.
4. To liaise with the Electronic Products manufacturers for the import of the raw materials like tapes, CDs, radios, transistors, and tape-recorders either gratis or at cost-effective terms.
5. To procure bay-offset printing machinery to produce the Printed Materials of the Broadcast programme for given range of courses in the formal and non-formal education either by gratis or at low cost terms.
6. To maintain a watch for the different donor agencies' objectives and goals and plan the appropriate proposals for proper utilization of the opportunity.
7. To maintain good diplomatic ties with all the multi-national and donor nation agencies for deriving maximum benefit.

Administrative Functions

1. To recruit such staff who are good in marketing and low cost procurement methods, besides export and import policies of the other and local governments.
2. To recruit such staff and assign them the tasks in developing proper diplomatic ties with the donor agencies, UN agencies and the World Bank for proper consideration of the import of adequate raw materials free from these.
3. To be able to develop proper proposals for the processing for legally obtaining copyright permissions free from other countries.
4. To plan the budget and submission of proper proposals for procuring a Baby-offset printing machine to print the broadcast materials.
5. To appoint such staff who would look into and monitor the quality of the raw materials imported or procured.
6. To assign the task of assuring the quality of the Video-cassettes copyrighted either indigenous or imported before the supply to the target institutions.
7. To assign the specific task of certifying the quality of raw materials procured or imported either at low cost or gratis.
8. To monitor the quality of printing including printing.

With the above objectives and specific administrative functions, the nodal institution must be in a position to fully press into service all its energies to obtain maximum procurement of raw materials in keeping with the national priorities and requirements.

Nodal Institution to Ensure Proper Supply of All Raw Materials to the Recipients

This is the institution, which would take the responsibility of equitable distribution of the raw materials zoba-wise to all the intended target groups. It also does the function of auditing the not only previously supplied stock but also takes fresh indents from the intended target institutions. It is the duty of this institution to ensure hundred per cent timely distribution to all the remote corners of the country. This is very essential for the success of the Media Education. The Educational programme produced by the Media Centre would achieve the intended targets only when they (institutions) are properly provided by all the equipment and raw materials.

Institutional Objectives

1. To provide all the targeted institutions the materials and equipment required from time-to-time.
2. To make the proper auditing of the stocks received and supplied to the targeted institutions.
3. To plan for the proper logistic support to ensure that the raw materials reach the intended target groups in time.

Administrative Functions

1. To appoint and recruit such personnel who are familiar with conservation strategies of the go down stocks of the electronic and stationery materials.
2. To appoint such personnel who would attend to the maintenance and wear and tear repairs of the stocks procured.
3. To appoint such personnel who are familiar with accounting, auditing and computing techniques.

The Media Education becomes comprehensive with the support of all these nodal institutions.

8

Funding—A Critical Review of Preparatory Requirements and Low Cost Strategies—Media Education as Balancing Act

A Critical Review of Ministry's Annual Budget Allocations – World Bank Report Recommendations

The World Bank document is a joint document prepared by both the Government of Eritrea and the World Bank and hence can be taken as a basis for any future planning of budget. In fact, the Government has come out with a simulation model in which it showed the possible input variables such as GDP Growth, Taxes, Budgetary Allocations from the State to the Sector of Education which would go into the system and emerge out as output variable such as a single entity enveloping the entire budget of basic and secondary education. This would contrast with the Projected Government spending on basic and secondary education. The model is a reiteration of the Government's firm commitment to keep the education sector as its priority area. It has also come out with a 3-cycle plan for each of the level basic, middle and secondary, to embrace the objectives of EFA. It is a long-term visualization. It also calls for drastic macro and micro changes in the structure and function of the present working of the Ministry of Education. Further a number of corollary changes should be done from top to bottom, apart from establishing some corollary institutions too. However, in any of its documents, there is no, even remotely, any proposed plan of action as to how the Government proposes to utilize the Media Education to hasten the programmes and reforms it has planned to launch. Thus the question of funding the Media Education becomes equally important as much as the establishment of a full-fledged Media Education.

In the first place, for a systematic approach, to build a sound and effective national plan for Media Education, and to determine the exact quantum of funding and to determine the exact number of the target groups and the populations to be benefited, the following steps should be taken care of. Without these steps, the possible expenditure data, coming as it does, would always look high. The actual aspects of fund raising for many of the projects and reforms the Government of Eritrea planned so far had already been discussed in the first chapter under the sub-heading–*Budgeting*. The scope of the present discussion is to take a critical review of the whole scenario of budgeting and funding the entire gamut of Educational Reforms, insofar integrating them with and relating them to the Media Education, that the Government of Eritrea has undertaken in the absence of certain foreground or preparatory steps, which are mentioned below, for such a huge exercise.

There is a famous adage known all over the world that *Money Saved is Money Earned*. It is also known in Economics that the investment in any sector including education sector must ensure always long-range plans and returns besides sustainability and viability. It must be based on realistic and actual mathematics than by mere speculative statistical models, which might often bloat, the funding required for a specific plan of action. Most of the Government documents including the World Bank document suffer fundamentally from this lacuna. It is not even known in any of the documents on how and when the demographic data are collected last. Even the theoretical calculations done on the basis of this data are mere statistical and speculative and do not really reflect or match the population systems, which is a living system, and are subject to enormous fluctuations and variations due to war, epidemics, and drought etc. Especially the data are silent about the physically disabled, psychically disturbed and deranged, and visually impaired people in the productive age group, who turned dependents for various reasons including war and 30 years of prolonged struggle for freedom. Further, the data do not speak of the educated elderly generation, some of who are very good in English and in mother tongue. Hence an effort is to be made to identify areas which have been neglected in the scientific treatment of all the policy documents laid so far.

Table–29
Government and Donor Contribution to Education and Training Expenditure in Eritrea 1993-2000 (Million, US$)

	Spending on Basic Secondary Education		*Donors' Contribution*			*University of Asmara*		
Year	*Total Spen-ding*	*Capital Spen-ding*	*Donors Contri-bution*	*% of Total spending*	*% of Capital spending*	*Total spen-ding*	*Donors' contri-bution*	*% Donors contri-bution*
1993	10.8	2.5	2.5	23.1	100.0	0.9	0.3	32
1994	13.6	3.8	2.8	20.6	73.7	1.1	0.1	12
1995	18.1	5.1	2.4	13.3	47.1	1.3	0.3	19
1996	15.9	5.0	2.5	15.7	50.0	3.1	0.9	29
1997	25.5	8.1	5.8	22.7	71.6	7.2	1.5	21
1998	33.9	9.3	7.1	20.9	76.3	3.6	1.7	46
1999	34.9	13.4	9.7	27.8	72.4	4.2	2.3	56
2000	26.8	8.3	7.1	26.5	85.5	3.5	1.8	51

Source: Ministry of Education and Ministry of Finance.

Notes: Total spending for basic and secondary education includes spending by the MOE and all other line ministries who are involved in education activities. Total spending by the University of Asmara includes funds from the general funds that come from Central Government allocations and special funds, obtained from numerous external linkages that the university maintains.

Note: World Bank Document.

Courtesy: Eritrea Education and Training Sector.

Further, these factors throw light on how to enable the Government to go for low cost alternatives without draining away the much-starved State exchequer. Further, prima facie, the women employment in certain sectors appears to be very high compared to many other developing nations or newly formed countries. Though the reasons for this, such as threat of war over, which engaged the majority of the male force in the military training for nation's defence and for regaining the disputed territories, are obvious, the women employment has certainly been a source of income to many thousands of families and the same has not been reflected under the data in the World Bank document. Consequently the data reflecting the percentage of dependents including the unemployed, disabled men and women, besides the data of the employed youth, the boys and the girls, who should be included for Adult Education and for Formal Stream of Education are blurred. This greatly hampers the planning and budgeting process of the Media Education too.

A. *Census Data*

A systematic and scientific population survey village-wise and zoba-wise is very essential to determine the exact target populations. In the absence of this data, all the calculations involving funding are vague, ambiguous and are likely to tend to deep errors. The major error of the World Bank document, though it says it has provided enough cushion to eliminate this error in its calculations, is exactly centred round this. In fact, all the documents of the Ministry of Education projecting the estimates of the expenditure for the possible reforms lasting upto 2010 suffer from this error. It is afraid that this might repeat with the planning of Media Education too.

It is not impossible to have scientific census operation conducted for nearly a population of 3.8 million in a month's time and all the teaching and the village staff together can accomplish this in one month's time given the political will and administrative support. It would bring out the exact population target that would fit in the range of educational reforms linked to the Media Education in the formal education sector, and the target groups that go into the TVET and Non-formal Sector. This would go a long way in making precise calculations sector-wise. Further, it would give us the precise data as to the productive age group, which would play a very critical role in assessing the future requirement of the number of schools, institutions of higher learning and TVET and Adult Education Centres. It will also give an insight into the number of teachers required at all levels and the number of teacher training institutions need to be established now. It will then give an insight as to the requirement of budget to go by conventional mode *vis-a-vis* an insight how cost effective would it be if Media Education is resorted to. A Census data taken once would be valid for 10 years for all precise scientific calculations.

B. *Demographic Distribution*

By virtue of a variety of reasons the population distribution in the entire State of Eritrea is greatly varied. So far no scientific study on this important and crucial aspect has been done. Particularly it helps establish the precise numbers of populations involved in nomadic and pastoral life. If it helps restrict the mobility of these populations, by alternative means of rehabilitation programmes, then the government would be in the know of precise parameters of its targets. This is very crucial to prioritize the establishment of the educational institutions and their link upto Media Education at all levels. Most crucially the important junction points where a cluster of institutions of higher learning could be placed with the access to Media, internet, telephone, transport and comfortable travel, both for the students and the teaching staff from within a radius of 30 to 40 kms on time. Further, such a study will give a precise data as to the numbers of the different age groups migrating from rural to urban centres for various reasons such as Education, Employment and Health.

C. *Risks in the Capacity Building and Investment*

The initial anxiety to recruit number of teachers for basic, middle and secondary schools as proposed in the National Policy of Education and the Rapid Transformation of Eritrean Education System with tremendous emphasis on expenditure including a recurrent heavy salary budget for local and expatriates along the sidelines of building-up an infrastructure for various levels of institutions including Teacher Training and Technical Schools at the present may prove counter-productive after a decade's time, due to the terrible changes that occur in human populations both in the sense of the birth rate as also in the sense of the distribution and migration. Further, if Media Education comes into play, as seen in many of the African and Asian nations, the transformation of education sector would be very fast and most of the institutions established today with heavy investment prove counter-productive and redundant soon. Of all, such a vision would immediately save the most important national fund from being drained. Most of the developing nations often land in this kind welter of confusion where it would become impossible for the State or the Government to get rid of the unwanted institutions later as it amounts to risking the careers of many persons employed in those institutions. Alternatively it would have to drain its very valuable resources for unproductive causes.

D. *Prioritization of Private and Public Sector Investment in Education*

The Government has committed in its policy documents on Education to go for privatization for which it agreed in principle to bring out a comprehensive legislation. At the rates of expenditure as a percentage of GDP it projected on education, the national income is not likely to grow-up. As a result there would be a yawning gap between the government projections and the real estimates. Further, all the variables mentioned above would play their own devastating effect, unless those studies are done, on the total estimates that Government project from now upto 2010. This might endanger the whole economic policy of the Government at a stage impeding the progress of the total programmes and reforms.

Alternatively, the Government can comfortably rely on the Media Education at less than one-fifth of the total budget it estimates covering all sectors of education. Thus, the prioritization and laying down a Media policy covering all sectors of education as an alternative means to investment on the recurrent and non-recurrent heads in the conventional mode of education is very essential. For instance if correspondence courses and the courses offered through National Open Schools by the Media Education can eliminate the establishment of a number of teacher training institutes and basic schools, would it not save the government a lot of money that could be otherwise used for some other priority areas. Hence, it is better if the government right now decides its priorities of the education in the public sector and relinquish the remaining to the private sector by going in for global notifications. This would reduce the degree of dependence on Donor Agencies and on foreign debts. For a developing nation both seem to be good initially but in the long run prove to be suicidal. Especially the debt trap brings another form of slavery to the developing nations from the Development Partners of the West. Lack of visualization of this risk at this stage spells doom for the future generations.

E. *Alternative Strategies to Investment—Efficient Utilization of Existing Man Power*

Under ordinary conditions, with all the above data, it would have been advisable to go for permanent infrastructure for most of the establishments in the education sector including the Teacher

Training and Technical and Vocational institutions. But, unfortunately, as fate would have it, the country of Eritrea has the perennial enemy perched on its southern borders who never allowed peace to descend down on this much ravaged nation in its decade's old existence. The country is not only beset with problems of the post conflict management but also with a state of ever being prepared to combat with the aggressors.

Both of these will place heavy constraints on the Government in terms of man power resources and funds, which a small nation like Eritrea could hardly afford or lift on its shoulders with its annual GDP being very less compared to its expenditure on these unproductive heads such as cited above. Hence, it is time for the Government to focus on alternative strategies involving more existing manpower and less economic investment.

(a) Dominant Role for Media Education

One idea to accomplish most of the goals and objectives of the planned reforms to achieve EFA is embracing the Media Education as a State Policy not as a supportive medium. It must be the main line of instrument for achieving macro and micro structural changes in the education sector on the preceding lines and through it in the economic sector.

(b) Utilization of Existing Teaching Force

Second is to utilize the existing teaching force, including the University of Asmara Staff down to Primary school teachers, voluntary agencies and the expatriates to help rapidly change the State Education Sector. These personnel could be inducted for obtaining the precise data mentioned above and to prepare the accurate statistical data to delineate the target groups at various levels, which are essential for Media Education. If necessary the vacation period could be utilized effectively for most of its Adult Education and Curriculum Planning Programmes of Media Education. No separate recruitment is necessary to accomplish this job for Media Education. The entire burden that is presently on the National Curriculum Development could be partly shared with these staff.

(c) Availing the Services of the Elder Generations

Third is to avail the services of literate elder generation, who are

Italian or British or Ethiopian educated and are hale and healthy for the adult education and non-formal sectors at rural level. They can be utilized for proper interaction and motivation at the Adult Literacy Learning Centres or Community Development Centres. They can be part of the manpower for the proposed recruitment of Adult Education Teachers or instructors or counselors under the New Policy laid down by the Government for 2004-08. (*Adult Literacy and Post-Literacy Programmes in Eritrea – 5 year Plan-2004-08, p.11*). Some of them may be receiving the pensions or funds from their kith and kin abroad. Only thing required is to know the precise number of this population and their identities. It is possible only by a scientific census data, which are not now immediately available. They can be trained easily both for Media Education and conventional Adult Education programmes.

(d) Utilizing the Services Physically Disabled or Visually Impaired Younger Generations

Fourth is to press into service the younger literate generation, who are unfortunately physically disabled or visually impaired due to war and the prolonged freedom struggle. Some of these may be even war veterans and may be of immense help at rural level in mobilizing the masses towards education. Even some among these may be getting some pensions on monthly basis. The data of these populations at the rural level are very useful to take them as coordinators for the Media Education. They could be trained to properly coordinate both the formal and non-formal streams. They could be of immense help in operating the Adult Learning Centres or Community Development Centres. They could be trained in operational techniques and methods of media and multi-media.

(e) Curriculum Reforms and Calling for the Scripts on a National Basis on the Guidelines of National Curriculum Development Board (For Formal and Non-Formal Sectors)

Fifth is to call for the nation-wide scripts for the curriculum development, enrichment and reforms both in native languages (for Primary level) and for English Medium at Middle and Secondary level, besides Adult Education curriculum. The syllabus could be prescribed by the National Curriculum Development Board for all the streams but the scripts could be developed for them by the outside department personnel. This would save a lot of money and time for the Government and the Ministry of Education in turn. The best scripts could be screened and awarded by the Government through its committee constituted by the Academics and the scriptwriters.

(f) Low Cost Printing: Baby Offset Printing

The printing costs of textbooks in bulk could be reduced by acquiring a Baby Offset Printing Machinery. Even many schools and colleges in developing countries like India could have their own baby offset printing machinery to produce their own study material. Alternatively cyclostyled material could be brought out in the form of Textbooks. It is not compulsory to have beautifully printed textbooks at the cost of the Government in the formative years of post-independent era. In fact, former Soviet Union and early China followed the same pattern for a quick development on the education sector. As the Media Education too can formulate its own curriculum, design its own primers and offer print materials for all the correspondence courses it would broadcast, acquiring this kind of machinery either indigenously or on donor cost would strengthen the very programmes.

(g) Supply of Paper for Print on Subsidy by the Development Partners

These apart there are some countries like the US in the West, which would supply the paper for the print materials free. It means the cost of the print production is likely to get subsidized. India received aid from the US for the supply of the paper for the production of textbooks for a decade. This was used to be printed on the textbooks and as a result the cost of the print production of textbooks had scaled down steeply. It is known that the success of Media Education depends by and large on the support materials like print materials. For all the wide ranges of programmes media could offer, the enormous paper and print costs could be subsidized by this kind of alternatives. Some European countries could even finance or supply free the baby offset printing machines to meet the print requirements in bulk. Without involving the investment of high infrastructure and capacity building, adult literacy and reforms in formal education could be achieved. The foreground could be kept ready for second phase of reforms. All this should be done in a national spirit, which must equal the spirit that was used for a 3 decades freedom struggle. Without availing these services for the preparation of the foreground any budgeting and financing for the capacity building and investment will have always its attendant consequences that sometimes may undermine the whole efforts of reforms.

F. *Streamlining the National Budgetary Process and Individual Line Ministry Budgets*

In the context of funding the Media Education, the Ministry of Education has to bear the entire onus either by itself or from donor funding. But at present state of vagueness and ambiguity, the funding process may appear either difficult or suffer from lack of precision. It may lead to either over estimations because of lack of precise data that are mentioned in the foregoing or under estimations.This is one of the important aspects that the World Bank looked into and has taken serious note of. It found the whole budgetary process of the Ministries lacking in Transparency. Especially the expenditure of funds and accountability at various levels of education sectors are very unclear to arrive at the exact expenditure on education as percentage of GDP. Further, the details of teachers on national service and the teachers on the contract basis are very misleading and confusing or sometimes not available. The expenditure of the University of Asmara is not completely available. Further, the World Bank noted that sometimes the University of Asmara and the Ministry of Education both are vying with each other and are working at cross-purposes. It therefore suggested the integration of budget for the entire sector of education including University of Asmara and streamlining the budget and accounting process.

One might argue that there is no relevance of this to the present situation, which is directly concerned, with the implementation of the reforms through the Media Education. But, the lack of precision will only camouflage the calculation of the actual growth rate of GDP obtained in the entire sector of education through the incessant efforts of the Ministry of Education and the Government of Eritrea. It will only lead to unilateral criticism of the progress achieved by it too. One-day or the other the above macro and micro changes are bound to be achieved to bridge the gap between the rest of the world and Eritrea. Without these it is not possible to know the actual expenditure as a percentage of GDP.

The World Bank suggested a number of reforms in the Education sector, which included removal of the disparities between the salaries of the teachers on the National Service and the others. It also suggested bringing down the expenditure on the non-teaching staff and also reduction in the high salaries of the teachers while enhancing the share of the Government expenditure or allocation for the Education. Both these changes seem not to be based on realistic considerations. If implemented, these decisions are likely to have far reaching consequences and are bound to have a negative impact and impeding effect on the whole sector. Further, the World Bank document calls for higher budgetary allocations for the education sector, while implementing its recommendations to bring down the gap expected. Yet the document shows the possible huge deficit, which needs to be, compensated by the donor agencies or by the Ministry of Education itself. Exactly it is here the Media Education may be brought in to perform the balancing act. With the introduction of Media Education most of the suggestions of the World Bank would automatically stand compensated. Rather the government must make a Media Policy in such a way that it would absorb all the suggestions by itself without disturbing the present situation. Hence, the above suggestions have been made to reduce burden on the State Exchequer.

G. Liberalization of Educational Options in Asmara University and EIT-Maynafhi-Link up with Media Education

The present watertight or airtight education packages may be very suffocating for different categories of the youth. The options available for different courses of education are very limited. For instance the options offered at EIT-Maynafhi are very limited. There are Engineering, Pure Sciences and Arts groups. But there are no options of inter-combinations among them. There are no options like Business Administration, Tourism and Travel, Hotel Management, Sculpture etc. This is quite contrary to the American System of Education, which offers a variety of combinations. This will not enhance any load work on the teaching staff. At the most it may add a little load on the Examination and Administration branch. Further, many staff members recruited as Expatriate Teacher Specialists for certain branches had to remain without work due to improper planning of Maynafhi-EIT. Most important omission is that the entire education at EIT is going on, with such a massive strength of students, without integration of Media Education. In fact, there are two important institutions in Eritrea now: one is University of Asmara and another one is the recent EIT. Unfortunately, both are operating with massive student strength without being supported or aided by the Media Education, let alone Media taking lead. Media Education with reference to the courses offered by these two institutions would have acted not only as agents of reinforcement and recapitulation, but also would have helped enrich the learning resources.

Whereas the Government is willing to mobilize thousands of soldiers towards higher education by starting the institutes like Maynafhi—Eritrean Institute of Technology, the massive admissions at this institute would surely rise a number of questions on the evaluation and the quality of the education administered. If the Government is planning every year to add thousands of students to this campus, one can imagine the decline of standards that the institute would serve at the best than improving the standards. Further questions arise as to the alternatives if the students studying in these courses have failed to come up to a certain level. Even if the educational institutions are established all over Eritrea at important places like Keren, Massawa and Anseba, there should be a lot of flexibility in the options and in the range of options. It is then a wide range of students would get motivated and benefited. Above all these institutions must be quickly supported by the Media Education like the British Open University if the Government's efforts should yield tangible results right from the day one.

Further, the present education is not inspiring the modern young generation as there are a few promises of bright future, if the Government intended to retain all of them in Eritrea itself. Many a talented youngmen aspire to go abroad for improving their qualifications or for gainful employment. Since the present policy of the Government, out of its own justified reasons, forbids it, the frustration in the youth is conspicuously writ large.

Unless this extremely motivating issue is not immediately attended to, many of the larger reforms may end up as croppers. The disenchantment and disillusion among youth is becoming more and more apparent with the passing of each day and negative indicators like sluggishness and lethargy are slowly creeping into every sector. The youth are turning more towards entertainment, drugs—such as alcohol, smoking which may one-day weaken the very backbone of the country.

Diaspora Donations

The World Bank Document has made a projection indicating that the Diaspora funds are likely to decrease in the next 10 years during which time the Ministry has planned to implement various reforms in different cycles or phases. There are various steps that Government can initiate on the sidelines of these reforms to ensure not only continued support of the Expatriate Eritreans abroad but also enhance its level. One is already discussed above to liberalize the movement of the educated youth to go abroad either for gainful employment or for higher studies. As the present expatriates, who moved out of Eritrea in the early 1960-90s, would grow older, younger generations must go out to replace them to continue and add to the present level of inflow of funds.

Alternatively they may come back with their new expertise and establish a number of organizations, including educational in the private sector. In the context of fast changing global scenario, where the European Union is expanding from its former 15 to 25, allowing the migration of skilled and semi-skilled labour entire Europe freely, it is a matter of pride that many expatriate Eritreans by now have already become citizens of these new countries of the European Union. As such their children stand excellent chances of higher education and there is every possibility of their returning to Eritrea one-day with newer ideas of development of motherland. This is currently the policy of all developing nations in Asia, such as South Korea, Taiwan, Japan including China and India where the youth of these countries now occupied almost every part of the continent in large numbers. As a result of these, both China and India are highly benefited in terms of foreign reserves.

Donor Nations Funds

From the close reading of the World Bank document, it becomes clear that there may be a few donor countries in future coming forward to offer funds liberally. As the Denmark and Italy, who are the biggest donor nations to Eritrea by far, would retreat, new donor nations might come forward. Each of these donor nations would lay conditions of its own and sometimes they may prove counter-productive. In this context it is better to think twice before seeking the donor funds. It is always better to rely on the indigenous resources, both man power and otherwise, than go for donor funds.

There are a number of alternatives and low cost suggestions given in this chapter which the Government may consider at the appropriate time for the funding of Media Education. Mere lack of budget allotment or donor nation should not be a constraint for initiating a full-fledged Media Education programme. Most of these suggestions were implemented by many developing countries in the Third World. Hence it is not wrong if Eritrean government also makes an effort to implement them.

Private Corporate Bodies Either by Tax or by Advertising

This has been discussed even in the earlier chapter. Though the business at the present times is still in a state of infancy and development, efforts to link corporate sector with the University Education is very much in the model suggested by the World Bank document (p. 66) under participation and partnerships. Therefore, provision must be made as a policy of State to begin commercial advertising which would fetch substantial revenue. Advertising need not be always electronic media based as both the Media in Eritrea are under State control.

The Government can encourage Advertising at low cost initially and may gradually extend the cost value of advertisements. At present the Advertising through hoardings, posters and bulletin boards or films appear to be very less. This is one area of revenue, which Government must explore to garner more resources on its own.

Local Taxes Local Bodies

The details of the Local Taxes being collected from the people by the Local Bodies are not clear except a passing reference to it in the World Bank document. Due to the poor income levels, probably the revenue coming to the Local Bodies in the form of Local Taxes may also be very less. Further, the regional parties and groups have different tax structures in different provincial areas. As such there should be a uniform local tax policy at national level. The rural electrification is certainly a great task to be achieved in Eritrea. There are low cost technologies available today to achieve 100 per cent rural electrification (*Uganda example which in collaboration with Shell Foundation and Ultra tech developed low cost power technology using Solar Panels: BBC Earth Report*). If the rural cooperatives form and establish such low cost technologies of power supply, this will greatly support the educational reforms undertaken by the Government. Further, this will support the Local Community Centres to be run by the Government for the adults and dropouts. Hence local tax structure is very vital instrument of revenue and the revenue it generates must meet all these demands without laying the burden on the national exchequer. Now that the Regional Assembly elections for entire Eritrea are just concluded, there should be a discussion to form rural cooperatives to meet the rural requirements out of these taxes. After all the discussion and consensus, a national tax law must emerge soon.

9
Decentralization—Priority Areas

Zoba-wise – Prioritization Based on Literacy Percentage of Adults, School Dropouts and Girls and Women

It has been well-established in all the documents of the Ministry as also the World Bank that the uniform access to and equity in education are in wanting in all the zobas of the State of Eritrea. It has also been clear that the capacity to plan and manage the education system was markedly deficient at both the national and zoba level. Access and inefficiency problems at primary and middle school levels are found to be the main causes in aggravating the inequity situation for rural schools and for gender. At primary school level the Gross Enrollment (57%) masks great disparities between zobas. It has also been found that the lowland zobas of Deb-Keih-Bahri (South Red Sea), Sem-Keih-Bahri (North Red Sea) and Gash-Barka have General Enrollment Rates far below the national average. The Red Sea Zobas have even worst enrollment and equity rates. On the other hand, Maekel and Debub Zobas have registered the enrollment ratios well above the national average. Enrollment rates for girls across all levels have remained lower than for boys throughout the 1990s to 2000s.

This apart within the regions, gender disparities are even more striking and pronounced. Girls' enrollment varies greatly from region to region. Excepting Maekel Zoba, where the girl enrollment is high, all the other zobas exhibit different patterns of female enrollments that change little over time. In some regions, the female enrollment rates are comparatively high at elementary schools but soon drop sharply at subsequent levels. In some zobas, gross and net enrollment rates are lower than average at all levels. If Maekel and Deb-Keih-

Bahri are excluded from secondary education analysis, female students represent only 27 per cent of the secondary student population. The World Bank document identified that the demands for girls to work at home, the difficulties involved in long walking to reach the schools, lack of safe boarding schools besides traditional beliefs are among others that are responsible for fairer sex to take part in education.

In addition to the above, the MOE is admitting to its lacking in the institutional capacity at all levels – Central, Zoba, sub-zoba and school management. Therefore, it has been planning to strengthen the institutional administration from top to down and is trying to find out long-term solutions.

In the process, the Ministry of Education has formulated two major documents as support documents of Action Plan for I-PRSP (Interim-Poverty Reduction Strategy Paper): One is Education Sector Improvement Programme (ESI) and Education Sector Development Program (ESDP). Though these two documents are replete with the calculations for building up infrastructure and investment, expanding access and equitable distribution in terms of establishing and constructing new schools and training institutions, development of manpower training and capacity building at all levels of education, a mention about Media Education as a substantial and viable alternative to many of these requirements has not been dealt with. The foregoing 8 chapters have extensively established embracing the myriad dimensions of the entire sector of Education that the Media Education can achieve a maximum target at lesser and non-recurrent investment than all these areas together could accomplish and in a shorter term than those.

Media Education would be easier to access to the girls and women logged in the houses due to the traditional beliefs than the establishment of additional schools or boarding institutions. So does the Media Education with reference to the under enrollment that is witnessed in zobas and sub-zobas down to rural level. If the need to achieve results in a short-term is to be realized, nothing short of Media Education can help it out. It would enable the Government to prioritize the zobas with less literacy and education rates than focusing them by investment and infrastructural development.

10
Administrative Hierarchy

Ministry of Education – Overall Administrative Body and the Line of Supervising Hierarchy for Media Education

In any country the overall administration of education is very crucial. Though the Ministry of Education of the concerned country would be the sovereign authority of administering the educational policies and the programmes, it is the lower rung of the structure that delivers it. Hence, the supervisory control must be vested with the local authority which should do frequent and periodical to inspect and ensure the quality of education. It is here the major lacuna exists and the quality assurance and supervision of education administered in all the educational institutions, including the Teacher Training Institutes, Technical Schools and institutes of higher learning leave much desired behind. The Ministry, which is over-burdened with the policy-framing job, cannot obviously perform the task of carrying out the quality assurance. Hence a hierarchy of structure for quality assurance and supervision which covers the Media Education too from top to down must be established.

When Media Education takes over the role of formal, non-formal and continuing education programmes as an independent body of education, there is an apparent need to establish a good number of corollary institutions. Obviously the Ministry must hold a grip on these line institutions to oversee that all these institutions act within the given mandate and perform the tasks with proper synchronization and integration. Therefore, it calls for a line hierarchy down the line to govern all these institutions of mutual cooperation and assistance.

Since this Media Education extends down to the rural level, there should be a Zobal Administrative Head to see the smooth transition down to sub-zobal level. Such an intermediary institution headed by the Governing Head of Zoba would indeed have a long arm to exercise and monitor the programmes beamed to the rural sector. The sub-zobal heads should contact the Zobal Head or MOE's Regional Apex Body Head with regard to the monitoring and pursuing the programmes. Thus, the sub-zobal Head, the MOE's Regional Apex Head and the Zobal Head all together can periodically review the implementation of the programmes of Media Education. This ensures the programs offered by the Media education reach the targets and help get a feedback too from time-to-time. It makes in other words the implementation of the Media Education meaningful and effective.

At the rural level the Community Development Centre or Adult Literacy Centre, which would be constituted by the local Village Committee, either by the elected representatives of the Regional Assemblies, or by the ad-hoc committees constituted by the Zobal Head keep regular schedule of the programmes offered through the centre. These rural committees must consist of all the school principals, directors including the heads of the training schools and centres. The committee must also comprise the local community leaders, war veterans. It is very essential to mobilizing and motivating the rural masses. They also help giving the feedback from the popular voice. They also help inform the line up, including the local committee about the special requirements, concerning to the areas they are in, for preparing appropriate programmes.

Recommendations

1. It is suggested to establish a full-fledged Radio and TV educational channel of beam educative and educational programmes for the benefit of the students and teachers in the formal education and for the benefit of the dropouts and adults in non-formal education. It is the first step in the right direction to reduce the present high budgetary investment on the Capital and Capacity building. This is also a right step in bringing about Rapid Transformation in Eritrean Education System as done by Kenya, Uganda, Papua New Guinea, Brazil, Mexico, China and India.

2. It is also recommended to establish Curriculum Department exclusively for the Media Education not only to help quickly bring curriculum reforms and development but also prepare scripts for the Ratio and TV Educative and Educational programmes.

3. It is further suggested to go for low cost strategies and alternatives on the lines of many developed and developing Third World countries. Establishing FM Radio Stations, low cost battery or Solar power or Wing power receiving Stations for Radio and TV transmissions along the sidelines of developing an electronic network is highly useful for the nation to make the courses offered by the Media Education meaningful.

4. It is further suggested to commence the Correspondence courses on the Radio and TV channel for quickly training the Teachers at low cost capital and capacity investment. Examples of Kenya, Niger and American Samoa, etc., are highly beneficial.

5. It is further recommended to conduct workshops and seminars to train the teachers and writers as a foreground for launching of the Educative and Educational broadcasting without much loss of time later.

6. The Radio and TV Educational channels can do multiple and varied functions such as Curriculum Reform to Content enrichment, and Teacher Education to Teacher Development and formulating the Curriculum for various categories of Adult learners. Futher, they can plan for the lifelong and continuing education programmes.

Bibliography

Abraham Moles: Media Systems and Educational Systems, UNESCO, 1984.

ADEA New Letter: Double Issue, 2003.

Adult Literacy and Post Literacy Programmes in Eritrea (2004-08). Ministry of Education, Government of Eritrea. March, 2003.

Alexandre P. Vladislavlev: The Conceptual Framework for the Development of Life Long Education in the USSR, UNESCO, 1987.

Amaneul Negassi, Estfamos Bein, Kifle Ghebru, Bo Tengnas: Soil and Water Conservation Manual for Eritrea (Technical Handbook No.29). RELMA, 2002.

Ana Maria Sandi: Mass Communication in Education: UNESCO, 1984.

Andrew Crisell: Understanding Radio, Methuen, London and NY, 1986

Anihony, W. B: Broadcasting in Education. Constable, London, 1984.

Baath, A.J.: A List of Ideas for the Construction of Distance Education Courses in D.Steward, D. Keegan and B.Holmberg (eds.) Distance Education: International Perspectives. London. Croom Helm and Routledge, pp. 272-289, 1984.

Badrul, H.K. and Vinod Joshi: E-Learning: Who, What and How? *Journal of Creative Communication,* Sage Publications 1:1, pp.1-14, 2006.

Bates TA: Trends in the use of audio-visual media in distance education system in D.Steward, D.Keegan and B.Holmberg (eds) Distance Education: International Perspectives. London Croom Helm and Routledge. pp. 227-242, 1984.

Bhola, H.S.: "Adult Education for Poverty Reduction. Political Economy Analysis from Systems Theory Perspective." *Journal of Adult Education and Development,* Vol. 62, IIZ/DVV 2004.

CIA: World Fact Book-Eritrea, 2006.

Cliffe, L. and Davidson, B.: The Long Struggle of Eritrea. Red Sea Press, USA, 1988.

Community: Radio Case Studies, UNESCO, 1988.

Concept Paper for a Rapid Transformation of the Eritrean Educational System: Ministry of Education, 2002.

D.Stewart, D. Keegan and B. Holmberg (eds.). Distance Education: International Perspectives. London, Croom Helm Routledge, 123-127, 2003.

Daniel, J.: "Education For All". *ADEA News Letter,* Double Issue. Vol 15, No. 2, 3.

Donald, P. Ely: The Two Worlds of Today's Learners, UNESCO, 1984.

Dwight, V. Swain: Scripting for Video and Audio-visual Media: Focal Press, London and Boston, 1981.

Education Sector Development Programme: Ministry of Education, Government of Eritrea. December, 2003.

Education Sector Improvement Programme: Ministry of Education, Government of Erirea, April 2003/4-2004/8.

Eritrea Education and Training Sector Note – No. 24448-ERI: A World Bank and MOE Document, Ministry of Education, Government of Eritrea. 2002.

Eritrea National Education Policy: Ministry of Education, February, 2003.

Eritrea: Basic Education Statistics 2000-01: Ministry of Education, November, 2001.

Eritrea: Education Sector: Interim Poverty Reduction Strategy Paper Second Draft, Ministry of Education, Government of Eritrea. June, 2003.

Eritrea: Demographic and Health Survey, 2002: National Statistics and Evaluation Office, Asmara, Eritrea: ORC Macro, Calverton, Maryland and USA, May, 2003.

Ernest Choat, Harry Griffin and Dorothy Hobart: Teachers and Television, Crooom Helm, London and NY, 1987.

ESDP: Education Sector Development Programme, Revised Draft, Ministry of Education, Government of Eritrea, 2003.

Fiske, J. and Hartley, J.: Reading Television, Methuen, London, 1978.

Friedrich-Ebert-Stiftung: Television and the Third World: 1987.

G.E.Ortner, K.Graff and H.Willnsderter (eds.). Distance Education as Two way Communication. Frankfurt, Verlagperter Lang, pp. 171-84. 1992.

Gaim Kibreab: People on the Edge in the Horn. The Red Sea Press, NJ, USA. 1996.

Gerhard, E.O.: "Does two-way communication require a new Distance Education Technology" in Gerhard E. Ortner, Kurt Graff and Harald Wilmerdoerfer (eds.) *Distance Education as Two Way Communication.* Frankfurt am Main: Verlag Peter Lang, pp. 148-170, 1992.

Goffman, E.: "The Radio Drama Frame" in *Communication Studies*. Eds. Corner J. and Hawthorn, J. Edward Arnold, London, 1980.

Guidelines on Learner Centered and Interactive Pedagogy in the National Curriculum. Ministry of Education, Government of Eritrea, November, 2003.

Holmberg, B.: Growth and Structure of Distance Education. London, Croom Helm, 1986.

Hussein M. Adam: "Eritrea, Somalia, Somaliland" – *in Eritrea and Ethiopia – From Conflict to Cooperation*. Ed. Amare Tekle.Red Sea Press, NJ, USA. 1994. IIZ/DVV.

Jakobson, R.: "Closing Statement: Linguistics and Poetics" in *Style in Language*. Ed. Sebeok TA. Cambridge, Mass, MIT Press, 1960.

Jose Maria De Vera: Educational Television in Japan, Sophia University, Tokyo and Charles E. Tuttle Co. Tokyo, 1967.

Keegan, D.: "Teaching and Learning by Satellites in a European Virtual classroom" in F. Lockwood (ed.) Open and Distance Learning. London. Routledge. pp. 108-118, 1995.

Keegan, D.: The Foundations of Distance Education. Croom Helm. London. 1986.

Liebert, R.M., Neale J.M. & Davidson, E.S.: The Early Window: Effects of Television on Children and Youth, Perfamon Press, NY, 1979.

Ljosa, E.: The Boundaries of Distance Education. *Journal of Distance Education*. III (1), Spring.1988.

Ljosa, E.: Understanding Distance Education in D.Keegan (ed.). Theoretical Principles of Distance Education, pp. 75-187, 1992.

Macropolicy: Major Policy Document of Government of Eritrea, 1994.

Manjulika, S. and Venugopal Reddy V.: Distance Education in India – A model for Developing Countries. Vikas Publishing House Pvt. Ltd., 1996.

Mc Anany, E.G. and Mayo J.: Communication Media in Education for Low Income Countries: Implications for Planning: International Institute for Educational Planning, Paris, 1979.

Miercea Malitza: Learning, Understanding and Communication Media: UNESCO, 1984.

Mohammed Hassen: "Eritrean Independence and Democracy in the Horn of Africa"- *in Eritrea and Ethiopia – From Conflict to Cooperation*. Ed. Amare Tekle, Red Sea Press, NJ, USA, 1994.

Mohanty, J.: Educational Broadcasting: Radio and Television in Education. Sterling Publishers, New Delhi, 1994.

Murthy, C.S.H.N: Designing Media and ICT Strategies for Non-formal Education in Eritrea. *Journal of Adult and Continuing Education,* Vol. 12 No. 1, pp. 45-75, 2006.

Murthy, C.S.H.N: Designing the Course and the Curricula for Teacher Development, Open School and Vocational Education through Media Education in Eritrea. *Educational Media International,* No. 43, Number 2, pp. 181-96, June 2006.

NEGP: Eritrea-National Education Gender Policy and Strategic Framework of Action. Ministry of Education, Government of Eritrea. 2004.

Peter Combes and JohnTiffin: TV Production for Education: A Systems Approach, Focal Press. London, NY, 1978.

Pierre Schaeffer: Mass Media and the School: Descartes or McLuhan? in *Media Education UNESCO,* 1984.

Randy, Garrison, D. and Dough Shale: Education at Distance: From Issues to Practice. Robert E. Krieger Publishing Co.Malabar, 1990.

Renaldo Infante Urivazo: Cuba-An Introduction to Radio Broadcasting, UNESCO, 1984.

R.H. Dave, A. Ouane, D.A. Perera Eds. Learning Strategies for Post Literacy and Continuing Education in China, India, Indonesia, Nepal, Thailand and Vietnam, UNESCO, 1986.

Robert, C. Hornick: Development Communication (Information, Agriculture and Nutrition in the Third World) Longman, NY & London, 1988.

Robert McLeish: Radio Production. 3rd. Ed. Butterworth-Heineman, Oxford, 1998.

Som Naidu: E-Learning. *CEMCA* 2006, New Delhi. pp. 1-100.

Sreedher, R.: Setting Up Community Radio Station, *CEMCA News Letter,* 18-20, 23.

Sydney, W. Head: World Broadcasting Systems, Wadsworth Publishing Co. US, 1985.

Torstein, R.: "Computer Mediated Communication in Distance Education" in G.E.Ortner, K.Graff and H.Wilmersderfer (eds.) Distance Education as Two-way Communication. Frankfurt-verl;ag Peter Lang, pp. 171-84, 1992.

Usha Vyasulu, R. and Sanjaya Mishra: (eds) Educational Multimedia A Hand book for Teacher Developers, *CEMCA,* March, 2003.

Usha Vyasulu, R.: Educational Broadcasting in Commonwealth with Special Reference to Educational Television, pp. 1-25, *CEMCA,* 2003.

Wedmeyer, C. Learning at the Backdoor: Reflections on Non-Traditional Learning in the life Span. Madison: University of Wisconsin Press, 1981.

Wedmeyer, C.A.: "Backdoor Learning in the Learning Society" in D. Stewart, D.Keegan and B.Holmberg (eds.), Distance Education: International Perspectives, London, Croom Helm and Routledge, pp. 123-27, 1984.

Wilbur Schramm: Big Media, Little Media, Sage, London, 1977.

Wilson, P. Dizard: Television – A World View, Syracuse University Press, 1966.

Wood James: Satellite Communications and DBS Systems, 1992.

World Education Forum: Education For All: 2000. An Assessment. Thematic Studies. Applying New Technologies and Cost Effective Delivery Systems in Basic Education, Paris, UNESCO, 2001.

World Education Forum: Thematic Studies: UNESCO, 2000.

Yuri Babansky: The Information Explosion and optimizing the Educational Process, UNESCO, 1984.

Index